THE RUSSIAN JOURNAL
AND OTHER SELECTIONS FROM THE WORKS
OF LEWIS CARROLL

EDITED AND WITH AN INTRODUCTION BY
JOHN FRANCIS McDERMOTT

DOVER PUBLICATIONS, INC.
NEW YORK

Published in Canada by General Publishing Com-
pany, Ltd., 30 Lesmill Road, Don Mills, Toronto,
Ontario.
Published in the United Kingdom by Constable
and Company, Ltd., 10 Orange Street, London
WC2H 7EG.

This Dover edition, first published in 1977, is an
unabridged, unaltered republication of the work
originally published by E. P. Dutton & Co., Inc.,
New York, in 1935. A new Preface to the Dover
Edition has been written especially for this edition.

International Standard Book Number: 0-486-23569-6
Library of Congress Catalog Card Number: 77-84529

Manufactured in the United States of America
Dover Publications, Inc.
180 Varick Street
New York, N.Y. 10014

PREFACE TO THE DOVER EDITION

Since this book was published in 1935 Lewis Carroll interpretation has become a popular industry. His diaries have been made public and studies of merit as well as a good bit of nonsense have poured from the pens of scholars pursuing the illusive Reverend Mr. Dodgson.

The most perceptive examination of the *Alice* stories is Martin Gardner's brilliant *Annotated Alice*. Mr. Gardner has written the book which, many years ago, I once dreamed of doing, before I became so engrossed with an entirely different field of research that, however reluctantly, my early interests had to be abandoned.

Some authors have made a great deal of Dodgson's neuroses, his celibacy, his dislike of boys, and his sensuous pleasure in little girls. Inevitably, Freudian analysts have applied techniques to his life and writings and have come up with some wonderfully strange theories. It is intriguing to imagine the enjoyment which Lewis Carroll would have found in satirizing the Freudians if they had been in full cry during his lifetime.

Lewis Carroll has gained in significance with the passing years. There is, indeed, scarcely a situation in life to which a quotation from one or other of his books is not appropriate. Certainly our world is that of the Red Queen where all must run "faster! faster!" just to keep up with the times. The philosophical implications of Carroll's fantasies and humorously presented problems of logic continue to fascinate scientists and philosophers. The lively glimpses of czarist Russia recorded in his travel diary grow in value as that regime recedes into history. With its quietly humorous observations of foreign scenes it is, perhaps, the most entertaining portion of all the diaries and is certainly essential to any study of the Dodgson-Carroll personality.

Carroll took great pleasure in contemplating a paradox but could not, of course, foresee that he would become one of literature's most baffling paradoxes, a proper Victorian churchman whose tales written for children reveal beneath the amusing accounts of magical adventures a profound skepticism about the validity of human reason. Lewis Carroll's "nonsense" is even more relevant (to use current jargon) to our era of uncertainty than it was to the more stable world of the Reverend Mr. Dodgson.

JOHN FRANCIS McDERMOTT

St. Louis, Missouri
30 June 1977

PREFACE TO THE FIRST EDITION

In this book I have brought together Carrolliana which I think should once more be made accessible. All of the pieces here included have been published at some time and in some form, but, with perhaps half a dozen exceptions (which I have added to round out the book, and, mostly, to please myself), the materials of the volume are long out of print, or otherwise inaccessible. The same sharpness of mind and cleverness of expression which are characteristic of *The Snark*, of the other poems, and of the *Alice* books the reader will find in this varied array of little-known writings.

In arranging the selections I have followed, roughly, a chronological order. The first group, Early Pieces, is made up of skits and sketches written for *The Rectory Umbrella*, one of his home magazines for the years 1849-1850, and for *Misch-Masch*, another family periodical running from 1855 to 1862 (though some of the pieces were published previously in other papers). In this group I have included also *Novelty and Romancement* which appeared in *The Train for October*, 1856 (the other Carroll writings from *The Train* have all been included in *The Collected Verse of Lewis Carroll*); a letter which contains a rhymed description of his work as a Tutor (this was written shortly after he obtained his Studentship); and *The Legend of "Scotland."* Most of this material I discovered in *The Lewis Carroll Picture Book*, a volume of Carroll writings compiled by Stuart Dodgson Collingwood (nephew and official biographer) a year after Carroll's death, never published in America, and very difficult of access. The pieces in this division of the book are nothing very subtle, but they are all amusing and are all indicative of the qualities which later became famous under the pen name of Lewis Carroll.

The manuscript notebooks of the *Journal of a Tour in Russia in 1867* are owned by Morris L. Parrish, Esq., of Dormer House, Pine Valley, New Jersey, who has kindly permitted me to include this very scarce and practically unknown item. Collingwood, in

5

the *Life*, quotes a good deal from this diary; Mr. Parrish published it in its entirety several years ago but only in a private edition limited to sixty-six copies; otherwise it has never appeared before the public. It is useful and desirable then to present it here—the only record of the only foreign travel by its author.

The *Oxford Papers* I have drawn from the *Notes by an Oxford Chiel* (also included in *The Lewis Carroll Picture Book*). The dates of first publication will be found on the title pages with each article; the author collected them himself in 1874 and published them under the title given above. The first of these papers, *The New Method of Evaluation*, I have omitted because it seemed difficult for the reader without an Oxford background to follow. The other five papers I have included, however; for, though sometimes the pages may appear alarming, the whole idea and the treatment are clear enough. And the reader will find in them many delightful evidences of Lewis Carroll. The identity of the principals is established in the notes accompanying the individual papers.

Next I have presented the essay which Carroll wrote for *The Theatre* in 1887, in which he told about Alice and the stage, about the origins of Alice, and about his idea of the characters in the book and the play. The Puzzles are a very few examples of the "brain-teasers" of which Lewis Carroll was very fond throughout his life.

In 1889 Carroll published *Sylvie and Bruno* and four years later *Sylvie and Bruno Concluded*. This pair of books never attained the popularity of the *Alice* books (the reasons for this I make apparent in the present Introduction) and for many years they have been out of print save in a much abridged form which omitted a great part of the most characteristic material. I have presented no narrative passages, though some are thoroughly delightful, because the material was by the very nature of the construction of the books scattered too widely; but I have lifted out a number of other passages each complete and each dealing with an idea or ideas in a typically Carrollan manner. To these excerpts I have given titles suggested by the context.

Since there are inseparable bits of verse and several complete poems embedded in the prose of this book I have put in the appendix a note on this material, and I have included also four separate poems, early material, which I think quite typical enough to preserve here. Two of these pieces have not been reprinted since *The Lewis Carroll Picture Book*, and, I believe, have never been published in America.

Unless otherwise indicated all footnotes are those of Lewis Carroll himself.

J. F. McD.

CONTENTS

A LIST OF THE VERSES TO BE FOUND
IN THIS VOLUME

INTRODUCTION

Priest without a parish, child-lover without children, recluse and reactionary, sentimentalist and scholastic, Charles Lutwidge Dodgson lived a strange and uneventful life. Born in a large family, living in the midst of the unceasing contacts of university life, having for friends many famous individuals, he was yet a recluse, hiding away all his life behind the protective walls of Christ Church. He loved little children with all the proper ideal love of a Victorian who did not have children and knew little about them. A thoroughly religious person, he preached very seldom in his life and made no attempt to obtain a living.

His father, Charles Dodgson, was in his way a distinguished scholar. Christ Church was his college and mathematics his favorite study. Among his other labors he translated Tertullian for the "Library of the Fathers." He took a prominent part in the controversy about Baptismal Regeneration, siding with the Tractarians ("though his views on some other points of Church doctrine were less advanced than those of the leaders of the Oxford movement"). He was, according to Stuart Dodgson Collingwood, his son's biographer, a man of deep piety and reserved and grave disposition. "His reverence for sacred things was so great that he was never known to relate a story which included a jest upon words from the Bible." The son of such a man as Archdeacon Dodgson must be either as thoroughly religious as the father or thoroughly irreligious. In this instance, the powerful and dominating character of the father caused the son to be both a profound religious and a satirist. The child of the Archdeacon freely accepted the influence about him, but at the same time unconsciously rose in rebellion.

The mother of Charles Lutwidge Dodgson was Frances Jane Lutwidge. C. L. D.'s biographer has little to say about her except to quote in admiration some words which are presumably those of her husband. She was "one of the sweetest and gentlest women that ever lived, whom to know was to love. The earnestness of her simple faith and love shone forth in all she did and said; she seemed to live always in the conscious presence of God." It is apparent then that the boy had a doubly religious background.

Charles was born January 27, 1832, at Daresbury, of which village his father was then incumbent. He spent here his first eleven years. Since the parsonage was a mile and a half from the village, the boy passed these years in complete seclusion, save for his family, which grew larger and larger (he was the oldest of eleven children) but did not necessarily provide variety or comradeship. In 1843 his father was given the living of Croft in Yorkshire (later becoming Archdeacon of Ripon and one of the Canons of Ripon Cathedral). At the age of twelve, Charles was sent to school at Richmond under a Mr. Tate. In 1846 he went to Rugby where A. C. Tait was his master. Two years later Mr. Tait could write to the elder Dodgson ". . . his examination for the Divinity prize was one of the most creditable exhibitions I have ever seen."

Charles matriculated at Oxford (Christ Church) on May 23, 1850, and came into residence January 24, 1851. Until his death forty-seven years later, he lived at Oxford. For his studiousness and his piety, he was a favorite with his masters. Presently, he was made a Student in Christ Church, the conditions of this office being that he remain unmarried and that he proceed to Holy Orders, two limitations that caused him no hesitation. He took his Bachelor of Arts, December 18, 1854. The next autumn he was made a "Master of the house," that is, he had all the privileges of an M.A., though he had not yet the official standing. The actual degree he took in 1857. He was made a Sub-Librarian, was given a scholarship, and settled down in his college as a lecturer. He was ordained December 22, 1861. After this he preached occasionally but he had no desire for the life of a preacher. An impediment in his speech had some influence on his decision. There is no question that he was very religious but his great desire was to do good rather than merely to preach beautiful sermons. His life was in general uneventful. He lectured at Oxford, he went occasionally to London, he went once (his only foreign travel) with Dean Liddon to Russia. He died in 1898.

His diary apparently was full of "modest deprecations of himself and his work, interspersed with earnest prayers . . . that God would forgive him the past, and help him to perform His holy will in the future" (so Collingwood assures us)—even though he was spending all his time doing what he thought were good deeds. He read *Alton Locke* and thought how it might stir up workers in the field of social betterment. "Oh that God, in His good providence, may make me hereafter such a worker!" The official biographer mentions as illustrative of his reverence an incident in connection with *Through the Looking-Glass:* in the original manuscript the bad-tempered flower was the passion flower; the religious connotation he did not see until it was pointed out to him by a friend, whereupon he substituted for it the tiger-lily. Collingwood also relates that, when a friend asked if the last scene of this book had been suggested by the conclusion of *Pilgrim's Progress*, strongly he denied the idea since he would consider highly irreverent the trespass on such holy ground. When, wishing to devote himself to special work, he sent in his resignation as a Lecturer, he noted the facts in his diary and added "May God bless the new form of life that lies before me, that I may use it according to His holy will." He requested Miss Thomson, who illustrated one of his books, to do no sketches or other work for him on Sunday, for "It is, in my view (of *course* I don't condemn any one who differs from me) inconsistent with keeping the day holy." Anecdotes upon sacred subjects he looked on with horror. When a friend repeated one which, innocently irreverent, dropped from a child, he was greatly pained. In writing to the friend about it, he added: "One further remark. There are quantities of such anecdotes going about. I don't in the least believe that 5 per cent. of them were ever said by *children.* I feel sure that most of them are concocted by people who *wish* to bring sacred subjects to ridicule—sometimes by people who *wish* to undermine the belief that others have in religious truths; for there is no surer way of making one's beliefs unreal than by learning to associate them with ludicrous ideas."

He was a recluse. He lived within Oxford for forty-seven years. He did there all his duties and mingled with his fellows, but he was not a person to cultivate outside interests (unless one considers his mania for amateur photography such an interest). It is true that he numbered among his acquaintance Tennyson, Ruskin, the Rossettis, and others, but his chief friendships were for little girls. He hated publicity and tried to avoid it. He always attempted to deny the Lewis Carroll identity, maintaining that he was Charles Dodgson, a lecturer on mathematics. He once requested a friend that if she saw him in the theatre, not to tell anyone. For years, when unknown correspondents wrote to him, either he did not answer or he wrote on the typewriter. Before he bought the machine, he would frequently have friends write out his answer and even sign it for him.

He was given also to writing serious verse. It is not now the time to enter into a critical discussion of this work. The reader may find some specimens of it in the appendix to *The Collected Verse of Lewis Carroll*. He will remember, perhaps, some of the introductory or dedicatory verse to the better-known books. Mr. Dodgson himself prepared, though he did not live to see published, a collection of serious verse which he entitled *Three Sunsets*. This work is competent versification but it is too insignificant or too sentimental to have value. He wrote occasionally on religious subjects; of all his sermon material we are told that he thought most highly of a paper on "Eternal Punishment" which he expected to issue in a volume of essays on religious subjects (he did not live to the completion of this project). He wrote also a considerable part of the *Sylvie and Bruno* which must be discussed at another time.

That Mr. Dodgson was a lover of children we have heard repeatedly. The origin of *Alice in Wonderland* is too well-known a story to bear repetition. His child friends began with the daughters of his friend Dean Liddell but they numbered many more before he died, for (though he lacked it with adults) he had a way of picking acquaintance with little girls and he was attentive to and thoughtful of them. In acknowledging the gift of a book containing a poem on Alice, he could write to the author, "Next to what conversing with an angel *might* be—for it is hard to imagine it—comes, I think, the privilege of having a real child's thoughts uttered to one." He was very fond of the acting of children and his greatest pleasure in the *Alice* productions was in the performances by child actors. Contrary to the attitude of many in his day, he did not object to children in the theatre; in fact, he thought that if they wanted to act, it was an excellent thing for them. If one enjoys the work he is doing, Dodgson held, then it does not hurt him but really benefits him. Although he had many little girl friends and some little boy ones, he was not friendly with everyone. A friend to whom he sent a copy of *Sylvie and Bruno* thanked him by letter, adding that he would bring his little boy to see him. But Dodgson wrote *no* to that and startled the man. "He thought I doted on *all* children. But I'm not omnivorous!—like a pig. I pick and choose...."

This man is Charles Lutwidge Dodgson.

I have said that the first eleven years of the life of Charles Dodgson were spent in practical seclusion. As the oldest of eleven children, he must, in one sense, have occupied an increasingly lonely position, for his mother's attention would necessarily be diluted as the family grew more numerous. As the oldest, he could not, by this very difference, find in the next of his brothers and sisters entirely satisfactory comrades, even if we discount the psychological struggle for position. He was forced to make his own amusement. But Lewis Carroll invented strange diversions for himself. He made pets of toads and snails and other unlikely animals. Collingwood tells us that he tried to encourage more modern and civilized warfare among earthworms by supplying them with small pieces of pipe with which to fight. He was fond of inventing games. At Croft he built in the Rectory gardens a crude railway with stations, refreshment stands, and so forth. He made a troupe of marionettes and a small theatre for them. He wrote all the plays himself and manipulated the strings.

There are other early indications of the presence and development of the Lewis Carroll personality. Mr. Tate, his master at the school to which he went at the age of twelve, wrote in his first report to the boy's father: "... whether in reading aloud or metrical compositions, he frequently sets at nought the notions of Virgil or Ovid as to syllabic quantity. He is moreover marvelously ingenious in replacing the ordinary inflexions of nouns and verbs as detailed in our grammars, by more exact analogues, or convenient forms of his own devising. This fault will in due time exhaust itself, though flowing freely at present . . ." Here is an early indication of Lewis Carroll's inventive powers and also of his particular sort of iconoclasm. (The prediction, of course, did not come true.)

During the Rugby holidays he edited "home" magazines. The best, apparently, of these was called *The Rectory Umbrella*. He supplied all the written matter and the illustrations as well. Although the work is not extraordinary, it is indicative of his early powers. For instance, one number contained caricatures of pictures in the Vernon gallery. He reproduced "The Age of Innocence" of Sir Joshua Reynolds. The picture, according to an editorial note, "representing a young Hippopotamus seated under a shady tree, presents to the contemplative a charming union of youth and innocence." In *The Rectory Umbrella* appeared also parodies of well-known poems. One, entitled "Lays of Sorrow No. 2," is a parody of Macaulay's lays. The poem, about a boy and a donkey, is just the subject to reduce the heroics of Macaulay (though it is possible that the boy did not have this directly in mind). The quotation of one stanza will show that the poem, though not very good, is not very bad. It illustrates the ease of parody which distinguished the work of Lewis Carroll but is without a great deal of satiric point.

> And now the road to Dalton
>   Hath felt their coming tread,
> The crowd are speeding on before
>   And all have gone ahead.
> Yet often look they backward,
>   And cheer him on, and bawl,
> For slower still, and still more slow,
> That horseman and that charger go,
>   And scarce advance at all.

"Lays of Sorrow No. 1" contains an example of one of Lewis Carroll's favorite tricks in his later work: the literal treatment of a common expression:

> And so it fell upon a day,
> (That is, it never rose again) . . .

Misch-Masch, a later "home" edition, covers the years from 1855 to 1862, and contains many pieces of prose and verse which had previously seen publication in periodicals such as *The Illustrated Times* and the *Whitby Gazette.* We find in this "magazine" the original version of the evidence contributed by the White Rabbit at the trial of the Knave of Hearts; here it is called "She's All My Fancy Painted Him." We find also "The Dear Gazelle" which was later included in the most comprehensive edition of his verse that Lewis Carroll issued, *Rhyme? and Reason?* But one of the best things in *Misch-Masch* is called "Photography Extraordinary." It is concerned with "the recent extraordinary discovery . . . which has reduced the art of novel-writing to the merest mechanical labor." The idea is that the flickerings of the feeblest intelligence can be " 'developed' up to any required degree of intensity." The inventor began on a person of the weakest possible powers, physical or mental. "On being asked what we thought of him, we candidly confessed that he seemed incapable of anything but sleep." The experiment is started, the subject insists that he is thinking of nothing, the paper is properly exposed, and at last examined. The result is astounding:

The eve was soft and dewy mild; a zephyr whispered in the lofty glade, and a few light drops of rain cooled the thirsty soil. At a slow amble, along the primrose-bordered path, rode a gentle-looking and amiable youth, holding a light cane in his delicate hand: the pony moved gracefully beneath him, inhaling as it went the fragrance of the roadside flowers: the calm smile, and languid eyes, so admirably harmonising with the fair features of the rider, showed the even tenor of his thoughts. With a sweet though feeble voice, he plaintively murmured out the gentle regrets that clouded his breast:

"Alas! She would not hear my prayer!
Yet it were rash to tear my hair;
Disfigured, I should be less fair.

"She was unwise, I may say blind;
Once she was lovingly inclined;
Some circumstance has changed her mind."

There was a moment's silence: the pony stumbled over a stone in his path, and unseated his rider. A crash was heard among the dried leaves; the youth arose; a slight bruise on his left shoulder, and a disarrangement of his cravat, were the only traces that remained of this trifling accident.

This is an example of the "milk-and-water School of Novels." The experiment is done over so as to produce the second time a sample of the writing of the "strong-minded or Matter-of-Fact School."

The evening was of the ordinary character, barometer at "change"; a wind was getting up in the wood, and some rain was beginning to fall; a bad look-out for the farmers. A gentleman approached along the bridle-road, carrying a stout knobbed stick in his hand, and mounted on a serviceable nag, possibly worth some 40 or so; there was a settled business-like expression on the rider's face, and he whistled as he rode; he seemed to be hunting for rhymes in his head, and at length repeated, in a satisfied tone, the following composition:

> "Well! so my offer was no go!
> She might do worse, I told her so;
> She was a fool to answer 'No.'
>
> "However, things are as they stood;
> Nor would I have her if I could,
> For there are plenty more as good."

At this the horse set his foot in a hole, and rolled over; his rider rose with difficulty; he had sustained several severe bruises and fractured two ribs; it was sometime before he forgot that unlucky day.

In order to show that this sort of thing might be developed to the greatest degree of intensity, the experiment is continued to the recasting of this passage in the "Spasmodic or German School":

The night was wildly tempestuous—a hurricane raved through the murky forest—furious torrents of rain lashed the groaning earth. With a headlong rush—down a precipitous mountain gorge—dashed a mounted horseman armed to the teeth—his horse bounded beneath him at a mad gallop, snorting fire from its distended nostrils as it flew. The rider's knotted brows—rolling eyeballs—and clenched teeth—expressed the intense agony of his mind—weird visions loomed upon his burning brain—while with a mad yell he poured forth the torrent of his boiling passion:

> "Firebrands and daggers! hope hath fled!
> To atoms dash the doubly dead!
> My brain is fire—my heart is lead!
>
> "Her soul is flint, and what am I?
> Scorched by her fierce, relentless eye,
> Nothingness is my destiny!"

There was a moment's pause. Horror! his path ended in a fathomless abyss. . . . A rush—a flash—a crash—all was over. Three drops of blood, two teeth, and a stirrup were all that remained to tell where the wild horseman met his doom.

Among other interesting pieces of work in *Misch-Masch* we find the "Stanza of Anglo-Saxon Poetry" (later the first stanza of "Jabberwocky," with explanations of the fantastic terms used) and "The Palace of Humbug," a parody of "I dreamt I dwelt in marble halls."

At Christ Church, he edited *College Rhymes*, to which he made a number of contributions; though he did not use his name, he did sign these by various initials that suited his fancy. He started also to contribute to general magazines. The first of these publications was called *The Comic Times* (1855) of which Edmund Yates was editor. In 1856 Yates founded *The Train* and took to it the old contributors to the first magazine. It was at this time that Yates picked, from a submitted list, the pseudonym "Lewis Carroll." Among Carroll's contributions was "Novelty and Romancement" (a sort of short story the very crux of which was a play on the second term in the title, an amusing sketch of a romantic aesthete who was almost worthy of a place in *The Snark*); also, "The Three Voices" (an excellent parody of Tennyson); "Hiawatha's Photographing" (a parody of Longfellow), and some other entertaining things.

From this time on Lewis Carroll was established as a definite and recognized personality. The first telling of *Alice's Adventures Underground* occurred in 1862. The publication of *Alice's Adventures in Wonderland* was in 1865. *Phantasmagoria* (1869) he called a collection "grave and gay"; that is, it is a mixture of Dodgson and Carroll. It was a collection of magazine reprints. *Through the Looking-Glass* appeared in 1871 and *The Hunting of the Snark* in 1876. *Rhyme? and Reason?* (1883) was a volume made up of the lighter pieces from *Phantasmagoria*, to which were added some other poems. It is the last volume that is almost pure Carroll.

It will hardly be necessary to enlarge on the later works of Lewis Carroll, especially those best examples and most widely known ones, the two *Alice* books and the *Snark*. It is quite clear that, though they are superficially children's books and dedicated to children, they are nevertheless very much more than that. They are satire. I have gone into some detail concerning the earlier work of Lewis Carroll to indicate the continuity of the satirical element. If this is true, then we have inhabiting one body two widely different and strangely assorted men. The remaining sections of this paper will be devoted to a tracing out of the connecting element between Charles Lutwidge Dodgson and Lewis Carroll.

In the long vacation of 1867 Carroll-Dodgson (if I may so call him for convenience) went abroad with his friend Dr. Liddon. In the day-by-day notebooks which he filled on this tour, the Oxford Don gives us glimpses of both Dodgson and Carroll. We may say that it was Dodgson who took such a great interest in the churches everywhere he went. The churchman traveling missed seeing no church if he could help it; yet the accounts we have before us are only mildly Dodgsonian, if we are to use as a guide the sort of religious feeling which we are shown later in the *Sylvie and Bruno* books. The comments here are merely those of a pleasantly alert traveler with a special interest in church architecture and in foreign variation in church services. It is an interesting and a copious record made with surprisingly little prejudice. On the other hand, we see Lewis Carroll wandering about, looking out continually for a theatre. Almost anything in stage performance is worth seeing for him, whether there is a language barrier or not.

Among the most entertaining features of this very interesting journal is the typical Carrollan comment upon his contacts with the native culture and the natives themselves. Like a proper traveling Englishman, he is interested in culture; he must see the art museums, all of them if physically possible. But, being Carroll, here is a typical opinion:

. . . The amount of art lavished on the whole region of Potsdam is marvelous; some of the tops of the palaces were like forests of pedestals. In fact the two principles of Berlin architecture appear to me to be these— "On the housetops, whenever there is a convenient place, put up the figure of a man; he is best placed standing on one leg. Whenever there is room on the ground, put either a circular group of busts on pedestals, in consultation, all looking inwards—or else the colossal figure of a man killing, about to kill, or having killed (the present tense is preferred) a beast; the more prickles the beast has, the better—in fact a dragon is the correct thing, but if that is beyond the artist, he may content himself with a lion or a pig."
The beast-killing principle has been carried out everywhere with a relent-

less monotony, which makes some parts of Berlin look like a fossil slaughter house. . . .

His contacts with hotel-keepers, servants, and the ubiquitous fraternity of waiters are reported in typical Carrollan fashion. There is, for instance, the affair of the hieroglyphics used in the recovering of Dr. Liddon's coat. He tells us of their hotel in Königsberg that

By staying at the "Deutsches Haus," we enjoy one unusual privilege—we may ring our bells as much and as often as we like: no measures are taken to stop the noise. . . .

Waiters, he records, are equally difficult to deal with wherever they are found. At Dover

We breakfasted, as agreed, at 8—or at least we then sat down and nibbled bread and butter till such time as the chops should be done, which great event took place about ½ past. We tried pathetic appeals to the wandering waiters, who told us "they are coming, Sir" in a soothing tone—and we tried stern remonstrance, & they then said "they are coming, Sir" in a more injured tone; & after all such appeals they retired into their dens, and hid themselves behind sideboards and dish-covers, still the chops came not. We agreed that of all virtues a waiter can display, that of a retiring disposition is quite the least desirable. Then I made 2 great propositions, both rejected on the first reading—one that we should desert the table, & refuse to pay for the chops, the other that I should search out the proprietor and lodge a formal complaint against all the waiters, which would certainly have produced a general row, if not the chops. . . .

But waiters are always waiters; let the world wag as it will:

And then we moved on to Giessen & put up at the "Rappe Hotel," for the night, & ordered an early breakfast of an obliging waiter who talked English. "Coffee!" he exclaimed delightedly, catching at the word as if it were a really original idea, "ah, Coffee—very nice. And eggs. Ham with your eggs? Very nice"—"If we can have it broiled" I said. "Boiled?" the waiter repeated with an incredulous smile. "No, not *boiled*," I explained, "*broiled*." The waiter put aside the distinction as trivial, "yes, yes, ham," he repeated, reverting to his favorite idea. "Yes, ham," I said, "but how cooked?" "Yes, yes, how cooked," the waiter replied, with the careless air of one who assents to a proposition more from good nature than from a real conviction of its truth. . . .

In this journal, then, we find a mingling of the Carroll and Dodgson elements; though neither one is as pronounced as we find it in other work, yet we can recognize each. But the evidence here is not sufficient alone to link up such divergent qualities as we find marking Dodgson and Carroll separately. When we turn, however, to the remaining publications we discover the connecting element.

There was a boy at Daresbury who found a book of logarithms and insisted that his father explain them to him, even after his father said that it was a subject too difficult for one so young to understand. Of this same boy, at the age of twelve, his master Mr. Tate (already quoted) had this to say: ". . . his reason is so clear and so jealous of error that he will not rest satisfied without a most exact solution of whatever appears to him obscure. He passed an excellent examination in mathematics, exhibiting at times an illustration of that love of precise argument, which seems to him natural."

At Oxford he obtained First Class Honors in the Final Mathematical School and soon after was appointed to a Lectureship in mathematics in his college. Collingwood reports that about this time he took sufficient interest in betting, from a mathematical point of view, to write a letter to *Bell's Life* explaining a method whereby a man might be sure of winning any race. The scheme was to back every horse or to bet against every horse, as the odds added up.

Though his teaching field was mathematics, this man was essentially a logician. All his life he took delight in noting flaws in logic. On one occasion after he had heard a lecture on the Arctic regions he wrote his impressions of the lecture to his sister. He quoted, " 'though he did not suffer all the hardships the others did, *yet* he came to an untimely end (of course one would think in the Arctic regions), *for instance*, (what follows being, I suppose, one of the untimely ends he came to), being engaged in a war of the Portuguese against the Prussians, while measuring the ground in front of a fortification, a cannon-ball came against him, with the force with which cannon-balls in that day *did* come, and killed him dead on the spot.' How many instances of this kind would you demand to prove that he did come to an untimely end? One of the ships was laid up three years in the ice, during which time, he told us, 'Summer came and went frequently.' This, I think, was the most remarkable phenomenon he mentioned in the whole lecture, and gave *me* quite a new idea of those regions."

A favorite problem of his, with which he loved to pose people, was the determination of the starting point of day. If a man could travel around the world so fast that the sun would be always overhead, and if he started at midday on Tuesday, he would be home again in twenty-four hours and find that it was now Wednesday. But where did Wednesday begin? Another problem which he invented to puzzle his friends was this: if a rope is hung over a wheel fixed to the top of a roof and at one end a weight is fixed to counterbalance exactly the weight of a monkey on the other end of the rope, what happens when the monkey begins to climb the rope? Will the weight go up or down?

This Oxford lecturer published a number of volumes strictly on mathematical subjects. *An Elementary Treatise on Determinants* was issued in 1867. The next year he published a simplified edition *of Euclid Book V* and a number of years later *Euclid I and II*. *Curiosa Mathematica* and *Pillow Problems* were other contributions to scholarship. For our purpose, however, there are four books by this logician-mathematician which have especial interest in that they combine the student, the logician, and the satirist. These books are *Notes by an Oxford Chiel, Euclid and His Modern Rivals, A Tangled Tale,* and *The Game of Logic.*

Notes by an Oxford Chiel (1874), issued anonymously, is a collection of papers written during the nine years previous on Oxford matters. The separate articles had appeared singly and were at last collected for the edition of 1874. Among these papers we find a parody of "The Deserted Village" written on a proposal to convert certain parks into cricket-grounds. *The Vision of the Three T's* (1873) and *The New Belfry* (1872) both deal with architectural improvements in Christ Church which our writer thought particularly hideous. The last-named pamphlet went rapidly through five editions in Oxford. The first portion of this pamphlet will be sufficient to characterize it.

§ 1. *On the etymological significance of the new Belfry, Ch. Ch.* The word "Belfry" is derived from the French *bel,* "beautiful, becoming, meet," and from the German *frei*, "free, unfettered, secure, safe." Thus the word is strictly equivalent to "meatsafe," to which the new belfry bears a resemblance so perfect as almost to amount to coincidence.

In both of these papers he vigorously attacks everyone, even his friends, who had anything to do with the monstrosities which offend him. He is particularly savage with the architect in charge:

The head of the House, and the architect, feeling a natural wish that their names should be embodied, in some conspicuous way, among the alterations then in progress, conceived the beautiful and unique idea of representing, by means of the new Belfry, a gigantic copy of a Greek Lexicon. But, before the idea had been reduced to a working form, business took them both to London for a few days, and during their absence, somehow (*this* part of the business has never been satisfactorily explained) the whole thing was put into the hands of a wandering architect, who gave the name of Jeeby. As the poor man is now incarcerated at Hanwell, we will not be too hard upon his memory, but will only say that he professed to have originated the idea in a moment of inspiration, when idly contemplating one of those high coloured, and mysteriously decorated chests which, filled with dried leaves from gooseberry bushes and quickset hedges, profess to supply the market with tea of genuine Chinese growth. . . .[1]

The Vision of the Three T's is in form a parody of *The Compleat Angler*, but in matter is a further ridiculing of the "architectural improvements" that so greatly upset Carroll. In Chapter II Jeeby appears in wild garb, a lunatic, boasting of the three great achievements on the Quadrangle, which Carroll has immortalised as the Trench, The Tunnel, and the Tea-chest.

PISCATOR: And the design of that Tunnel is—
LUNATIC: Is mine, Sir! Oh, the fancy! Oh, the wit! Oh, the rich vein of humor! When came the idea? I' the mirk midnight. Whence came the idea? From a cheese-scoop! How came the idea? In a wild dream. Hearken, and I will tell. Form square, and prepare to receive a canonry! All the evening long I had seen lobsters marching around the table in un- broken order. Something sputtered in the candle—something hopped among the tea-things—something pulsated, with an ineffable yearning, beneath the enraptured hearthrug! My heart told me something was coming—and something came. A voice cried "Cheese-scoop!" and the Great Thought of my life flashed upon me! Placing an ancient Stilton cheese, to represent this venerable Quadrangle, on the chimney-piece, I retired to the further end of the room, armed only with a cheese-scoop, and with a dauntless courage awaited the word of command. Charge, Cheesetaster, charge! On, Stilton,

[1] *The New Belfry*, section 3.

on! With a yell and a bound I crossed the room, and plunged my scoop
into the very heart of the foe! Once more! Another yell—another bound—
another cavity scooped out! The deed was done! . . .

The reader will discover for himself all the delightful variations
Carroll could work out for the relief of his feelings. Certainly there
is evidence enough here of the sharp wit and the delightful railing
we associate with our satirist, but it is rather surprising to find even
in brief passages the sort of savagery which we associate with
Jonathan Swift.

On another occasion when the expending of certain funds for
improved accommodations for Physics was under discussion, our
lecturer in Mathematics wrote a letter putting forward certain
requirements for accommodations "for carrying on the calculations necessary in that important branch of science." The five most
pressing needs are for:

A. A very large room for calculating Greatest Common Measure. To this
a small room might be attached for Least Common Multiple; this, however,
might be dispensed with.

B. A piece of open ground for keeping Roots and practicing their extraction: it would be advisable to keep Square Roots by themselves, as their
corners are apt to damage others.

C. A room for reducing Fractions to their Lowest Terms. This should
be provided with a cellar for keeping the Lowest Terms when found. . . .

D. A large room, which might be darkened, and fitted up with a magic
lantern for the purpose of exhibiting Circulating decimals in the act of circulation. This might also contain cupboards, fitted with glass doors, for
keeping the various Scales of Notation.

E. A narrow strip of ground, railed off and carefully leveled, for investing
the properties of Asymptotes, and testing practically whether Parallel Lines
meet or not: for this purpose it should reach, to use the expressive language
of Euclid, "ever so far." . . .

One of the best of these papers is entitled "The Dynamics of a
Parti-cle." It is concerned with a much talked of Parliamentary
election at Oxford and is done up in mathematical style. The
political satire may be illustrated by this postulate: "That a controversy may be raised about any question, and at any distance
from that question"; or this definition: "PLAIN SUPERFICIAL-
ITY is the character of a speech, in which any two points being
taken, the speaker is found to lie wholly with regard to those two
points." The introduction to this paper is very definitely Carrollan:

It was a lovely Autumn evening, and the glorious effects of chromatic aberration were beginning to show themselves in the atmosphere as the earth revolved away from the great western luminary, when two lines might have been observed wending their weary way across a plain superficies. The elder of the two had by long practice acquired the art, so painful to young and impulsive loci, of lying evenly between her extreme points; but the younger, in her girlish impetuosity, was ever longing to diverge and become an hyperbola or some such romantic and boundless curve. They had lived and loved: fate and the intervening superficies had hitherto kept them asunder, but this was no longer to be: *a line had intersected them, making the two interior angles together less than two right angles.* It was a moment never to be forgotten, and, as they journeyed on, a whisper thrilled along the superficies in isochronous waves of sound, 'Yes! We shall at length meet if continually produced!' " (Jacobi's Course of Mathematics, Chap. I.)

We have commenced with the above quotation as a striking illustration of the advantage of introducing the human element into the hitherto barren region of mathematics. Who shall say what germs of romance, hitherto unobserved, may not underlie the subject? Who can tell whether the parallelogram, which in our ignorance we have defined and drawn, and the whole of whose properties we profess to know, may not be all the while panting for exterior angles, sympathetic with the interior, or sullenly repining at the fact that it cannot be inscribed in a circle? What mathematician has ever pondered over an hyperbola, mangling the unfortunate curve with lines of intersection here and there, in his effort to prove some property that perhaps after all is a mere calumny, who has not fancied at last that the ill-used locus was spreading out its asymptotes as a silent rebuke, or winking one focus at him in contemptuous pity? . . .

But I must go on to the next of these books. In *Euclid and His Modern Rivals* (1879?)—signed by Dodgson—the author again offers us a very definite instance of the doubling of the personalities. The book is a defense of Euclid against a host of modern books on geometry and is a serious advancement of this Oxford Don's idea on the subject—ideas, according to some mathematicians, which have value and show the acuteness of the author's mind. But he presents his material in a way which he thinks will most interest the greatest number of readers. I quote from the preface:

It is presented in a dramatic form, partly because it seemed a better way of exhibiting in alternation the arguments on the two sides of the question; partly that I might feel myself at liberty to treat it in a rather lighter style than would have suited an essay, and thus to make it a little less tedious and a little more acceptable to unscientific readers.

In one respect this book is an experiment, and may chance to prove a

failure: I mean that I have not thought it necessary to maintain throughout
the gravity of style which scientific writers usually affect, and which has
somehow come to be regarded as an "inseparable accident" of scientific
teaching. I never could quite see the reasonableness of this immemorial
law. . . . I have permitted myself a glimpse of the comic side of things only
at fitting seasons, when the tired reader might well crave a moment's breath-
ing space, and not on any occasion where it could endanger the continuity
of a line of argument.

Pitying friends have warned me of the fate upon which I am rushing. . . .
But it must be borne in mind that, if there is a Scylla before me, there is also
a Charybdis—and that, in my fear of being read as a jest, I may incur the
darker destiny of not being read at all. . . .

Two snatches will illustrate the assisting hand of Lewis Carroll.
This bit of logic is one:

> . . . So far as I can make it out, Mr. Cooley quietly assumes that a Pair of
> Lines, which make equal angles with *one* Line, do so with *all* Lines. He
> might just as well say that a young lady, who was inclined to *one* young man,
> was 'equally and similarly inclined' to *all* young men!

Again,—at the end of Act I, the ghost of Euclid, on making his farewell speech, looks about for the customary music for the exit of
ghosts but not finding it he "vanishes without slow music."

A Tangled Tale was published in 1885, signed by Lewis Carroll.
This is a book of "knots" in each of which is buried (L. C. says
"like the medicine so dexterously, but ineffectually, concealed in
the jam of our early childhood") one or more mathematical problems of various sorts. Each of the knots is a brief story, with the
participants of the series being either the same persons or people
related to them. In this fashion, the readers of the magazine in
which the knots appeared might obtain both edification and amusement. This gives a hint of Dodgson who was strong on edification,
it is quite representative of the middle logico-mathematical person-
age, and in method of writing it is the work of Lewis Carroll. A
few excerpts will illustrate this.

Hugh and Lambert, two brothers, rechristened their old tutor
Balbus.

> They had named him after the hero of their Latin exercise-book, which
> overflowed with anecdotes of that versatile genius—anecdotes whose vague-
> ness in detail was more than compensated by their sensational brilliance.
> "Balbus has overcome all his enemies" had been marked by their tutor, in the

margin of the book, "Successful Bravery." In this way he had tried to exact a moral from every anecdote about Balbus—sometimes one of warning, as in "Balbus had borrowed a healthy dragon," against which he had written "Rashness in Speculation"—sometimes of encouragement, as in the words "Influence of Sympathy in United Action," which stood opposite to the anecdote "Balbus was assisting his mother-in-law to convince the dragon"— and sometimes it dwindled down to a single word, such as "Prudence," which was all that he could extract from the touching record that "Balbus, having scorched the tail of the dragon, went away. . . ."

This gentle form of amusement with his own profession is touched on again and again. The three are looking for living quarters in town. They come to the Square for which they are searching and Balbus is overwhelmed.

"It is a Square!" was Balbus' first cry of delight, as he gazed around him. "Beautiful! Beau-ti-ful! Equilateral! *And* rectangular! . . . See, boys. . . . Twenty doors on a side! What symmetry! Each side divided into twenty-one equal parts! It's delicious!"

Mad Mathesis, who is Clara's aunt (and the aunt of the boys, her brothers), is a character such as we expect of Lewis Carroll.[1] She admits that she is queer, and, in explaining her name, says:

You see, I never do what sane people are expected to do now-a-days. I never wear long trains (talking of trains, that's the Charing Cross Metropolitan Station—I've something to tell you about *that*), and I never play lawn-tennis. I can't cook an omelette. I can't even set a broken limb! There's an ignoramus for you!

Mad Mathesis had her own ideas about the place of woman. "Let a woman be meek and lowly! None of your high Schools for me!" Clara, for her part, does a bit of reasoning at school:

. . . Our excellent preceptress always says 'When in doubt, my dears, take an extreme case. . . . One day she was telling the little girls—they make such a noise at tea, you know—"The more noise you make, the less jam you'll have, and *vice versa*." And I thought they wouldn't know what '*vice versa*' meant: so I explained it to them. I said 'If you make an infinite noise, you get no jam: and if you make no noise, you'll get an infinite lot of jam.' . . .

The fourth of these mid-personality books is *The Game of Logic* (signed Lewis Carroll—1886). This is an elementary book on logic and is arranged, for more satisfactory consumption, in the

[1] He found her, apparently, in Pope's *Dunciad*, IV, 31-34.

form of a game. That does not, however, prevent the author from advancing seriously enough his ideas of logic. I am not concerned here with the soundness of his disquisition on logic: it is simply my purpose to point out the combination of the method and the material. To illustrate that the style of the book is much that of Lewis Carroll, I quote one syllogism from the explanatory first chapter:

> All Dragons are uncanny;
> All Scotchmen are canny.
> ∴ All Dragons are not-Scotchmen
> All Scotchmen are not-Dragons.

Another typical bit of writing we find at the end of the first chapter, when the author speaks of Logicians who have "a nervous dread of beginning with a negative particle," and addresses the reader:

> ... Let us quietly take our broader system: and, if they choose to shut their eyes to all these useful forms, and to say "They are not Syllogisms at all!" we can but stand aside, and let them Rush upon their Fate! There is scarcely anything of yours, upon which it is so dangerous to Rush, as your Fate. You may Rush upon your Potato-beds or your Strawberry beds, without doing much harm: you may even rush upon your Balcony (unless it is a new house, built by contract, and with no clerk of the works) and may survive the fool-hardy enterprise: but if you once Rush upon your *Fate*—why, you must take the consequences!

Thus we see that even when he wrote upon such subjects as mathematics and logic, he still called in Lewis Carroll.

We have, then, something like three personalities established, two at apparent extremes connected quite satisfactorily by the third. It is not, of course, to be held that each of these divisions is often distinct and separate. In the sermons and the serious poetry we find unmixed Dodgson, in the *Alice* books and the *Snark* we discover almost no Dodgson but a great deal of the other two. In the volume entitled *Rhyme? and Reason?* we see all three represented. And in the two-volume work, which is almost his last, the *Sylvie and Bruno* books, we have all three definitely interwoven—a final and most excellent example of the three-part character of this person. Since the two books are comparatively unknown, I shall enter into some detail in discussing them.

In 1867 Lewis Carroll contributed to *Aunt Judy's Magazine* a fairy tale entitled "Bruno's Revenge." In 1873 the idea occurred to him that he might make this the nucleus of a new book. From that time on he jotted down in his notebooks every notion that came into his head. By 1885 he had accumulated a sufficient mass and he determined to put it into a form which would be as original in its way as *Alice* had previously been in hers. The result is perhaps the strangest medley, the most fantastic book ever printed as fiction. This "huge unwieldy mass of litterature," as he calls it, he found "only needed stringing together upon the thread of a consecutive story, to constitute the book I hoped to write. Only!" After ten years of classification and struggle he had evolved first *Sylvie and Bruno* in 1889 and then *Sylvie and Bruno Concluded* (1893) to use up the remaining part of the material and to complete the story.

What was this story? Well, there were several of them twisted up together. First, there is a novel concerned with the life of a very noble young doctor who is greatly in love with the daughter of an Earl. She gives him no hope; in fact, she becomes engaged to her soldier-cousin. It turns out, however, that these two differ on some point of church doctrine, and their engagement is off. After a time, the girl recognizes the true nobility of soul of the Doctor and they are married. But (the worst is yet to come) on their wedding day an epidemic breaks out in the village and the Doctor, of course, kisses his new-wed love and leaves her, though the chances are he will not return. He doesn't—at least, not until all the agonies of death are gone through for everyone. At last it turns out that the doctor was not really buried, but had been carried off unconscious and nursed back to life. So all ends happily. I am afraid that the novel itself is actually worse than this sketch may convey. I will add that it is a religious novel; the whole thing is full of lessons. One cannot turn without having some moral pointed out or some religious truism offered. This obviously is the work of Dodgson,—of a Dodgson powerful enough to lay a most emphatic hand upon work that is not all his.

In addition there is the fairy tale. This is really in and of two parts. The sticky sweetness of Bruno's talk and the sweet virtuous-

ness of Sylvie—all the story of their relations with each other and
with the people of the real world—this too is Dodgson.

But then there is the other and, I think, main part of the fairy
tale: the political drama of Outland. Theoretically, this is the
story of the children; actually, they serve as binder for the narrative
but little more. The machinery is that common in folk-story: the
good but naively simple old man who, wandering away, leaves his
children in the care of his brother and the latter's wife. These two
are, of course, villainous and would do the children out of their
rightful inheritance, in favor of their own darling, who, in contrast
to the others, is ugly and stupid. In Carroll's hands this becomes
a drama of conspiracy and revolution. Sibimet, a leaner and hun-
grier villain than usual, plans to seize the control of, and have
himself made Emperor over Outland during the absence of his
brother, the Warden. A man of less than no conscience, he is
personally capable of engineering his own revolutions, if any. However, since he is endowed with some sharpness of mind, he knows
how much better it is to have some stupider person obviously direct
the upheaval and for this enviable position he has picked the
Chancellor, who through his pompous assurance and his thick-
wittedness is well qualified, if need be, to hold the bag. Though
the Chancellor is rather a mismanager than otherwise, the affair
comes off well enough. There are, to be sure, a few little hitches:
the mob does persist for a while in shouting "less bread! more
taxes!" until it is re-instructed. When the Warden protests that
he has instructed the Government bakery to sell bread at cost, he
is informed by the able chancellor that by the Warden's own
orders the bakery has been closed; and when the Warden insists
that he has personally abolished the last of the taxes a month
previously, removing the last possible cause of unrest, the Chancellor replies that again by the Warden's own order (through his
brother and by his signature) the taxes were replaced.

The Chancellor informs the Warden that the "seedling" discontent of the people is approaching the dimensions of a revolution (though, when the Warden asks humorously just what are
the dimensions of a revolution, the Chancellor is at a loss for an
answer) and suggests that they will probably be appeased by a

government measure abolishing the Sub-Wardenship and sub-
stituting for it the office of Vice-Warden, the said Sibimet in such
capacity to exercise the full powers of the Warden in the latter's
absence. To this the most naïve Warden consents. Later, the
Chancellor presents for his signature the papers of the new edict,
which our wily plotter, under the guise of making corrections,
has covered with blotting paper so that only the place for signa-
tures is to be seen. The Warden departs and we discover what
dastardly deeds have been transpiring before our very eyes. The
most astounding clause is one providing for the election of an
Emperor. So the subtle intrigue progresses.

It will, of course, be necessary to spread a rumor of the Warden's death (for, naturally, he is very popular with the people)
before trying to hold the election. This involves more conspiracy, than which nothing could more delight my Lady Tabitha,
the Vice-Wardenness. With all her heart and soul she enters into
the affair.

... She had got one of the cupboards open, and stood with her back to him,
smoothing down a sheet of brown paper on one of the shelves, and whispering to herself "So, so! Deftly done! Craftily contrived!"

Her loving husband stole behind her on tiptoe ... and playfully shouted
in her ear. ...

My Lady wrung her hands. "Discovered!" she groaned, "yet no—he is
one of us! Reveal it not, oh Man! Let it bide its time!"

"Reveal what not?" her husband testily replied, dragging out the sheet of
brown paper. "What are you hiding here, my Lady? I insist upon knowing!"

My Lady cast down her eyes, and spoke in the littlest of little voices.
"Don't make fun of it, Benjamin!" she pleaded. "It's—it's—don't you understand? It's a DAGGER!"

"And what's that for?" sneered His Excellency. "We've only got to make
people think he's dead. We haven't got to kill him. And made of tin, too!"
he snarled, contemptuously bending the blade round his thumb. "Now,
Madam, you'll be be good enough to explain. First, what do you call me
Benjamin for?"

"It's part of the Conspiracy, Love! One must have an alias, you know—"

"Oh, an alias, is it? Well! And next, what did you get this dagger for?
Come, no evasions! You ca'n't deceive me!"

"I got it for—for—for—" the detected Conspirator—stammered, trying her
best to put on the assassin-expression that she had been practicing at the
looking-glass. "For—"

"For what, Madam!"

"Well, for eighteenpence, if you must know, dearest! That's what I got
it for, on my—"

"Now don't say your Word and Honour!" groaned the other Conspirator.
"Why they aren't worth half the money, put together!"

"On my birthday," my Lady concluded in a meek whisper. "One must
have a dagger, you know. It's part of the—"

"Oh, don't talk of Conspiracies!" her husband savagely interrupted, as he
tossed the dagger into the cupboard. "You know about as much how to
manage a Conspiracy as if you were a chicken. Why, the first thing is to get
a disguise. Now, just look at this!"

And with pardonable pride he fitted on the cap and bells, and the rest
of the Fool's dress, and winked at her, and put his tongue in his cheek. "Is
that the sort of thing, now?" he demanded.

My Lady's eyes flashed with all a Conspirator's enthusiasm. "The very
thing!" she exclaimed, clapping her hands. "You do look, oh, such a perfect
Fool!"

The Fool smiled a doubtful smile. He was not quite clear whether it was
a compliment or not, to express it so plainly. "You mean a Jester? Yes, that's
what I intended. And what do you think your disguise is to be?" And he
proceeded to unfold the parcel, the lady watching him in rapture.

"Oh, how lovely!" she cried, when at last the dress was unfolded. "What
a splendid disguise! An Esquimaux peasant-woman!"

"An Esquimaux peasant, indeed!" growled the other. "Here, put it on,
and look at yourself in the glass. Why, it's a Bear, ca'n't you use your
eyes?" . . . .

Eventually the death of the Warden is accepted (the rumour
has been spread by a mysteriously appearing and disappearing
Jester who wandered about with a bear) and Sibimet is elected
Emperor. It is to consolidate his position with the people that
the Emperor puts into effect the famous Money Act that he in-
duced the Court Professor to work out for him (incidentally
arranging so that any blame will fall upon the Professor) whereby
everyone is made twice as rich as he had been by the simple device
of doubling the value of each banknote and coin in the realm.
The Emperor then gives a magnificent banquet and entertainment,
which had long been planned, to celebrate his new greatness. It is
truly a marvelous affair. Suddenly, in the midst of the festivities,
the elder brother appears and the guilty one is heartstricken. However, all is well. The Warden, now King of Fairyland, has a better
Kingdom, and gladly forgives his brother and confirms him as
Emperor of Outland.

Though the contrition of the evil brother is quite unbelievable and is evidently the work of Dodgson, the engineering of the whole wild political extravaganza is always Carroll and often Carroll of the very best grade. It is not possible here to go into proper detail pointing out all the typical Carrollan touches with which this work abounds, for there is much of it in spite of the heavy and frequently felt hand of Dodgson. But I must be forgiven if I quote one more passage out of this drama, a bit of pure farce:

"What's all this noise about?" the Vice-Warden angrily enquired, as he strode into the room. "And who put the hatstand here?" And he hung his hat up on Bruno, who was standing in the middle of the room. . . .
The Professor mildly explained that His Highness [Uggug] had been graciously pleased to say that he wouldn't do his lessons.
"Do your lessons this instant, you young cub!" thundered the Vice-Warden. "And take *this!*" and a resounding box on the ear made the unfortunate Professor reel across the room.
"Save me!" faltered the poor old man, as he sank half-fainting at my Lady's feet.
"Shave you? Of course, I will!" my Lady replied, as she lifted him into a chair, and pinned an anti-macassar around his neck. "Where's the razor?"
The Vice-Warden meanwhile had got hold of Uggug, and was belabouring him with an umbrella. "Who left this loose nail in the floor?" he shouted. "Hammer it in, I say! Hammer it in!" Blow after blow fell upon the writhing Uggug, till he dropped howling to the floor.
Then his father turned to the "shaving" scene which was being enacted, and roared with laughter. "Excuse me, dear, I can't help it," he said as soon as he could speak, "you *are* such an utter donkey! Kiss me, Tabby!"
And he flung his arms around the neck of the terrified Professor, who raised a wild shriek. . . .

The characters are most of them fine examples of Carrollan workmanship: the mad Gardener, who is a combination of the wise fool, the faithful retainer, and the mysterious and philosophic lunatic of the old drama and old fiction (for Carroll is really satirising many old dramatic and fictional conventions as well as political ones). Though his songs are cut to the same pattern, each time he appears he has a different one.

> He thought he saw an Elephant,
> That practised on the fife:
> He looked again and saw it was

A letter from his wife.
"At length I realize," he said,
"The bitterness of Life."

He is one of Carroll's most perfect creations. But there are many
more amusing characters chief among whom are the two Professors
and Mein Herr (some of whose ideas on education and politics
are given in this book). Carroll enjoyed satirising his own profession as much as anything else. If we want examples of the logico-
mathematical middle-self we can find it where we will look: the
gardener waters the flowers with an empty sprinkling-can. Why?
Because "it's lighter to hold. A lot of water in it makes one's arms
ache." The Professor is the inventor of that marvelous portable
bath of which the reader may find a report in this book. The
Professor has discovered how to meet creditors. The Professor
has invented a machine for carrying oneself: "whatever fatigue
one incurs by *carrying*, one saves by being *carried*." Well? The
Other Professor, too, is a great scholar: while he is discussing
with the Professor the coming Banquet and Lecture, he occupies
himself "in taking the books out, one by one, and turning them
upside-down. An easel, with a blackboard on it, stood near him:
and, every time he turned a book upside-down, he made a mark
on the board with a piece of chalk." His only remark to Sylvie,
his dinner companion, throughout the course of the famous Banquet is this: "What a comfort a Dictionary is!" And then there
is his delightful "Pig-Tale" with its especially fine introductory
verses that have nothing to do with the narrative thread of that
poem and which not only introduce it but also reappear in the
middle and again at the end.

Little Birds are teaching
    Tigresses to smile,
    Innocent of guile:
Smile, I say, not smirkle—
Mouth a semicircle,
    That's the proper style!
        *   *   *   *   *
Little Birds are writing
    Interesting books,
    To be read by cooks:

Read, I say, not roasted—
Letterpress, when toasted,
Loses its good looks.

* * * * *

Little Birds are bathing
Crocodiles with cream,
Like a happy dream:
Like, but not so lasting—
Crocodiles, when fasting,
Are not all they seem!

Each man in his time plays many parts. Dodgson is a religious person, a recluse; Carroll is an observer, a satirist; with them is an Oxford Don, a mathematical Lecturer who delights in logic. Each one we can see, and we can see that each one is bound to the others. This is the fascinating person usually called Lewis Carroll.

JOHN FRANCIS MCDERMOTT.

EARLY PIECES
chiefly from
The Rectory Umbrella
and
Misch-Masch

DIFFICULTIES [1]

NO. I

Half of the world, or nearly so, is always in the light of the sun: as the world turns round, this hemisphere of light shifts round too, and passes over each part of it in succession.

Supposing on Tuesday, it is morning at London; in another hour it would be Tuesday morning at the west of England; if the whole world were land we might go on tracing [2] Tuesday morning, Tuesday morning all the way round, till in 24 hours we get to London again. But we *know* that at London 24 hours after Tuesday morning it is Wednesday morning. Where then, in its passage round the earth, does the day change its name? where does it lose its identity?

Practically there is no difficulty in it, because a great part of its journey is over water, and what it does out at sea no one can tell: and besides there are so many different languages that it would be hopeless to attempt to trace the name of any one day all round. But it is the case inconceivable that the same land and the same language should continue all round the world? I cannot see that it is: in that case either [3] there would be no distinction at all between each successive day, and so week, month, &c., so that we should have to say, "The Battle of Waterloo happened to-day, about two million hours ago," or some line would have to be fixed, where the change should take place, so that the inhabitant of one house would wake and say "Heigh-ho,[4] Tuesday morning!" and the inhabitant of the next (over the line), a few miles to the west would wake a few minutes afterwards and say "Heigh-ho! Wednesday morning!" What hopeless confusion the people who happened

---

[1] From *The Rectory Umbrella.—McD.*

[2] The best way is to imagine yourself walking round with the sun and asking the inhabitants as you go "What morning is this?" If you suppose them living all the way round and all speaking one language, the difficulty is obvious.

[3] This is clearly an impossible case, and is only put as an hypothesis.

[4] The usual exclamation at waking; generally said with a yawn.

41

to live *on* the line would always be in, it is not for me to say. There would be a quarrel every morning as to what the name of the day should be. I can imagine no third case, unless everybody was allowed to choose for themselves, which state of things would be rather worse than either of the other two.

I am aware that this idea has been started before, namely, by the unknown author of that beautiful poem beginning "If all the world were apple pie, &c." [5] The particular result here discussed, however, does not appear to have occurred to him, as he confines himself to the difficulties in obtaining drink which would certainly ensue.

Any good solution of the above difficulty will be thankfully received and inserted.

[5] If all the world were apple pie,
And all the sea were ink,
And all the trees were bread and cheese,
What *should* we have to drink?

DIFFICULTIES [6]

Which is the best, a clock that is right only once a year, or a clock that is right twice every day? "The latter," you reply, "unquestionably." Very good, reader, now attend.

I have two clocks: one doesn't go *at all*, and the other loses a minute a day: which would you prefer? "The losing one," you answer, "without a doubt." Now observe: the one which loses a minute a day has to lose twelve hours, or seven hundred and twenty minutes before it is right again, consequently it is only right once in two years, whereas the other is evidently right as often as the time it points to comes round, which happens twice a day. So you've contradicted yourself *once*. "Ah, but," you say, "what's the use of its being right twice a day, if I can't tell when the time comes?" Why, suppose the clock points to eight o'clock, don't you see that the clock is right *at* eight o'clock? Consequently when eight o'clock comes your clock is right. "Yes, I see *that*," you reply.[7] Very good, then you've contradicted yourself *twice*: Now get out of the difficulty as you can, and don't contradict yourself again if you can help it.

[6] From *The Rectory Umbrella.*—McD.
[7] You *might* go on to ask, "How am I to know when eight o'clock *does* come? My clock will not tell me." Be patient, reader: you know that when eight o'clock comes your clock is right; very good; then your rule is this: keep your eye fixed on your clock, and *the very moment it is right* it will be eight o'clock. "But—" you say. There, that'll do, reader; the more you argue the farther you get from the point, so it will be as well to stop.

PREFACE

[to *Misch-Masch*]

"Yet once more" (to use the time-honoured words of our poet Milton) we present ourselves before an eager and expectant public, let us hope under even better auspices than hitherto.

In making our bow for the—may we venture to say so?—fourth time, it will be worth while to review the past, and to consider the probable future. We are encouraged to do so by Mrs. Malaprop's advice: "Let us not anticipate the past; let all our retrospections be to the future," and by the fact that our family motto is "*Respiciendo prudens.*"

We purpose then to give a brief history of our former domestic magazines in this family, their origin, aim, progress, and ultimate fate, and we shall notice, as we go on, the other magazines which have appeared, but not under our own editorship. We commence our history, then, with

Useful and Instructive Poetry

This we wrote ourselves about the year 1845, the idea of the first poem being suggested by a piece in the "Etonian": it lasted about half a year, and was then very clumsily bound up in a sort of volume: the binding, however, was in every respect worthy of the contents: the volume still exists.

The Rectory Magazine

This was the first started for general contribution, and at first the contributions poured in in one continuous stream, while the issuing of each number was attended by the most violent excitement through the whole house: most of the family contributed one or more articles to it. About the year 1848 the numbers were bound into a volume, which still exists.

The Comet

This was started by us about the year 1848. It was the same shape as the former, but, for the sake of variety, opened at the

44

end instead of the side. Little interest attended this publication, and its contents were so poor, that, after 6 numbers were out, we destroyed all but the last, and published no more. The last number, we believe, is still in existence.

The Rosebud

This was started in imitation of the Comet, but only reached a second number: the cover of each number was tastefully ornamented with a painted rosebud: the two numbers do not contain much worth notice, but are still preserved.

The Star

Another imitator of the Comet, on a less ambitious scale even than the last: the manuscript and illustrations decidedly below par: some half-dozen numbers still survive.

The Will-o-the-Wisp

Even inferior to the last: the numbers were cut in a triangular shape: we believe some numbers are still to be found.

The Rectory Umbrella

This we started, we believe, in 1849 or 1850, in a ready bound square volume. It was admired at the time, but wholly unsupported, and it took us a year or more to fill the volume by our own unaided efforts. The volume exists, and in good preservation, and therefore any further account of it is needless.

We will here notice one or two of our own writings, which have seen more extended publicity than the above mentioned. In the summer of 1854 we contributed two poems to the "Oxonian Advertiser," neither at all worth preservation; and in the Long Vacation of the same year, when staying with a reading party at Whitby, we contributed "The Lady of the Ladle" and "Wilhelm von Schmitz," to the weekly Gazette of that place. Both will be found inserted in this volume. From this subject we hasten to the consideration of the present magazine.

Misch-Masch

The name is German, and means in English "midge-madge," which we need not inform the intelligent reader is equivalent to "hodge-podge": our intention is to admit articles of every kind, prose, verse, and pictures, provided they reach a sufficiently high standard of merit.

The best of its contents will be offered at intervals to a contemporary magazine of a less exclusively domestic nature: we allude to the Comic Times; thus affording to the contributors to this magazine an opportunity of presenting their productions to the admiring gaze of the English Nation.

Croft, Aug. 13, 1855.

PHOTOGRAPHY EXTRAORDINARY [8]

The recent extraordinary discovery in Photography, as applied to the operations of the mind, has reduced the art of novel-writing to the merest mechanical labour. We have been kindly permitted by the artist to be present during one of his experiments; but as the invention has not yet been given to the world, we are only at liberty to relate the results, suppressing all details of chemicals and manipulation.

The operator began by stating that the ideas of the feeblest intellect, when once received on properly prepared paper, could be "developed" up to any required degree of intensity. On hearing our wish that he would begin with an extreme case, he obligingly summoned a young man from an adjoining room, who appeared to be of the very weakest possible physical and mental powers. On being asked what we thought of him, we candidly confessed that he seemed incapable of anything but sleep; our friend cordially assented to this opinion.

The machine being in position, and a mesmeric rapport established between the mind of the patient and the object glass, the young man was asked whether he wished to say anything; he feebly replied "Nothing." He was then asked what he was thinking of, and the answer, as before, was "Nothing." The artist on this pronounced him to be in a most satisfactory state, and at once commenced the operation.

After the paper had been exposed for the requisite time, it was removed and submitted to our inspection; we found it to be covered with faint and almost illegible characters. A closer scrutiny revealed the following:—

"The eve was soft and dewy mild; a zephyr whispered in the lofty glade, and a few light drops of rain cooled the thirsty soil. At a slow amble, along the primrose-bordered path rode a gentle-looking and amiable youth, holding a light cane in his delicate

8 From *Misch-Masch.—McD.*

47

hand; the pony moved gracefully beneath him, inhaling as it went the fragrance of the roadside flowers: the calm smile, the languid eyes, so admirably harmonising with the fair features of the rider, showed the even tenor of his thoughts. With a sweet though feeble voice, he plaintively murmured out the gentle regrets that clouded his breast:—

> 'Alas! she would not hear my prayer!
> Yet it were rash to tear my hair;
> Disfigured, I should be less fair.
>
> 'She was unwise, I may say blind;
> Once she was lovingly inclined;
> Some circumstance has changed her mind.'

There was a moment's silence; the pony stumbled over a stone in the path, and unseated his rider. A crash was heard among the dried leaves; the youth arose; a slight bruise on his left shoulder, and a disarrangement of his cravat, were the only traces that remained of this trifling accident."

"This," we remarked, as we returned the papers, "belongs apparently to the milk-and-water School of Novels."

"You are quite right," our friend replied, "and, in its present state, it is of course utterly unsaleable in the present day: we shall find, however, that the next stage of development will remove it into the strong-minded or Matter-of-Fact School." After dipping it into various acids, he again submitted it to us: it had now become the following:—

"The evening was of the ordinary character, barometer at 'change': a wind was getting up in the wood, and some rain was beginning to fall; a bad look-out for the farmers. A gentleman approached along the bridle-road, carrying a stout knobbed stick in his hand, and mounted on a serviceable nag, possibly worth some £ 40 or so; there was a settled business-like expression on the rider's face, and he whistled as he rode; he seemed to be hunting for rhymes in his head, and at length repeated, in a satisfied tone, the following composition:—

> 'Well! so my offer was no go!
> She might do worse, I told her so;
> She was a fool to answer 'No.'

'However, things are as they stood;
Nor would I have her if I could,
For there are plenty more as good.'

At this moment the horse set his foot in a hole, and rolled over; his rider rose with difficulty; he had sustained several severe bruises and fractured two ribs; it was some time before he forgot that unlucky day."

We returned this with the strongest expression of admiration, and requested that it might now be developed to the highest possible degree. Our friend readily consented, and shortly presented us with the result, which he informed us belonged to the Spasmodic or German School. We perused it with indescribable sensations of surprise and delight:—

"The night was wildly tempestuous—a hurricane raved through the murky forest—furious torrents of rain lashed the groaning earth. With a headlong rush—down a precipitous mountain gorge— dashed a mounted horseman armed to the teeth—his horse bounded beneath him at a mad gallop, snorting fire from its distended nostrils as it flew. The rider's knotted brows—rolling eye-balls—and clenched teeth—expressed the intense agony of his mind—weird visions loomed upon his burning brain—while with a mad yell he poured forth the torrent of his boiling passion:—

'Firebrands and daggers! hope hath fled!
To atoms dash the doubly dead!
My brain is fire—my heart is lead!

'Her soul is flint, and what am I?
Scorch'd by her fierce, relentless eye,
Nothingness is my destiny!'

There was a moment's pause. Horror! his path ended in a fathomless abyss. . . . A rush—a flash—a crash—all was over. Three drops of blood, two teeth, and a stirrup were all that remained to tell where the wild horseman met his doom."

The young man was now recalled to consciousness, and shown the result of the workings of his mind; he instantly fainted away.

In the present infancy of the art we forbear from further

comment on this wonderful discovery; but the mind reels as it contemplates the stupendous addition thus made to the powers of science.

Our friend concluded with various minor experiments, such as working up a passage of Wordsworth into strong, sterling poetry: the same experiment was tried on a passage of Byron, at our request, but the paper came out scorched and blistered all over by the fiery epithets thus produced.

As a concluding remark: *could* this art be applied (we put the question in the strictest confidence)—*could* it, we ask, be applied to the speeches in Parliament? It may be but a delusion of our heated imagination, but we will still cling fondly to the idea, and hope against hope.

HINTS FOR ETIQUETTE: OR, DINING OUT MADE EASY [9]

As caterers for the public taste, we can conscientiously recommend this book to all diners-out who are perfectly unacquainted with the usages of society. However we may regret that our author has confined himself to warning rather than advice, we are bound in justice to say that nothing here stated will be found to contradict the habits of the best circles. The following examples exhibit a depth of penetration and a fulness of experience rarely met with.

V

In proceeding to the dining-room, the gentleman gives one arm to the lady he escorts—it is unusual to offer both.

VIII

The practice of taking soup with the next gentleman but one is now wisely discontinued; but the custom of asking your host his opinion of the weather immediately on the removal of the first course still prevails.

IX

To use a fork with your soup, intimating at the same time to your hostess that you are reserving the spoon for the beefsteaks, is a practice wholly exploded.

XI

On meat being placed before you, there is no possible objection to your eating it, if so disposed; still in all such delicate cases, be guided entirely by the conduct of those around you.

XII

It is always allowable to ask for artichoke jelly with your boiled venison; however there are houses where this is not supplied.

XIII

The method of helping roast turkey with two carving-forks is practicable, but deficient in grace.

[9] From *Misch-Masch.—McD.*

XVII

We do not recommend the practice of eating cheese with a knife and fork in one hand, and a spoon and wine-glass in the other; there is a kind of awkwardness in the action which no amount of practice can entirely dispel.

XXVI

As a general rule, do not kick the shins of the opposite gentleman under the table, if personally unacquainted with him; your pleasantry is liable to be misunderstood—a circumstance at all times unpleasant.

XXVII

Proposing the health of the boy in buttons immediately on the removal of the cloth, is a custom springing from regard to his tender years, rather than from a strict adherence to the rules of etiquette.

STANZA OF ANGLO-SAXON POETRY [10]

```
TWAS BRYLLYG, AND ye SLYTHY COVES
DID GYRE AND GYMBLE IN ye WABE:
ALL MIMSY WERE ye BOROGOVES;
AND ye MOME RATHS OUTGRABE.
```

This curious fragment reads thus in modern characters

> TWAS BRYLLYG, AND THE SLYTHY TOVES
> DID GYRE AND GYMBLE IN THE WABE'
> ALL MIMSY WERE THE BOROGOVES;
> AND THE MOME RATHS OUTGRABE.

The meanings of the words are as follows:

BRYLLYG. (derived from the verb to BRYL or BROIL). "the time of broiling dinner, i.e., the close of the afternoon."

SLYTHY. (compounded of SLIMY and LITHE). "smooth and active."

TOVE. a species of Badger. They had smooth white hair, long hind legs, and short horns like a stag. Lived chiefly in cheese.

GYRE. verb (derived from GYAOUR or GIAOUR, "a dog.") "to scratch like a dog."

GYMBLE. (whence GIMBLET) to screw out holes in anything.

WABE. (derived from the verb to SWAB or SOAK) "the side of hill." (from its being *soaked* by the rain)

MIMSY. (whence MIMSERABLE AND MISERABLE) "unhappy"

BOROGOVE. An extinct kind of Parrot. They had no wings, beaks turned up, and made their nests under sun-dials, lived on veal.

MOME. (hence SOLEMOME, SOLEMONE and SOLEMN). "grave"

RATH. A species of land turtle. Head erect, mouth like a shark, the fore legs curved out so that the animal walked on its knees, smooth green body, lived on swallows and oysters.

[10] From *Misch-Masch.—McD.*

OUTGRABE. past tense of the verb to OUTGRIBE. (it is connected with the old verb to GRIKE or SHRIKE, from which are derived "shriek" and "creak.") "squeaked."

Hence the literal English of the passage is
"It was evening, and the smooth active badgers were scratching and boring holes in the hill side' all unhappy were the parrots, and the grave turtles squeaked out."

There were probably sun dials on the top of the hill, and the "borogoves" were afraid that their nests would be undermined. The hill was probably full of the nests of "raths," which ran out squeaking with fear, on hearing the "toves" scratching outside. This is an obscure, but yet deeply affecting, relic of ancient Poetry.

Croft, 1855   Ed [11]

[11] The stanza quoted, of course,· Lewis Carroll later developed into the "Jabberwocky" ballad of *Through the Looking-Glass*. It is interesting to compare the explanations given here with those of Humpty-Dumpty published sixteen years later. (See Chapter VI of *Through the Looking-Glass* or Appendix B of the *Collected Verse of Lewis Carroll*.) —McD.

NOVELTY AND ROMANCEMENT [12]

A Broken Spell

I had grave doubts at first whether to call this passage of my life "A Wail," or "A Paean," so much does it contain that is great and glorious, so much that is sombre and stern. Seeking for something which should be a sort of medium between the two, I decided, at last, on the above heading—wrongly, of course; I am always wrong: but let me be calm. It is a characteristic of the true orator never to yield to a burst of passion at the outset; the mildest of commonplaces are all he dare indulge in at first, and thence he mounts gradually;—*"vires acquirit eundo."* Suffice it, then, to say, in the first place, that *I am Leopold Edgar Stubbs.* I state this fact distinctly in commencing, to prevent all chance of the reader's confounding me either with the eminent shoemaker of that name, of Pottle-street, Camberwell, or with my less reputable, but more widely known, namesake, Stubbs, the light comedian, of the Provinces; both which connexions I repel with horror and disdain: no offence, however, being intended to either of the individuals named—men whom I have never seen, whom I hope I never shall.

So much for commonplaces.

Tell me now, oh! man, wise in interpretation of dreams and omens, how it chanced that, on a Friday afternoon, turning suddenly out of Great Wattles-street, I should come into sudden and disagreeable collision with an humble individual of unprepossessing exterior, but with an eye that glowed with all the fire of genius? I had dreamed at night that the great idea of my life was to be fulfilled. What was the great idea of my life? I will tell you. With shame and sorrow I will tell you.

My thirst and passion from boyhood (predominating over the love of taws and running neck and neck with my appetite for toffy) has been for poetry—for poetry in its widest and wildest sense—for poetry untrammelled by the laws of sense, rhyme, or

[12] First published in *The Train* for October, 1856.—*McD.*

rhythm, soaring through the universe, and echoing the music of the spheres! From my youth, nay, from my very cradle, I have yearned for poetry, for beauty, for novelty, for romancement. When I say "yearned," I employ a word mildly expressive of what may be considered as an outline of my feelings in my calmer moments: it is about as capable of picturing the headlong impetuosity of my life-long enthusiasm as those unanatomical paintings which adorn the outside of the Adelphi, representing Flexmore in one of the many conceivable attitudes into which the human frame has never yet been reduced, are of conveying to the spectaculative pit-goer a true idea of the feats performed by that extraordinary compound of humanity and Indian-rubber.

I have wandered from the point: that is a peculiarity, if I may be permitted to say so, incidental to life; and, as I remarked on an occasion which time will not suffer me more fully to specify, "what, after all, *is* life?" nor did I find any one of the individuals present (we were a party of nine, including the waiter, and it was while the soup was being removed that the above-recorded observation was made) capable of furnishing me with a rational answer to the question.

The verses which I wrote at an early period of life were eminently distinguished by a perfect freedom from conventionalism, and were thus unsuited to the present exactions of literature: in a future age they will be read and admired, "when Milton," as my venerable uncle has frequently exclaimed, "when Milton and such like are forgot!" Had it not been for this sympathetic relative, I firmly believe that the poetry of my nature would never had come out; I can still recall the feelings which thrilled me when he offered me sixpence for a rhyme to "despotism." I never succeeded, it is true, in finding the rhyme, but it was on this very next Wednesday that I penned my well known "Sonnet on a Dead Kitten," and in the course of a fortnight had commenced three epics, the titles of which I have unfortunately now forgotten.

Seven volumes of poetry have I given to an ungrateful world during my life; they have all shared the fate of true genius—obscurity and contempt. Not that any fault could be found with their contents; whatever their deficiencies may have been, *no reviewer has yet dared to criticize them.* This is a great fact.

The only composition of mine which has yet made any noise in the world, was a sonnet I addressed to one of the Corporation of Muggleton-cum-Swillside, on the occasion of his being selected Mayor of that town. It was largely circulated through private hands, and much talked of at the time; and though the subject of it, with characteristic vulgarity of mind, failed to appreciate the delicate compliments it involved, and indeed spoke of it rather disrespectfully than otherwise, I am inclined to think that it possesses all the elements of greatness. The concluding couplet was added at the suggestion of a friend, who assured me it was necessary to complete the sense, and in this point I deferred to his maturer judgment:—

> "When Desolation snatched her tearful prey
> From the lorn empire of despairing day;
> When all the light, by gemless fancy thrown,
> Served but to animate the putrid stone;
> When monarchs, lessening on the wildered sight,
> Crumblingly vanished into utter night;
> When murder stalked with thirstier strides abroad,
> And redly flashed the never-sated sword;
> In such an hour thy greatness had been seen—
> That is, if such an hour had ever been—
> In such an hour thy praises shall be sung,
> If not by mine, by many a worthier tongue;
> And thou be gazed upon by wondering men,
> When such an hour arrives, but not till then!"

Alfred Tennyson is Poet Laureate, and it is not for me to dispute his claim to that eminent position; still I cannot help thinking, that if the Government had only come forward candidly at the time, and thrown the thing open to general competition, proposing some subject to test the powers of the candidate ("say Frampton's Pill of Health, an Acrostic"), a very different result might have been arrived at.

But let us return to our muttons (as our noble allies do most unromantically express themselves), and to the mechanic of Great Wattles-street. He was coming out of a small shop—rudely built it was, dilapidated exceedingly, and in its general appearance seedy—what did I see in all this to inspire a belief that a great epoch in my existence had arrived? Reader, I saw the signboard!

Yes. Upon that rusty signboard, creaking awkwardly on its one hinge against the mouldering wall, was an inscription which thrilled me from head to foot with unwonted excitement. "Simon Lubkin. Dealer in Romancement." Those were the very words.

It was Friday, the fourth of June, half-past four p.m.

Three times I read that inscription through, and then took out my pocketbook, and copied it on the spot; the mechanic regarding me during the whole proceeding with a stare of serious and (as I thought at the time) respectful astonishment.

I stopped that mechanic, and entered into conversation with him; years of agony since then have gradually branded that scene upon my writhing heart, and I can repeat all that passed, word for word.

Did the mechanic (this was my first question) possess a kindred soul, or did he not?

Mechanic didn't know as he did.

Was he aware (this with thrilling emphasis) of the meaning of that glorious inscription upon his signboard?

Bless you, mechanic knew all about that 'ere.

Would mechanic (overlooking the suddenness of the invitation) object to adjourn to the neighbouring public-house, and there discuss the point more at leisure?

Mechanic would *not* object to a drain. On the contrary.

(Adjournment accordingly: brandy-and-water for two: conversation resumed.)

Did the article sell well, especially with the "*mobile* vulgus"?

Mechanic cast a look of good-natured pity on the questioner; the article sold well, he said and the vulgars bought it most.

Why not add "Novelty" to the inscription? (This was a critical moment: I trembled as I asked the question.)

Not so bad an idea, mechanic thought: time was, it might have answered; but time flies, you see.

Was mechanic alone in his glory, or was there any one else who dealt as largely in the article?

Mechanic would pound it, there was none.

What was the article employed for? (I brought this question out with a gasp, excitement almost choking my utterance.)

It would piece a'most anything together, mechanic believed, and make it solider nor stone.

This was a sentence difficult of interpretation. I thought it over a little, and then said, doubtfully, "you mean, I presume, that it serves to connect the broken threads of human destiny? to invest with a—with a sort of vital reality the chimerical products of a fertile imagination?"

Mechanic's answer was short and anything but encouraging: "mought be—, I's no scollard, bless you."

At this point conversation certainly began to flag; I was seriously debating in my own mind whether this could really be the fulfilment of my life-cherished dream; so ill did the scene harmonize with my ideas of romance, and so painfully did I feel my companion's lack of sympathy in the enthusiasm of my nature—an enthusiasm which has found vent, ere now, in actions which the thoughtless crowd have too often attributed to mere eccentricity.

I have risen with the lark—"day's sweet harbinger"—(once, certainly, if not oftener), with the aid of a patent alarum, and have gone forth at that unseemly hour, much to the astonishment of the housemaid cleaning the door steps, to "brush with hasty steps the dewy lawn," and have witnessed the golden dawn with eyes yet half-closed in sleep. (I have always stated to my friends, in any allusion to the subject, that my raptures at that moment were such that I have never since ventured to expose myself to the influence of excitement so dangerous. In confidence, however, I admit that the reality did not come up to the idea I had formed of it over night, and by no means repaid the struggle of getting out of bed so early.)

I have wandered in the solemn woods at night, and bent me o'er the moss-grown fountain, to lave in its crystal stream my tangled locks and fevered brow. (What though I was laid up with a severe cold in consequence, and that my hair was out of curl for a week? Do paltry considerations such as these, I ask, affect the poetry of the incident?)

I have thrown open my small, but neatly furnished, cottage tenement, in the neighbourhood of St. John's Wood, and invited an aged beggar in to "sit by my fire, and talk the night away." (It was immediately after reading Goldsmith's "Deserted Village." True it is that he told me nothing interesting, and that he took the hall-clock with him when he departed in the morning; still my uncle has always said that he wishes he had been there, and that it displayed in me a freshness and greenness of fancy (or "disposition," I forget which) such as he had never expected to see.)

I feel that it is incumbent on me to enter more fully into this latter topic—the personal history of my uncle: the world will one day learn to revere the talents of that wonderful man, though a want of funds prevents, at present, the publication of the great system of philosophy of which he is the inventor. Meanwhile, out of the mass of priceless manuscripts which he has bequeathed to an ungrateful nation, I will venture to select one striking specimen. And when the day arrives that my poetry is appreciated by the world at large (distant though it now appear!) then, I feel assured, shall his genius also receive its meed of fame!

Among the papers of that respected relative, I find what appear to have been a leaf torn from some philosophical work of the day: the following passage is scored. "Is this your rose? It is mine. It is yours. Are these your houses? They are mine. Give to me (of) the bread. She gave him a box on the ear." Against this occurs a marginal note in my uncle's handwriting; "some call this unconnected writing: I have my own opinion." This last was a favourite expression of his, veiling a profundity of ethical acumen on which it would be vain to speculate; indeed, so uniformly simple was the language of this great man, that no one besides myself ever suspected his possessing more than the ordinary share of human intellect.

May I, however, venture to express what I believe would have been my uncle's interpretation of this remarkable passage? It appears that the writer intended to distinguish the provinces of Poetry, Real Property, and Personal Property. The inquirer touches first on flowers, and with what a gush of generous feeling does the answer break upon him! "It is mine. It is yours." That is the beautiful, the true, the good; these are not hampered by petty consideration of "meum" and "tuum"; these are the common property of men. (It was with some such idea as this that I drew up the once celebrated bill, entitled "An Act for exempting Pheasants from the operation of the Game Laws, on the ground of Beauty"—a bill which would doubtless, have passed both Houses in triumph, but that the member who had undertaken the care of it was unfortunately incarcerated in a Lunatic Asylum before it had reached the second reading.) Encouraged by the success of his first question, our inquirer passes on to "houses" ("Real Property," you will observe); he is here met by the stern, chilling answer, "They are mine"—none of the liberal sentiment which dictated the former reply, but in its place a dignified assertion of the rights of property.

Had this been a genuine Socratic dialogue, and not merely a modern imitation, the inquirer would have probably here interrupted with "To me indeed," or, "I, for my part," or "but how otherwise?" or some other of those singular expressions, with which Plato makes his characters display at once their blind acquiescence in their instructor's opinions, and their utter inability to express themselves grammatically. But the writer takes another line of thought; the bold inquirer, undeterred by the coldness of the last reply, proceeds from questions to demands, "give me (of) the bread"; and here the conversation abruptly ceases, but the moral of the whole is pointed in the narrative: "she gave him a box on the ear." This is not the philosophy of one individual or nation, the sentiment is, if I may so say, European; and I am borne out in this theory by the fact that the book has evidently been printed in three parallel columns, English, French, and German.

Such a man was my uncle; and with such a man did I resolve to confront the suspected mechanic. I appointed the following morning for an interview, when I would personally inspect "the article" (I could not bring myself to utter the beloved word itself). I passed a restless and feverish night, crushed by a sense of the approaching crisis.

The hour came at last—the hour of misery and despair; it always does so, it cannot be put off forever; even on a visit to a dentist,

as my childhood can attest with bitter experience, we are not forever getting there; the fatal door too surely dawns upon us, and
our heart, which for the last half hour has been gradually sinking
lower and lower, until we almost doubt its existence, vanishes
suddenly downward into depths hitherto undreamed of. And so,
I repeat it, the hour came at last.

Standing before that base mechanic's door, with a throbbing and
expectant heart, my eye chanced to fall once more upon that signboard, once more I perused its strange inscription. Oh! fatal
change! Oh! horror! What do I see? Have I been deluded by
a heated imagination? A hideous gap yaws between the N and
the C, making it not one word but two!

And the dream was over.

At the corner of the street I turned to take a sad fond look at
the spectre of a phantom hope, I once had held so dear. "Adieu!"
I whispered; this was all the last farewell I took, and I leant upon
my walking stick and wiped away a tear. On the following day
I entered into commercial relations with the firm of Dumpy and
Spaag, wholesale dealers in the wine and spirit department.

The signboard yet creaks upon the mouldering wall, but its
sound shall make music in these ears nevermore—ah! nevermore.

TO MISS HENRIETTA, AND MASTER EDWIN DODGSON [13]

"Ch. Ch., Jan. 31st.

"My Dear Henrietta,

"My Dear Edwin,

"I am very much obliged by your nice little birthday gift—it was much better than a cane would have been—I have got it on my watch-chain, but the Dean has not yet remarked it.

"My one pupil has begun his work with me, and I will give you a description how the lecture is conducted. It is the most important point, you know, that the tutor should be *dignified* and at a distance from the pupil, and that the pupil should be as much as possible *degraded*.

"Otherwise, you know, they are not humble enough.

"So I sit at the further end of the room; outside the door (*which is shut*) sits the scout: outside the outer door (*also shut*) sits the sub-scout: half-way downstairs sits the sub-sub-scout; and down in the yard sits the *pupil*.

"The questions are shouted from one to the other, and the answers come back in the same way—it is rather confusing till you are well used to it. The lecture goes on something like this:—

"Tutor. What is twice three?
"Scout. What's a rice tree?
"Sub-Scout. When is ice free?
"Sub-Sub-Scout. What's a nice fee?
"Pupil (*timidly*). Half a guinea!
"Sub-Sub-Scout. Can't forge any!
"Sub-Scout. Ho for Jinny!
"Scout. Don't be a ninny!
"Tutor (*looks offended, but tries another question*). Divide a hundred by twelve!
"Scout. Provide wonderful bells!
"Sub-Scout. Go ride under it yourself!

---

[13] This letter L. C. wrote to his sister and his brother shortly after getting his studentship, Collingwood tells us.—*McD.*

63

"Sub-Sub-Scout. Deride the dunder-headed elf!
"Pupil (*surprised*). Who do you mean?
"Sub-Sub-Scout. Doings between!
"Sub-Scout. Blue is the screen!
"Scout. Soup-tureen!

"And so the lecture proceeds.

"Such is Life.

"from

"Your most affect. brother,

"Charles L. Dodgson.

THE LEGEND OF "SCOTLAND" [14]

Being a true and terrible report touching the rooms of Auckland Castell, called Scotland, and of the things there endured by Matthew Dixon, Chaffer, and of a certain Ladye, called Gaunless of some, there apparent, and how that none durst in these days sleep therein, (belike through fear,) all which things fell out in ye days of Bishop Bec, of chearfull memorie, and were writ down by mee in the Yeere One Thousand Three Hundred and Twenty Five, in the Month February, on a certayn Tuesday and other days.

EDGAR CUTHWELLIS.

Now the said Matthew Dixon, having fetched wares unto that place, my Loords commended the same, and bade that hee should be entertained for that night, (which in sooth hee was, supping with a grete Appetite,) and sleep in a certayn roome of that apartment now called Scotland—From whence at Midnight hee rushed forth with so grete a Screem, as awaked all men, and hastily running into those Passages, and meeting him so screeming, hee presentlie faynted away.

Whereon they hadde hym into my Loorde's parlour, and with much ado set hym on a Chaire, wherefrom hee three several times slipt even to the grounde, to the grete admiration of all men.

But being stayed with divers Strong Liquors, (and, chiefest, with Gyn,) hee after a whyle gave foorth in a lamentable tone these following particulars, all which were presentlie sworn to by nine painful and stout farmers, who lived hard by, which witness I will heare orderlie set downe.

Witness of Matthew Dixon, Chaffer, being in my right minde, and more than Fortie Yeeres of Age, though sore affrighted by

[14] "The Legend of 'Scotland' was written by Lewis Carroll for the daughters of Archbishop Longley, while he was, as Bishop of Durham, living at Auckland Castle, and between the years 1856-60. The legend was suggested by some markings upon the walls of a cellar in a part of the castle which, from its remoteness and chilliness, was, and perhaps still is, called 'Scotland' ". S. D. Collingwood: *Lewis Carroll Picture Book*, p. 331 (*McD.*).

reason of Sightes and Sounds in This Castell endured by mee, as touching the Vision of Scotland, and the Ghosts, all two of them, therein contayned, and of A certayn straunge Ladye, and of the lamentable thyngs by her uttered, with other sad tunes and songs, by her and by other Ghosts devised, and of the coldness and shakyng of my Bones, (through soe grete feer,) and of other things very pleasant to knowe, cheefly of a Picture hereafter suddenlie to bee taken, and of what shall befall thereon, (as trulie foreshowne by Ghosts,) and of Darkness, with other things more terrible than Woordes, and of that which Men call Chimera.

Matthew Dixon, Chaffer, deposeth: "that hee, having supped well over Night on a Green Goose, a Pasty, and other Condiments of the Bishop's grete bountie provided, (looking, as hee spake, at my Loorde, and essaying toe pull offe hys hatte untoe hym, but missed soe doing, for that hee hadde yt not on hys hedde,) soe went untoe hys bedde, where a long tyme hee was exercysed with sharp and horrible Dreems. That hee saw yn hys Dreem a yong Ladye, habited, (not as yt seemed) yn a Gaun, but yn a certayn sorte of Wrapper, perchance a Wrap-Rascal." (Hereon a Mayde of the House affirmed that noe Ladye woold weare such a thing, and hee answered, "I stand corrected," and indeed rose from hys chaire, yet fayled to stand.)

Witness continued: "that ye sayde Ladye waved toe and froe a Grete Torche, whereat a thin Voyce shreeked 'Gaunless! Gaunless!' and Shee standyng yn the midst of the floor, a grete Chaunge befell her, her Countenance waxing ever more and more Aged, and her Hayr grayer, shee all that tyme saying yn a most sad Voyce, 'Gaunless, now, as Ladyes bee: yet yn yeeres toe come they shall not lacke for Gauns.' At whych her Wrapper seemed slowlie toe melte, chaunging into a gaun of sylk, which puckered up and down, yea, and flaunced itself out not a lyttle:" (at thys mye Loorde, waxing impatient, smote hym roundlie onne the hedde, bydding hym finish hys tale anon.)

Witness continued: "that the sayd Gaun thenne chaunged ytself into divers fashyons whych shall hereafter bee, loopying ytself uppe yn thy place and yn that, soe gyving toe View ane pettycote of a most fiery hue, even Crimson toe looke upon, at whych dismal and blode-thirstie sight hee both groned and wepte. That at the laste the shyrt swelled unto a Vastness beyond Man's power toe tell ayded, (as hee judged.) by Hoops, Cartwheels, Baloons, and the lyke, bearing yt uppe within. That yt fylled alle that Chamber, crushing hym flat untoe hys bedde, tylle such tyme as she appeared toe depart, fryzzling hys Hayre with her Torche as she went.

"That hee, awakyng from such Dreems, herd thereon a Rush, and saw a Light." (Hereon a Mayde interrupted hym, crying out that there was yndeed a Rush-Light burning yn that same room, and woulde have sayde more, but that my Loorde sheckt her, and sharplie bade her stow that, meening thereby, that she shoulde holde her peece.)

Witness continued: "that being muche affrited thereat, whereby hys Bones were, (as hee sayde,) all of a dramble, hee essayed to leep from hys bedde, and soe quit. Yet tarried hee some whyle, not, as might bee thought from being stout of Harte, but rather of Bodye; whych tyme she chaunted snatches of old lays, as Maister Wil Shakespeare hath yt."

Hereon my Loorde questioned what lays, byddyng hym syng the same, and saying hee knew but of two lays: " 'Twas wee Trafalgar's bay wee saw the Frenchmen lay," and "There wee lay all that day yn the Bay of Biscay—O," whych hee forthwyth hummed aloud, yet out of tune, at whych some smyled.

Witness continued: "that hee perchaunce coulde chaunt the sayde lays wyth Music, but unaccompanied hee durst not." On thys they hadde hym to the Schoolroom, where was a Musical Instrument, called a Paean-o-Forty, (meening that yt hadde forty Notes, and was a Paean or Triumph of Art,) whereon two yong Ladyes, Nieces of my Loorde, that abode there, (lerning, as they deemed, Lessons; but, I wot, idlynge not a lyttle,) did wyth much thumpyng playe certyn Music wyth hys synging, as best they mighte, seeing that the Tunes were such as noe Man had herde before.

"Lorenzo dwelt at Heighington,
    (Hys cote was made of Dimity,)
Least-ways yf not exactly there,
    Yet yn yt's close proximity.

> Hee called on mee—hee stayed to tee—
> Yet not a word hee ut-tered,
> Untyl I sayd, (D'ye lyke your bread
> Dry?' and hee answered 'But-tered.' "
> *(Chorus whereyn all present joyned with fervor).*
>> "Noodle dumb
>> Has a noodle-head,
>> I hate such noodles, *I* do."

Witness continued: "that shee then appeered unto hym habited yn the same loose Wrapper, whereyn hee first saw her yn hys Dreem, and yn a stay'd and piercing tone gave forth her History as followeth."

THE LADYE'S HISTORY

"On a dewie autum evening, mighte have been seen, pacing yn the grounds harde by Aucklande Castell, a yong Ladye of a stiff and perky manner, yet not ill to look on, nay, one mighte saye, faire to a degree, save that haply that hadde been untrue.

"That yong Ladye, O miserable Man, was I" (whereon I demanded on what score shee held mee miserable, and shee replied, yt mattered not). "I plumed myself yn those tymes on my exceeding not soe much beauty as liftinesse of Figure, and gretely desired that some Painter might paint my picture: but they ever were too high, not yn skyll I trow, byt yn charges." (At thys I most humbly enquired at what charge the then Painters wrought, but shee loftily affirmed that money-matters were vulgar and that shee knew not, no, nor cared.)

"Now yt chaunced that a certyn Artist, hight Lorenzo, came toe that Quarter, having wyth hym a merveillous machine called by men a Chimera (that ys, a fabulous and wholly incredible thing;) where wyth hee took manie pictures, each yn a single stroke of Tyme, whiles that a Man might name 'John, the son of Robin' (I asked her, what might a stroke of Tyme bee, but shee, frowning, answered not).

"He yt was that undertook my Picture: yn which I mainly required one thyng, that yt shoulde bee at full-length, for yn none other way mighte my Loftiness bee trulie set forth. Nevertheless, though hee took manie Pictures, yet all fayled yn thys: for some, beginning at the Hedde, reeched not toe the Feet; others, takyn yn the Feet, yet left out the Hedde; whereof the former were a grief unto myself, and the latter a Laughing-Stocke unto others.

"At these thyngs I justly fumed, having at the first been frendly unto hym (though yn sooth hee was dull), and oft smote hym gretely on the Eares, rending from hys Hedde certyn Locks, whereat crying out hee was wont toe saye that I made hys lyfe a burden untoe hym, whych thyng I not so much doubted as highlie rejoyced yn.

"At the last hee counselled thys, that a Picture shoulde bee made, showing so much skyrt as mighte reesonably bee gotte yn, and a Notice set below toe thys effect: 'Item, two yards and a Half Ditto, and then the Feet.' But thys no Whit contented mee, and thereon I shut hym ynto the Cellar, where hee remaned three Weeks, growing dayly thinner and thinner, till at the last hee floted up and downe like a Feather.

"Now yt fell at thys tyme, as I questioned hym on a certyn Day, yf hee woulde nowe take mee at full-length, and hee replying untoe mee, yn a little moning Voyce, lyke a Gnat, one chaunced to open the Door: whereat the Draft bore hym uppe ynto a Cracke of the Cieling, and I remaned awaytyng hym, holding uppe my Torche, until such tyme as I also faded ynto a Ghost, yet stickyng untoe the Wall."

Then did my Loorde and the Companie haste down ynto the Cellar, for to see thys straunge sight, to whych place when they came, my Loorde bravely drew hys sword, loudly crying "Death!" (though to whom or what he explained not); then some went yn, but the more part hung back, urging on those yn front, not soe largely bye example, as Words of cheer: yet at last all entered, my Loorde last.

Then they removed from the wall the Casks and other stuff, and founde the sayd Ghost, dredful toe relate, yet extant on the Wall, at which horrid sight such screems were raysed as yn these days are seldom or never herde: some faynted, others by large drafts of Beer saved themselves from that Extremity, yet were they scarcely alive for Feer.

Then dyd the Ladye speak unto them yn suchwise: —

"Here I bee, and here I byde,
Till such tyme as yt betyde
That a Ladye of thys place,
Lyke to mee yn name and face,
(Though my name bee never known,
My initials shall be shown,)
Shall be fotograffed aright—
Hedde and Feet bee both yn sight—
Then my face shall disappeer,
Nor agayn affrite you heer."

Then sayd Matthew Dixon unto her, "Wherefore holdest thou
uppe that Torche?" to whych shee answered, "Candles Gyve
Light": but none understood her.

After thys a thyn Voyce sang from overhedde:—

"Yn the Auckland Castell cellar,
Long, long ago,
I was shut—a brisk yong feller—
Woe, woe, ah woe!
To take her at full-lengthe
I never hadde the strengthe
Tempore (and soe I tell her,)
Praeterito!

(Yn thys Chorus they durst none joyn, seeing that Latyn was
untoe them a Tongue unknown.)

"She was hard—oh, she was cruel—
Long, long ago,
Starved mee here—not even gruel—
No, believe mee, no!—
Frae Scotland could I flee,
I'd gie my last bawbee,—
Arrah, bhoys, fair play's a jhewel,
Lave me, darlints, goe!"

Then my Loorde, putting bye hys Sworde, (whych was layd up
thereafter, yn memory of soe grete Bravery,) bade hys Butler fetch
hym presentlie a Vessel of Beer, whych when yt was broughte at
hys nod, (nor, as hee merrily sayd, hys "nod, and Bec, and wreathed
smyle,") hee drank hugelie thereof: "for why?" quoth hee, "surely
a Bee ys no longer a Bee, when yt ys Dry."

JOURNAL OF A TOUR IN RUSSIA IN 1867

JOURNAL OF A TOUR IN RUSSIA IN 1867

JULY 12 (F.) The Sultan & I arrived in London almost at the same time, but in different quarters—*my* point of entry being Paddington, and *his* Charing Cross: I must admit that the crowd was greatest at the latter place. A third centre of attraction was the Mansion House, where the Belgian volunteers were entertained, & from which, at about 6, a steady stream of omnibuses, laden with heroes, was setting in eastwards. This delayed my shopping a good deal & I did not get off from Charing X for Dover till 8/30, & on arriving at the "Lord Warden" I found Liddon already there.

JULY 13 (SAT.) We breakfasted, as agreed, at 8—or at least we then sat down & nibbled bread & butter till such time as the chops should be done, which great event took place about 1/2 past. We tried pathetic appeals to the wandering waiters, who told us "they are coming, Sir" in a soothing tone—and we tried stern remonstrance, & they then said "they are coming, Sir" in a more injured tone; & after all such appeals they retired into their dens, & hid themselves behind sideboards and dish-covers, & still the chops came not. We agreed that of all virtues a waiter can display, that of a retiring disposition is quite the least desirable. Then I made 2 great propositions, both rejected on the first reading—one that we should desert the table, & refuse to pay for the chops, the other that I should search out the proprietor & lodge a formal complaint against all the waiters, which would certainly have produced a general row, if not the chops.

However by 9 we found ourselves on board the boat, & after 2 trains had been emptied into it, & a very successful imitation of the Great Pyramid had been made on deck, to which interesting work we were proud to contribute a couple of portmanteaus, we got under weigh. The pen refused to describe the sufferings of some of the passengers during our smooth trip of 90 minutes: my own sensations—it was not for *that* I paid my money. It rained hard most of the way, making our private cabin (which we were luxurious enough to hire) a great comfort, sheltered, and yet airy,

73

as it was on deck. We landed at Calais in the usual swarm of friendly natives, offering services & advice of all kinds: to *all* such remarks I returned one simple answer "Non!" It was probably not strictly applicable in all cases, but it answered the purpose of getting rid of them; one by one they left me, echoing the "Non!" in various tones, but all expressive of disgust. After Liddon had settled about the luggage, &c. we took a stroll in the market-place, which was white with the caps of the women, & full of their shrill jabbering. . . .

The journey to Brussels was flat & monotonous, the tower of St. Omer, & the five-towered cathedral of Tournay, being about the only buildings of note on the way. From Lille to Tournay we had the company of a family-party, the 2 children being about 6 & 4, & the younger one hardly ceased talking a moment the whole way. I made a drawing of the little creature, which was inspected by the family, & freely (& I think favorably) criticised by the original. She was sent back again by her mother, as they were leaving the carriage, to bid us "Bon soir" & to be kissed.

At Blandain, on the Belgian frontier, our luggage was bundled out, searched—or rather peeped into—and bundled in again: no charge, being the first examination I have passed without a fee.

Thence to Brussels with German travelling companions. The chief feature I remarked in the scenery was the way the trees were planted, in straight lines miles in length: as they generally all leaned one way, they seemed to me like long files of wearied soldiers marching hither and thither across the plains: some were drawn up in square, some standing at "Attention!", but most of them were plodding hopelessly on, bending as they went, as if under the weight of ghostly knapsacks.

At Brussels we put up at the "Hotel Bellevue," & after a little dinner, "tres-simple," & therefore consisting of only 7 courses— we went out for a turn, & hearing music going on in the Public Park, we turned in there: & there we sat an hour or more, listening to some capital orchestral music, in a sort of Cremorne, with hundreds of people sitting at little tables about among the trees, & the whole place lit up with lamps.

JULY 14. (SUN.) We went to the church of S. Gudule, the finest in Brussels, at 10. I did not like it much, for though one could have joined in much of the service, if audible, it was only possible to catch a word here & there: besides, there were generally 2 things going on at once: the choir were generally singing anthems, &c. while the priest went on, quite independently, with his part of the service—and the whole body of priests, &c. were continually going up in little processions, kneeling for about a second before the altar (quite too short a time for any act of devotion) & returning to their places. Attention was called to the chief points in the service by a shrill bell, which drowned everything else while it lasted. The people about us were some of them going on with their own devotions—(the man next me, not having a chair to kneel on, was kneeling on the pavement, & counting off his prayers with a string of beads)—some merely looking on, & people going in & out all the while. I joined in the service, whenever I could make out what was going on, but even with Liddon to find the places, it was generally impossible to catch the words, but it was very difficult to realise it as a service for the congregation to join in—it all seemed to be done *for* them. The music was very beautiful, & the swinging the censers of incense had a most picturesque effect—two boys, dressed in scarlet & white, standing in front of the altar & facing it, & swinging the censers exactly together, in time with the music. Afterwards took place a ceremony that only happens once a year, the grand procession of the "host" through the town: we watched it out, & waited for its return, which was not for more than an hour. They were preceded by a troop of cavalry! Then came a long series of little boys, most of them in scarlet & white, & some of them with wreaths of paper flowers round their heads, carrying banners, & some with baskets full of bits of coloured paper, which I suppose they strewed on the way—then a long train of little girls dressed in white, with long white veils: then numbers of singing men, priests, &c. all in splendid dresses, and carrying banners which got larger & more gorgeous down the procession: then a large figure of the Virgin Mary, with the Holy Child, was carried by— the figure stood on a large pedestal, shaped like a hemisphere, but flatter, and covered with artificial flowers—then more banners— then a large canopy on 4 poles, under which walked the priests who carried the host: many of the people knelt as they passed. It was far the most splendid ceremonial I have ever seen, and had a most beautiful effect, but it was terribly theatrical & unreal. The crowds were enormous, but quite orderly—there must have been many thousands present.

In the afternoon Liddon called on some friends, & I took a stroll to the "Grande Place," & had a good look at the beautiful "Hotel de Ville"; the square is said to be the finest specimen of domestic Gothic in the world. We went to the English church in the evening, but the service had been changed to the afternoon.

JULY 15. (MON.) Left at 9.40 for Cologne, which we reached (with no adventures by the way) at 4. Here the luggage underwent a second examination, even more cursory than the last; as *my* portmanteau was not even opened. We spent about an hour in the cathedral, which I will not attempt to describe further than by saying it was the most beautiful of all churches I have ever seen, or can imagine. If one could imagine the spirit of devotion embodied in any material form, it would be in such a building.

We took another stroll in the evening, crossing the river, & so getting a magnificent view of the whole town. This was after an excellent dinner (all the dinners &c. hitherto have been so), & a bottle of Rudescheimer, which fully deserved the remark with which the cheerful little waiter introduced it to our notice—"that is good wine, I suppose!" Our Hotel was "du Nord."

JULY 16. (TU.) We made a round of several of the churches, the effect of which was that I have no very definite idea of any one of them. They were: "The church of St. Ursula & of the 11,000 virgins," whose bones are stored away in cases with fronts of glass, through which they are hardly visible—"St. Gereon's"—another ossuary, with a curious ten-sided dome—"The Apostles' Church"—"St. Peter's" containing an altar-piece by Rubens, representing the crucifixion of St. Peter—(near this we found a house with a tablet attesting that Rubens was born there)—"St. Mary in Capitolio."

Liddon went to the table d'hote at 1 1/2, & I took the opportunity of returning to the Apostles' Church to witness a wedding. There were a good many people there, & many children, who ran about

the church as they liked, but quietly & very unlike English children. The wedding party all went within the rails, where they
knelt, (the whole time) at movable desks. The service began, I
think, with prayers & some questions & answers, after which the
priest, leaning comfortably against the altar, shut his book & gave
them a long address, extempore seemingly—then he waved over
them what looked like a vessel of holy water—then the clerk
brought, & placed on the altar, a book with pen & ink, & the priest
was occupied for a long time in making entries in it, during which
2 of the gentlemen came & whispered to him, I suppose giving
their names as witnesses—then the priest made a little bow to the
bridal party, & the thing was over. In going the round of the
churches, I was much struck by the numbers of the people we
found in them, engaged in private devotions. In one of them there
were 3 women confessing at the same time at 3 different confes-
sionals: they hid their faces in their hands, & the priest held a hand-
kerchief in front of his face, but there were no curtains. The
number of children, who seemed to have come by themselves to
pray, was very remarkable: some of them had books, but not all—
most of them, I think, looked at us as we walked about, but they
soon went back to their devotions, & one by one they got up &
went out again, evidently coming & going just when they liked.
I noticed no men or boys engaged in these devotions (though there
were many at the Sunday service in Brussels) . . . In the afternoon
we went up to the top of the cathedral, & had a glorious view of the
town with its mass of white walls & grey roofs, & many miles of
the Rhine. We had agreed to try the journey to Berlin by night &
accordingly took our seats at 7.15 p. m. & got to Berlin about 8 in
the morning. The seats in the carriage were made to draw out till
they met & formed a very fair bed, & there was a green silk shade
to draw over the lamp when we wanted the carriage dark, & we
managed to pass a very comfortable night, though I am sorry to
say Liddon did not sleep.

JULY 17. (w.) At Berlin, when we wanted a cab (here called
a droschky) to take us to the "Hotel de Russie," they gave us a
ticket with a number on it, & we were *obliged* to take the cab,
which had that number, on the stand—a regulation that would not

long be endured in England. In the course of the day we examined the splendid equestrian statue of Frederick the Great (by Rauch), and the famous "Amazon & Tiger" (by Kiss), and paid rather hasty visits to 2 picture-galleries, both of which we must examine in detail if possible. We dined at 3, at the table d'hote. (mem: that "potage à la Flamande" means mutton-broth, that duck is eaten with cherries, & that it is *not* the thing to wish for a clean knife & fork during the repast), & in the evening we strolled about, & finding service going on at St. Peter's (Evangelical) we went in & heard about 20 minutes of a very fluent extempore sermon, in German: the preacher ended with a long extempore prayer & the Lord's prayer—then rose, (all rising with him), & gave the blessing with his arms extended—then the organ struck up, the preacher retired, & the congregation seated themselves again & sang a long & very melodious hymn.

JULY 18. (TH.) We paid a second and longer visit to the great picture-gallery (containing 1243 pictures), arranged by the great art-critic, Waagen. His catalogue, however, contains little if any criticism, but merely enumerates what is to be seen in each picture. The majority of the pictures are on sacred subjects, & there are a great number of the "Madonna & Child," treated in a great variety of styles: in many of them St. Sebastian is introduced (already pierced with the arrows)—in some, Mary has placed the Child on the ground, & is kneeling before Him in prayer—& in one, a very fine piece of colouring, Joseph is represented asleep, with the angel whispering in his ear. There is a fine picture of the Tower of Babel, with thousands of figures—another of the garden of Eden, crowded with all manner of beasts & birds—& several well known from engravings, such as St. Anthony's temptation. One of the most wonderful pieces of *finish* I ever saw is a triptych by Van Weyden, representing scenes after the death of our Lord—in one where Mary is weeping, each tear is carefully painted hemisphere (or rather more) with its own point of light & its own shadow—& there is a book lying on the floor with the leaves a little fluttered open, where one of the clasps hangs so that its shadow crosses the edges of the leaves, & tho' the shadow is perhaps not an inch long altogether, wherever there is the least opening between the leaves, the artist has carefully carried the shadow in along the surface of the lower leaf. In taking a general view of the pictures one did not get much impression of beauty, but one could hardly pick out any picture where a little examination did not reveal marvels of execution. It would take many days to do anything like justice to the whole gallery. After the table d'hote it rained too much for us to do more than take a short stroll & look at the ancient church of St. Nicholas.

JULY 19. (F.) We got up (by help of the alarum), at 6 1/2, & breakfasted soon after 7 1/2. In the morning we visited S. Nicholas', which contained a feature new to me—an aisle, completely screened off, running round the apse at the east end, outside a circle of pillars, the altar being within the circle, with the usual pile of marble-work behind, & behind that again, a screen covered with old paintings (chiefly scripture subjects) each put up to the memory of someone deceased. Here too we saw the tomb of Puffendorf. From this we went to the Schloss, or King's Palace, & were guided, with a crowd of other sight-seers, through a series of gorgeous rooms, & a large circular chapel: throughout, everything capable of being gilt, was gilt. The grand staircase by which we entered was not in steps, but a sort of paved street rising gently, & reminding me much of some of the streets of Whitby, but, after we had seen the rooms & paid our guide, no further attention was paid us, & we were left to get out as best we could, down a winding back-stair, among buckets & workmen doing repairs—wherein lies a deep moral, beginning "Such is the fate of princes—." The rest of the morning we gave to the 2 picture-galleries.

After dinner we went, on the roof of the omnibus, to Charlottensburg (about 4 miles west), getting a grand panoramic view of the "Unter den Linden" as we went. There is another palace there, & some very pretty grounds, but the only thing really remarkable is the chapel where the Princess [1] lies buried. Her tomb consists of an exquisitely carved marble figure lying on a couch—a most marvellous effect is produced by filling some of the windows in the roof with violet-coloured glass, which gives an indescribable softness & dreaminess to the marble.

[1] Von Liegnitz.

Later in the evening we strolled out & looked at the Jewish Synagogue, said to be well worth inspection—this we were told by a New York gentleman, whom we had met (with his wife) at the table d'hote & who seem to be very pleasant people. They have come here without knowing a word of German, & so find life rather a complicated affair.

JULY 20. (SAT.) We began the day by visiting the Jewish Synagogue, where we found service going on, and remained till it was over: the whole scene was perfectly novel to me, & most interesting. The building is most gorgeous, almost the whole interior surface being gilt or otherwise decorated—the arches were nearly all semi-circular, tho' there were a few instances of the shape sketched here—the east end was roofed with a circular dome, & contained a smaller dome on pillars, under which was a cupboard (concealed by curtain) which contained the roll of the Law: in front of this was a reading-desk, facing east, & in front of that again a small desk facing west—the latter was only once used. The rest of the building was fitted up with open seats. We followed the example of the congregation in keeping our hats on. Many of the men, on reaching their places, produced white silk shawls out of embroidered bags, & these they put on square fashion: the effect was most singular—the upper edge of the shawl had what looked like gold embroidery, but was probably a phylactery. These men went up from time to time & read portions of the lessons. What was read was all in German, but there was a great deal chanted in Hebrew, to beautiful music: some of the chants have come down from very early times, perhaps as far back as David. The chief Rabbi chanted a great deal by himself, without music. The congregation alternately stood & sat down: I did not notice any one kneeling.

We spent the afternoon at Potsdam, a region of palaces and gardens. The New Palace (where our own Crown Princess lives) was even more splendid than the Schloss at Berlin. Here we saw the rooms of Frederick the Great, his writing-table, a chair with the cover nearly torn to pieces by the claws of his dogs, &c. We also visited the church which contains his tomb—plain & with no inscription, according to his wish. The gem of the place is "Sans Souci," his favorite palace: we roamed about the gardens, laid out in the old formal style, with straight avenues of trees, radiating from centres, & a most beautiful series of terrace gardens rising one above the other, & full of orange trees. The amount of art lavished on the whole region of Potsdam in marvellous; some of the tops of the palaces were like forests of pedestals. In fact the two principles of Berlin architecture appear to me to be these—"On the house-tops, whenever there is a convenient place, put up the figure of a man; he is best placed standing on one leg. Whenever there is room on the ground, put either a circular group of busts on pedestals, in consultation, all looking inwards—or else the colossal figure of a man killing, about to kill, or having killed (the present tense is preferred) a beast; the more prickles the beast has, the better—in fact a dragon is the correct thing, but if that is beyond the artist, he may content himself with a lion or a pig."

The beast-killing principle has been carried out everywhere with a relentless monotony, which makes some parts of Berlin look like a fossil slaughter house. The Potsdam expedition occupied 6 hours.

JULY 21. (SUN.) Liddon went to the German services at the Dom-Kirche. I attended the only English service (a morning one) in a room, lent for the purpose, in the Monbijon Palace. While Liddon was at the evening service, I strolled about in the Lust-Garten, where were knots of people seated on the benches & on the steps of the Museum, and numbers of children at play: their favorite amusement being dancing round in a ring, holding hands & facing outwards, while they sang, a little song, the words of which I could not catch. Once they found a large dog lying down, & at once arranged their dance round it, & sang their song to it, facing inwards for that purpose: the dog looked thoroughly puzzled at this novel form of entertainment, but soon made up his mind that it was not to be endured, & must be escaped from at all costs. I also met, lounging about like myself, a very pleasant German gentleman, & had a sort of conversation with him: he was most good-natured in guessing at my meaning, & helping me out with my sentences of what would have been very bad German, if it had deserved the name of German at all. Nevertheless, the German I talk is about as good as the English I hear—at breakfast this morning, for which I had ordered some cold ham, the waiter, when he had brought the other things, leant across the table, & said to me in a confidential under-tone "I brings in minutes ze cold ham."

At 10.15 we left for Danzig, which we reached in very fair condition by 10 in the morning.

JULY 22. (M.) We spent the rest of the day in seeing the Dom-Kirche, & exploring the rest of this fantastic & most interesting old town. The streets are narrow & winding, the houses very tall, & nearly every one is topped by a queer ornamental gable, full of strange curves & zigzags. The Dom-Kirche was a very great treat. We spent 3 hours in the church, & another on the top of the tower, which is 328 feet high, giving a magnificent view of the old town, the windings of the Moldan & the Vistula, & a long reach of the Baltic. In the church we saw the great picture, by Memling, of the Last Judgement, one of the greatest marvels I have ever seen: it contains almost hundreds of figures, & almost every face is as minutely finished as if it were a miniature portrait; some of the evil spirits prove an unbounded power of imagination in the artist, but are too grotesque to be horrible. The church was full of altars & altar-pieces (though it is now Lutheran) whose general character was to have folding doors with illuminations on the outside & inside, & behind them an alto-relievo, coloured & gilt almost to excess, & generally representing the crucifixion. In one, where Our Lord is bearing the cross, I noticed a novel idea: a post is fixed in the ground, ending in a screw, which passes through the end of the cross that is highest, & there is a nut on the end of this screw, which an imp is trying to turn round, & so to increase the labour of bearing the cross. Nearly up in the roof of the chancel is an enormous crucifix standing on a beam, with figures of the weeping women, all more than life size.

In two sacristies we found a splendid collection of old vestments, relics, musical instruments & of chasubles alone I counted 75! There were also 2 "vesicas" (very rare)—that is, a hollow case made of curved bars, & containing a figure of the Virgin Mary. Every pair of opposite bars is supposed to represent a fish (ΙΧΘΥΣ). These were hung by chains, from the roof of the chancel. The whole church is white & gold inside, very lofty, & full of tall, splendid pillars.

We took a stroll in the evening, &, coming home in the dusk through a narrow alley, passed a little soldier on guard in the middle of the street with fixed bayonet: he looked fiercely at us, but let us pass unmolested.

At the hotel was a green parrot on a stand: we addressed it as "Pretty Poll," & it put its head on one side & thought about it, but wouldn't commit itself to any statement. The waiter came up to inform us of the reason of its silence—"Er spricht nicht English: er spricht nicht Deutsch." It appeared that the unfortunate bird could speak nothing but Mexican! Not knowing a word of that language, we could only pity it.

JULY 23. (TU.) We strolled about and bought a few photographs, and at 11.39 left for Königsberg. On our way to the station, we came across the grandest instance of the "Majesty of Justice" that I have ever witnessed—A little boy was being taken to the magistrate, or to prison (probably for picking a pocket). The achievement of this feat had been entrusted to two soldiers in full uniform, who were solemnly marching, one in front of the poor little creature, and one behind; with bayonets fixed of course, to be ready to charge in case he should attempt an escape . . . .

The scenery between Danzig & Königsberg is very dull. We passed a cottage near Danzig, with a nest on the roof, inhabited by some large long-legged birds—cranes, I suppose, as the German children's books tell us they build on houses, & fulfil a deep moral purpose by carrying off naughty children.

We reached Königsberg about 7, & put up at the "Deutsches Haus."

10 1/2 p.m. Hearing a squeaking noise in the street, I have just looked out, & observed a policeman (or a being of that kind) on his beat. He marches slowly down the middle of the street, & every few yards he stops, puts a musical instrument to his mouth, and produces a sound exactly like a child's penny-trumpet. I noticed the same noise at Danzig, about mid-night, & attributed it to wandering boys.

JULY 24. (W.) I went out & roamed over the place alone, as Liddon was not well enough to go too, & among other things went up to the top of the tower of the Aldstadt Kirche, & got a very good general view of the place.   The hunting up the sexton with the key, & questioning him, when we had mounted the tower, about the different objects in sight, was a severe tax on my very slender stock of German.   The parts of the town I visited were common-place enough, but I found afterwards that I had missed the oldest portion.

In the evening we sat for more than 2 hours in the Bürse-Garten, listening to some capital music, & watching the natives enjoying themselves, which they did most thoroughly.   The elder folk settled themselves round the little tables (each holding 4 or 6), the women bringing their work, while the children wandered everywhere, generally in sets of 4 or 5 together, all holding hands. Waiters were roaming about, on the watch for orders, but there seemed to be but little drinking going on.   All were as quiet & courteous as in a London drawing room.   Everybody seemed to know everybody else, & the whole thing was a much more domestic scene than what we witnessed at Brussels.

By staying at the "Deutsches Haus," we enjoy one unusual privilege—we may ring our bells as much & as often as we like: no measures are taken to stop the noise.   The average time it takes to get a bell answered is from 5 to 10 minutes, & to get the required article from 1/2 to 3/4 of an hour.

JULY 25. (TH.) A day of walking about, but there is nothing to record, except that some of the shops have the German inscriptions repeated in Hebrew characters.   In the evening I visited the theatre, which was fairly good in every way, & very good in the singing & some of the acting.   The play was "Anno 66," but I could only catch a few words here & there, so have very little idea of the plot. One of the characters was a "correspondent of an English newspaper."   This singular being came on in the midst of a soldiers' bivouac (before Sadowa), dressed very nearly in white—a very long frock-coat, & a tall hat on the back of his head—both nearly white.   He said "morning," as a general remark, when he first came on, but afterwards talked what I suppose was broken German.   He appeared to be regarded as a butt by the soldiers, & ended his career by falling into a drum.

The 2 things most sold in Königsberg *ought* to be (as they occupy about half the shops) gloves & fireworks. Nevertheless, I have met many gentlemen walking about without gloves: perhaps they are only used to guard the hands when letting off fireworks.

JULY 26. (F.) In the morning we visited the Dom-Kirche, a fine old building, and by the 12.54 train we left for St. Petersburg (or Petersburg, as it seems to be generally called), which we reached punctually at 5.30 p.m. next day, being a run of 28 1/2 hours! Unfortunately, the seats of the carriage we were in only allowed room for four to lie down, & as there were 2 ladies & another gentleman besides ourselves, I slept on the floor, with a carpet-bag & coat for a pillow, &, though not in great luxury, was quite comfortable enough to sleep soundly all night. The other gentleman we found to be an Englishman, who had lived in Petersburg for 15 years, & was returning from a visit to Paris & London. He was most kind in answering our questions, & in giving us a great many hints as to seeing Petersburg, pronouncing the language, &c. but gave us rather dismal prospects of what is before us, as he says very few speak any language but Russian. As an instance of the extraordinary long words which the language contains, he spelt for me the following:—

ЗАЩИЩАЮЩИХСЯ

which, written in English letters, is Zashtsheeshtshayoushtsheekhsya:—this alarming word is the genitive plural of a participle, and means "of persons defending themselves."

He proved a very pleasant addition to our party, & he & I had 3 games of chess in the course of the second day, which it is perhaps as well that I did not record, as they all ended in my defeat.

The whole of the country from the Russian frontier to Petersburg, was perfectly flat & uninteresting, except for the occasional apparition of a peasant, in the usual fur cap, tunic & belt, & now & then a church with a circular dome and four little domes set round it, the tops painted green & the whole thing looking (as our friend said) very like a cruet-stand.

At one station where we paused for lunch, there was a man playing a guitar with panpipes fixed at the top, & bells somewhere about it, all of which he managed to play in tune & time: this place was also remarkable for our first tasting the native soup, Щи (pronounced shtshee), which was quite drinkable, though it contained some sour element, which perhaps is necessary for Russian palates . . . Before arriving, we got our friend to teach us the Russian name of our hotel, Gostinritsa Klee, as he thought we should probably have to take a Russian driver, but we were relieved of all trouble by finding that there was a man in waiting, belonging to the "Hotel de Russie," who accosted us in German, put us into their omnibus, & fetched the luggage.   We had only time for a short stroll after dinner, but it was full of wonder and novelty.   The enormous width of the streets (the secondary ones seem to be broader than anything in London), the little droshkies that went running about, seemingly quite indifferent as to running over anybody, (we soon found it was necessary to keep a very sharp lookout, as they never shouted, however close they were upon us)— the enormous illuminated signboards over the shops, & the gigantic churches, with their domes painted blue & covered with gold stars— & the bewildering jabber of the natives—all contributed to the wonders of our first walk in St. Petersburg.   We passed a shrine on our way, beautifully ornamented & gilt inside & out, & containing a crucifix, pictures, &c.   Nearly all the poor who went by uncovered their heads, bowed towards it, & crossed themselves many times— a strange sight in the midst of busy crowds.

   JULY 28. (SUN.) We went in the morning to the great Isaac-Church, but the service, being in Sclavonic, was beyond all hope of comprehension.   There were no musical instruments whatever to aid in the chants, but they managed to produce a wonderful effect with voices alone.   The church is a huge square building, running out into 4 equal pieces for the chancel, nave, & transepts, the middle being roofed by a great dome (which is gilt all over outside), & there are so few windows that it would be nearly dark inside, if it were not for the many Eikons that are hung round it with candles burning before them.   Each Eikon seems to have only 2 large candles supplied to begin with, but there are numbers of holders for little candles, & these are supplied by those who pray before them, each of whom brings one with him, & lights it & sticks it in. The only share the congregation had in the service was to bow and cross themselves, & sometimes to kneel down & touch the ground with their foreheads. One would hope that this was accompanied by some private prayer, but it could not have been so in all cases: I saw quite young children doing it, with no expression on their faces which even hinted that they attached any meaning to it, & one little boy (whom I noticed in the afternoon in the Kazan Cathedral), whose mother made him kneel down & put his forehead to the ground, could not have been more than 3 years old. They were doing all the bowing & crossing before the Eikons as well, & not only that, but when I was waiting outside for Liddon (I went out when the sermon began) I noticed great numbers do it while passing the church-door, even when they were at the opposite side of an enormously broad street. A narrow piece of pavement ran from the entrance right across, so that every one driving or walking by could tell the exact moment when they were opposite.

The crossing, by the way, is hardly to be so called, as it consists of touching, with the right forefinger, the forehead, breast, right shoulder, & left shoulder: this is generally done 3 times, followed by a low bow each time, & then a 4th time without a bow.

The dresses of the officiating ministers were most splendid, & the processions & incense reminded me of the Roman Catholic Church at Brussels, but the more one sees of these gorgeous services, with their many appeals to the senses, the more, I think one learns to love the plain, simple (but to my mind far more real) service of the English church.

I found out too late that the only English service here is in the morning, so in the afternoon we walked here & there about this marvellous city. It is so utterly unlike anything I have ever seen, that I feel as if I could and should be content to do nothing for many days but roam about it. We walked the whole length of the Nevoki, which is about 3 miles long, with many fine buildings along it, & must, I should think, be one of the finest streets in the world: it terminates in (probably) the largest square in the world, the Admiralty Platz (Пл о Ща Аь) which is about a mile long, the front of the Admiralty occupying most of one side.

There is a fine equestrian statue of Peter the Great near the Admiralty. The lower part is not a pedestal, but left shapeless & rough like a real rock. The horse is rearing, & has a serpent coiled about its hind feet, on which, I think, it is treading. If this had been put up in Berlin, Peter would no doubt have been actively engaged in killing the monster, but here he takes no notice of it: in fact the killing theory is not recognized. We found two colossal figures of lions, which are so painfully mild, that each of them is rolling a great ball about, like a kitten.

We had a very good dinner at the table d'hote, beginning with Щи which I am much relieved to find is not always, & essentially, sour, as I had feared.

JULY 29. (M.) I began the day by buying a map of Petersburg, & a little dictionary & vocabulary. The latter seems pretty sure to be of great use to us—in the course of a day (a good deal of which went in ineffectual calls) we took 4 in droshkies—2 of them from the hotel, when we got the hall-porter to arrange with the driver for us, but the other 2 we had to arrange for ourselves. I give one of the preliminary conversations as a specimen:—

MYSELF. Gostonitia Klee—(Klees Hotel).

DRIVER. (utters a sentence rapidly of which we can only catch the words) Tri groshen—(Three groshen—30 kopecks?)

M. Doatzat kopecki? (20 kopecks?)

D. (indignantly) Tritzat! (30).

M. (resolutely) Doatzat.

D. (Coaxingly) Doatzat pait? (25?).

M. (with the air of one who has said his say, & wishes to be rid of the thing) Doatzat. (Here I take Liddon's arm, & we walk off together, entirely disregarding the shouts of the driver. When we have gone a few yards, we hear the droshky lumbering after us: he draws up alongside, & hails us).

M. (gravely) Doatzat?

D. (with a delighted grin). Da! Da! Doatzat! (and in we get).

This sort of thing is amusing for once in a way, but if it were a necessary process in hiring cabs in London, it would become a little tedious in time.

After dinner we visited the markets, which are great blocks of building surrounded by little shops under a colonnade. I should think there must have been 40 or 50 consecutively which sold gloves, collars & such things. We found here dozens of shops devoted to the sale of Eikons, ranging from little rough paintings an inch or two in length, up to elaborate pictures a foot or more in length, where all but the faces & hands consisted of gold. They will be no easy things to buy, as we are told the shop-keepers in that quarter speak nothing but Russian.

JULY 30. (TU.) We took a long walk about the place, probably 15 or 16 miles altogether—the distances here are enormous: it is like walking about in a city of giants. We paid a visit to the Cathedral Church in the fortress, which is a grand array of gold & jewels, & marble: magnificent rather than beautiful. Our guide was a Russian soldier (most official business seems to be done by soldiers) whose explanations, in his native tongue, were of no particular use. The tombs of all the emperors since Peter the Great (but one) are here: all exactly alike, of white marble, with a gold ornament at each corner, a massive gold cross lying on the top, & the inscription on a gold plate—no other ornament.

There were many Eikons all round the Church, with candles burning in front, & boxes to receive offerings. I saw one poor woman go up to the picture of St. Peter, with her sick baby in her arms: she first gave a piece of money to the soldier on duty, who put it in the box for her, & then began a long series of bowing & crossing herself, all the time talking soothingly to the poor little baby. One could almost read in her worn, anxious face, that she believed what she was doing would in some way propitiate St. Peter to help her child.

From the fortress we crossed to the Wassili Ostrov (Isle of Basil) & walked over a good deal of it: the names of the shops, &c. were almost entirely Russian. Accordingly, in order to get some bread & water at a little shop we passed, I hunted out the 2 words in a vocabulary, "khlaib" and "vadáh," & these we found enough for the transaction.

Tonight, on coming up to my room, I found there was no water for the morning, & no towel—and to add to the excitement of the position, the bell (which would have summoned a German waiter) refused to ring. In this pleasing emergency, I had to go down, & found a servant, luckily the man belonging to my passage. Him I addressed hopefully in German, but it was no use—he only shook his head wildly: so I was reduced (after a hasty consultation of the vocabulary) to make my request in Russian, which I did in a severely simple style, ignoring all but principal words.

JULY 31. (w.) Our fellow-traveller, Mr. Alexander Muir, called on us, & invited us to come over and lionise Peterhof tomorrow, (under the escort of his partner), and to dine with him. We gave the day to visiting the "Hermitage," (i.e., the collection of pictures, &c. at the Winter Palace), & the Alexander Nevoki Monastery.

At the Hermitage, where we had intended to confine ourselves entirely to the pictures, we fell into the hands of the guide who showed the sculpture, &c. & who, disregarding all hints of our wish to get up to the gallery, insisted on taking us through his department, & so earning his fee. It is nevertheless a magnificent collection of ancient art, collected at an almost incalculable expense.

The pictures we could only see partially & hurriedly, but they formed, like the sculpture, quite a priceless collection. One of the large rooms contained mostly Murillos—one a most lovely "Assumption of the Virgin"—another "Jacob's Vision" (Qu. the one engraved in D'Oyly and Mart?). Another room was full of Titians. Not having time for all, or even half the collection, we passed on to the Dutch School, to see Paul Potter's "Masterpiece," a picture described by Murray, representing, with extraordinary skill & humor, in compartments, hunting-scenes of various kinds of game, the lion, boar, &c.—and the final combination of all the animals to try & execute the hunter and his dogs.

The picture I chiefly remember was a circular "Holy Family" by Raphael, quite exquisite.

From the Winter Palace we took a droshky to the Monastery. Here we only succeeded in seeing the church, which contains great wealth of gold, silver, & jewels, in the form of shrines, &c. We remained through the evening service, which was much like that at the Isaac-Church, though of course with a very small congregation.

AUG. 1. (TH.) About 1/2 past 10 Mr. Merrilies called for us, & with really remarkable kindness gave up his day to taking us down to Peterhof, a distance of about 20 miles, & showing us over the place. We went by steamer, down the tideless, saltless Gulf of Finland: the first peculiarity extends through the Baltic, & the second through a great part of it. The piece we crossed some 15 miles from shore to shore is very shallow, in many parts only 6 or 8 feet deep, & every winter it is entirely frozen over with ice 2 feet thick, & when this is covered with snow it forms a secure plain, which is regularly used for travelling on—though the immense distance, without means of food or shelter, is dangerous for poorly-clad foot-passengers. Mr. Merrilies told us of a friend of his who, in crossing last winter, passed the bodies of 8 people who had been frozen. . . . We had a good view, on our way, of the coast of Finland & of Cronstadt. . . . When we landed at Peterhof, we found Mr. Muir's carriage waiting for us, & with its assistance, getting out every now & then to walk through portions where it could not go, we went over the grounds of 2 imperial palaces, including many little summer-houses, each of which would make a very good residence in itself, as, though small, they were fitted up & adorned in every way that taste could suggest or wealth achieve. For varied beauty, & perfect combination of nature & art, I think the gardens eclipse those of "Sans Souci." At every corner, or end of an avenue or path, where a piece of statuary *could* be introduced with effect, there one was sure to find one, in bronze or in white marble—many of the latter had a sort of circular niche built behind, with a blue background to throw the figure into relief. Here we found a series of shelving ledges made of stone, with a sheet of water gliding down over them—here a long path, stretching down slopes & flights of steps, and arched over all the way with trellises & creepers—here a huge boulder, hewn, just as it lay, into the shape of a gigantic head & face, with mild Sphinx-like eyes, as if some buried Titan were struggling to free himself—here a fountain, so artfully formed of pipes set in circles, each set shooting the water higher than those outside as to form a solid pyramid of glittering spray—here a lawn, seen through a break in the woods below us, with threads of scarlet geraniums running over it, and looking in the distance like a huge branch of coral—and here & there long avenues of trees, lying in all directions, sometimes three or four together side by side, and sometimes radiating like a star, and stretching away into the distance till the eye was almost weary of following them.

All this will rather serve to remind me, than to convey any idea, of what we saw.

We just called at the house on our way for lunch, & saw Mrs. Muir & some charming little children, & went there again about 5, when we met Mr. Muir. Other friends came in for dinner, & we finally returned to Petersburg with the indefatigable Mr. Merrilies, who crowned the many services he had done us during the day by procuring a droshky & making the indispensable bargain with the driver, a feat we might well have despaired of by ourselves, in the dark, hustled about in a mob of drivers and a perfect Babel of uncouth noises.

AUG. 2 (FRI.) Left by the 2.30 train for Moscow, which we reached about 10 next morning. We took "sleeping-tickets" (2 roubles extra) which resulted in the guard coming in & performing an elaborate conjuring-trick at about 11 p.m. What had been the back of the seat revolved upwards & became a shelf; the seats & the divisions melted away; cushions & pillows made their appearance—& finally we put ourselves away on the said shelves, which we found to be very comfortable beds. The floor would have accommodated 3 other sleepers, but luckily none made their appearance. I staid up till about 1 in the morning, & was most of the time the sole occupant of the outside platform at the end of the carriage: it had a handrail & a roof, and afforded a splendid view of the country as we flew through it—its disadvantages being that the vibration & noise were much worse than inside. The guard came out now & then, & during the hours of darkness raised no objection to my being there—perhaps he felt lonely: but when I tried it again the next morning he was soon seized with a despotic fit, & drove me into the carriage again.

At Moscow we found a carriage & porter waiting for "Dusaux Hotel," to which we were bound.

We gave 5 or 6 hours to a stroll through this wonderful city, a

city of white & green roofs, of conical towers that rise one out of
another like a fore-shortened telescope; of bulging gilded domes,
in which you see as in a looking-glass, distorted pictures of the
city; of churches which look, outside, like bunches of variegated
cactus (some branches crowned with green prickly buds, others
with blue, & others with red & white), & which, inside, are hung
all round with Eikons & lamps, & lined with illuminated pictures up
to the very roof; & finally of pavement that goes up & down like a
ploughed field, & droshky-drivers who insist on being paid 30 per
cent extra today, "because it is the Empress' birthday."

After dinner we drove to the "Sparrow Hills," whence we had
a grand panoramic view of the forest of spires & domes, with the
river Moskva winding in front—the same hills from which Napo-
leon's army first caught sight of the city.

AUG. 4. (SUN.)   In the morning we had a long & unsuccessful
search for the English Chapel.   Afterwards I went alone, & luckily
fell in with a Russian gentleman who could speak English, & who
kindly went with me to the place.   Mr. Penny, the Chaplain, was
at home, & I presented an introductory note from Burgon, & was
received most heartily by himself & his wife.

Liddon came with me to the evening service there, & we spent
the evening with them, & received many valuable suggestions as
to our plans here, & kind offers to assist us in making purchases of
curiosities, &c.

AUG. 5. (M.)   A day of sight-seeing.   We began by getting up at
5, & going off to the 6 o'clock service at the Petrovski Monastery, it
being the anniversary of the consecration, & therefore a service
of peculiar magnificence.   It was most beautiful in music & scenic
effect, but much of the ceremonial was to me unintelligible.   Bishop
Leonide (?) was present, & took the principal part in the Com-
munion, of which one infant partook, but no others of the congregation.   It was a very interesting sight when the service was over,
& the bishop, having been disrobed of the gorgeous vestments
before the altar, came out in a plain black gown, while the people
crowded round him as he went, to kiss his hand.

After breakfast, as the day seemed to have set in for steady rain,
we devoted ourselves to seeing interiors, of which it is quite impos-

sible to give any adequate idea by mere words. We began with St. Basil's church, which is as quaint (almost grotesque) within as it is without, & which is shown by undoubtedly the most atrocious guide I have yet met with. His original theory was that we were to walk through the place at the rate of about 4 miles an hour. Finding it quite impossible to get us along at that rate, he resorted to rattling his keys, fidgeting noisily about, singing loud, abusing us violently in Russian—in fact doing everything short of taking us by the collar & dragging us along. By dint of pure obstinacy, and a convenient deafness, we managed to see the church, or rather group of churches under one roof, in tolerable comfort. Each had its own peculiarities, though the golden screen, & illuminated frescoes all over the walls & up into the dome were common to all.

Next we went to the Treasury & saw thrones, & crowns, & jewels—until one began to think that those three articles were rather more common than blackberries. On some of the thrones, &c. the pearls were literally showered like rain.

Then we were shown through the palace, after which, I think, all other palaces must seem dwarfed & poor. I measured one of the reception rooms by stepping, & made it 80 yards long, & I should think, it would be 25 or 30 broad. There were at least 2 of this size, and many other large rooms—all lofty, all decorated elaborately, from the floor inlaid with satin-wood, &c. up to the frescoed ceilings—all profusely gilded—the dwelling-rooms furnished with silk or satin instead of wall-paper—& all furnished & decorated as if the wealth of the owner were simply boundless. Thence we went to the sacristy, which, besides untold wealth in vestments, thick-set with pearls & jewels, crucifixes, & Eikons, contains the 3 enormous silver chaldrons in which the holy oil is made, used in baptism, &c. which is supplied from here to the 16 bishoprics . . . After dinner we went by arrangement to Mr. Penny & accompanied him to see a Russian wedding—it was a *most* interesting ceremony.

There was a large choir from the cathedral, who sang a long & beautiful anthem, before the service began—& the deacon (from the Church of the Assumption) delivered several recitative portions of the service in the most magnificent bass voice I ever heard, rising gradually (I should say by less than half a note at a time, if that is possible), & increasing in volume of sound as he rose in the scale, until his final note rang through the building like a chorus of many voices. I could not have conceived that one voice could have produced such an effect.

One part of the ceremony, the crowning the married couple, was very nearly grotesque. Two gorgeous golden crowns were brought in, which the officiating priest first waved before them, & then placed on their heads—or rather, the unhappy bridegroom had to wear *his*, but the bride, having prudently arranged her hair in a rather complicated manner with a lace veil, could not have hers put on, but had it held above her by a friend. The bridegroom, in plain evening dress, crowned like a king, holding a candle, & with a face of resigned misery, would have been pitiable if he had not been so ludicrous. When the people had gone, we were invited by the priest to see the east end of the church, behind the golden gates, & were finally dismissed with a hearty shake of the hands, and the "kiss of peace," of which even I, though in lay costume, came in for a share. We spent the rest of the evening with our friends, Mr. and Mrs. Penny.

AUG. 6. (TU.) Mr. Penny kindly came with us round the Dvor (or Market) to show us where to get the best Eikons, &c. Before this we had been up the Ivan Tower & had a beautiful view of Moscow, lying around us on all sides, its spires & golden domes all flashing in the sun. At 1/2 past 5 we set off with the two Wares for Nijni Novgorod, & found the expedition well worth all the discomfort we had to endure from first to last. Our friends brought their "commissionaire," who can talk French & Russian, & who was of great use to us in making purchases in the fair. Sleeping carriages are unknown luxuries on this line, so that we had to make the best we could of the ordinary second-classes. I slept on the floor both going & returning. The only thing that occurred to vary (I can hardly say relieve) the monotony of a journey that lasted from 7 one evening till past noon the next day was our having to get out & walk over a temporary foot-bridge over a river, the railway bridge having been washed away. This entailed on some 200 or 300 passengers a trudge of about a mile in pelting rain.

There had been an accident, which delayed our train, & the result was that if we had kept to our first plan of returning that afternoon, we should have had about 2 1/2 hours in the world's fair. We agreed that this was not worth while, considering the trouble & expense we were put to, & that we would engage beds & remain till next day. So we went to the Smernovaya (or some such name) Hotel—a truly villainous place, though no doubt the best in the town. The feeding was very good, & everything else very bad. It was some consolation to find that as we sat at dinner we furnished a subject of the liveliest interest to 6 or 7 waiters, all dressed in white tunics, belted at the waist, & white trousers, who ranged themselves in a row & gazed in a quite absorbed way at the collection of strange animals that were feeding before them . . . Now & then a twinge of conscience would seize them, that they were after all not fulfilling the great object of life as waiters, & on these occasions they would all hurry to the end of the room, & refer to a great drawer, which seemed to contain nothing but spoons & forks. When we asked for anything, they first looked at each other in an alarmed way—then, when they had ascertained which understood the order best, they all followed his example, which always was to refer to the big drawer . . . we spent most of the afternoon wandering through the fair, & buying Eikons, &c.

It was a wonderful place. Besides there being distinct quarters for Persians, the Chinese, & others, we were constantly meeting strange beings, with unwholesome complexions and unheard-of costumes. The Persians, with their gentle intelligent faces, the long eyes set wide apart, the black hair, & yellow brown skin, crowned with a black woollen fez something like a grenadier, were about the most picturesque we met—but all the novelties of the day were thrown into the shade by our adventure at sunset, when we came upon the Tartar Mosque (the only one in Nijni), exactly as one of the officials came out on the roof to utter the [1] or call to prayer. Even if it had been in no way singular in itself, it would have been deeply interesting from its novelty & uniqueness—but the cry itself was quite unlike anything I have ever heard before. The beginning of each sen-

[1] These blank spaces are in the original.—*McD.*

tence was uttered in a rapid monotone, & towards the end it rose gradually till it ended in a prolonged shrill wail, which floated overhead through the still air with an indescribably sad & ghost-like effect: heard at night it would have thrilled one like the cry of the Banshee.

Presently the worshippers came trooping in, obedient to the call, each laying aside his shoes as he entered: we were allowed by the chief minister to stand in the doorway & watch. The form of devotion seemed to be standing facing to Mecca, suddenly kneeling down & touching the carpet with the forehead, rising & repeating it once or twice, then again standing motionless for a few minutes, & so on. On the way home we visited a church & found vespers going on, with all the usual accompaniments of Eikons, candles, crossing & bowing, &c.

In the evening I went, with the younger of the two Wares, to the Nijni Theatre, which was the plainest I ever saw—the only decoration inside being white wash. It was very large, & not more than a tenth full, so that it was remarkably cool & comfortable. The performance, being entirely in Russian, was a little beyond us, but by working away diligently at the play bill, with a pocket dictionary, at all intervals, we got a tolerable idea of what it was all about. The first & best piece was "Aladdin and the Wonderful Lamp," a burlesque that contained some really first-rate acting, & very fair singing and dancing. I have never seen actors who attended more thoroughly to the drama & the other actors, & looked less at the audience. The one who took the part of "Aladdin," named "Ленскій," [2] & one of the actresses in another piece, who was named "Соронина," [3] were about the best. The other pieces were "Cochin China," "The Hussar's Daughter."

AUG. 7. (WED.) After passing the night on beds consisting of boards covered with a mattress about an inch thick, a pillow, one sheet & a quilt—and a breakfast whose chief feature was a large delicious-tasting fish, almost entirely without bones, called a Stir-let—we visited the Cathedral and the Minin Tower. In the Cathedral we found a great Mass going on, & the white building

[2] Lyensky.   [3] Soronina.

crowded with military: we waited some while & heard some splendid singing.

From the Minin Tower we had a glorious view of the whole town & the Volga winding away into the dim distance. Then after another visit to the Dvor, we set out about 3 on our homeward journey, if possible a more uncomfortable one than the former, and reached Moscow again, tired but delighted with all we had seen, at about 9 in the morning.

AUG. 9. (F.) The only great event of the day was our visit, (again in company with the Wares), to the Semonof Monastery, where from the top of a tower, in climbing which we counted 380 steps, we had a nearer, & to my mind better, view of Moscow than that from the Sparrow Hills. We visited the chapels, cemeteries, & dining-hall: the chapels were beautifully decorated with frescoes &c. & one of them contained a curious picture, almost grotesque, of the beam & the mote—and we tasted the monks' brown bread, which was certainly eatable, though not inviting . . . The elder of the Wares accompanied me in the evening to the "Little Theatre" of Moscow—really a large handsome building. There was a very good audience, and the pieces "The Burgomaster's Wedding" and "A Woman's Secret," won great applause, but neither pleased me so much as "Aladdin." It was all in Russian.

AUG. 10. (SAT.) We gave the morning to calls with letters of introduction, but did not succeed in finding any one at home. In the afternoon we drove to the Petrovski Palace, & walked about in the park there. The palace is bright red & white—the result being decidedly ugly. On our way back I took a copy of the inscription over the Toer Gate, which forms the entrance to the Park

PIAE MEMORIAE

ALEXANDRI I

Ob Restitutam E Cine Ribus
Multisque Paternae Curae Monumentis Auctam
Antiquam Hanc Metropolin

FLAGRANTE BELLO GALLICO ANNO MDCXII FLAMMIS DATAM.

We dined with Mr. Penny to meet Mr. and Mrs. Combe & their niece Miss Nathalie, and afterwards we all went together to the

Semonof Monastery, & heard a very long but very beautiful service, which contained one feature quite new to me: the chief minister brought forwards the book of the Gospels, & held it while all the others, & then all the monks, came forwards, two by two, & kissed it. He then placed it on a desk, & stood by it while the rest of the congregation came up & kissed, first the book, & then his hand.

AUG. 11. (SUN.) We attended the English church in the morning, as Liddon had undertaken to preach. Thence with Mr. Penny, to call on Bishop Leonide, suffragan bishop of Moscow, to whom Liddon had an introduction from Prince Orloff. We were quite delighted with his reception of us, and his gentle winning manner —the sort of manner that puts people at their ease in a moment. I think the visit must have lasted an hour and a half; before leaving we arranged to go with him over to Troitsa tomorrow, in hopes that a visit to the Metropolitan, Archbishop Philoret, may be possible . . . . We then went back to dine with our hospitable friends, & to accompany them to the Strasnoi Nunnery, where the singing is all done by the nuns themselves—though portions of the service are of course taken by the priest. The reader however was in every case a nun: there were many readings in the course of the service, & for some of them the nuns left their places in the choir, & ranged themselves in a circle round the reader. Some of them looked quite young: one, I should think, could not have been 12. The musical parts of the service seemed to be much the same as in other churches we have visited, but the effect of the women's voices, unaccompanied, was singularly beautiful . . . We had tea with the Pennys, & attended evening service there, ending with a walk along the Kremlin terrace, where the cool evening, & the splendid view—a perfect panorama of beautiful buildings lying around us—were most enjoyable.

AUG. 12. (M.) A most interesting day. We breakfasted at 5 1/2, & soon after 7 left by railway, in company with Bishop Leonide and Mr. Penny, for Troitska Monastery. We found the Bishop, in spite of his limited knowledge of English, a very conversational & entertaining fellow-traveller. The service at the cathedral had already begun when we reached it, & the Bishop took us in with him, through a great crowd which thronged the building, into a

side-room which opened into the chancel, where we remained
during the service, & enjoyed the unusual privilege of seeing the
clergy communicate—a ceremony for which the doors of the
chancel are always shut, & the curtains drawn, so that the congregation never witness it. It was a most elaborate ceremony, full of
crossings, & waving of incense before every thing that was going
to be used, but also clearly full of much deep devotion. Towards
the end of the service one of the monks brought round a dish of
little loaves, & gave us each one: these had been blessed, & their
presenting the loaves to us was to signify that we had been re-
membered in their prayers. On leaving the cathedral, we were
ushered by one of the monks through the sacristy, & the rooms
for painting & photography (a number of boys are taught these
2 arts, which are used entirely for ecclesiastical purposes), and
we were accompanied by a Russian gentleman who had been with
us in the cathedral, & who was most kind in explaining the various
objects to us in French, &, when we wanted to purchase Eikons,
&c., in enquiring the prices & counting the change. It was only
when he had wished us good day & left us, that we discovered who
it was that had shown us so much attention—more, I am afraid, than
most Englishmen would show to foreigners—Prince Chirkoff.

In the painting-room we found so many exquisite Eikons, done
some on wood, & some on mother-of-pearl, that the difficulty was
to decide, not so much what to buy as what to leave unbought.
We ultimately left with three each, the limit being produced by
shortness of time rather than by any prudential considerations.

The sacristy was a perfect mine of wealth—jewels, embroidery,
crosses, chalices, &c. We saw there the renowned stone, polished
& set as an Eikon, which contains in its strata (apparently at least)
the picture of a monk praying before a crucifix. I looked at it
carefully, but could not in the least believe in the naturalness of so
complicated a phenomenon.

In the afternoon we went down to the Archbishop's palace, &
were presented to him by Bishop Leonide. The Archbishop could
only talk Russian so that the conversation between him & Liddon—
(a most interesting one, which lasted more than an hour)—was

conducted in a very original fashion—the Archbishop making a remark in Russian, which was put into English by the Bishop: Liddon then answered the remark in French, & the Bishop repeated his answer, in Russian, to the Archbishop. So that a conversation, entirely carried on between two people, required the use of three languages!

The Bishop had kindly got one of the Theological students who could talk French to conduct us about, which he did most zealously, taking us, among other things to see the subterranean cells of the hermits, in which some of them live for many years. We were shown the doors of two of the inhabited ones: it was a strange & not quite comfortable feeling, in a dark narrow passage where each had to carry a candle, & to know that a human being was living within, with only a small lamp to give him light, in solitude and silence day and night . . . .

We returned with the Bishop by a late train, after one of the most memorable days of our tour.

At our dinner at the Troitska inn, we succeeded in obtaining two of the specialties of Russia—a sort of bitter wine, made of the berries of the mountain ash, of which they take a glass before dinner to give an appetite. It is called "P hoboe" (Ribinov). The other was the soup "III" (Shchi), with the proper accompaniment of a jug of sour cream to be stirred into it.

AUG. 13. (TU.) The day of the "blessing of the waters," a great ceremony performed, partly in the cathedral, & partly at the river-side. The service began at 9, & as I was not dressed till 1/2 past, I went off without breakfast. We made our way into the cathedral first, but the crowd was so great that I at once made my way out again, & went & took my place among the crowd waiting near the river-side, to see the procession pass. It did not come till about 11, & I then waited to see it return: the ceremony at the river-side I could not get a view of, but the procession itself was a very grand one. It began with a series of large banners—if they may be so called— each carried by 3 men: the poles being about 15 feet high, & the banner being more like a circular shield, built all over, generally with rays round the edge, & bearing in the centre a cross or eikon.

There must have been 30 or 40 of them. Then came a long train of priests, deacons, & other orders, all in embroidered copes with other decorations, some of them even wearing large eikons on their breasts—then large candles, eikons, &c.—then four bishops in full dress, with attendant priests, &c.—then crowds of singing men & boys in a sort of uniform of red & blue. There were very large crowds looking on, but all quite orderly & good humored: the only scene of confusion I noticed was caused by a vessel of water being brought back from the river by one of the deacons at the end of the procession. There was a wild rush made by every one near him to put their lips to it, & the result was that the water was dashed about in all directions over the bystanders, & nearly all of it spilt. It was 1/2 past 12 before I got back to my breakfast.

The whole day was observed as a grand holiday, & in the afternoon we walked through the fair. There was nothing specially Russian about it, unless it were in the ages of the people who partook of the charming but unintellectual amusement of riding on wooden horses suspended to the circumference of a great horizontal wheel. Grave middle-aged men, some of them soldiers in uniform, might be seen bestriding creatures that once looked like horses, & trying to fancy they enjoyed it. There were a number of little circuses, &c., with large pictures outside representing people going through performances that would have been very difficult even if arms & legs had not been, as most of them were represented to be, entirely out of joint. And there were booths where food was sold, from which it would seem that the proper food for a fête-day is raw fish & dried beans.

In the evening we visited the zoological gardens, where after visiting the birds & beasts we sat under the trees, among wreaths of coloured lamps, & listened to the "Tyrolien Singers," a very enjoyable performance.

AUG. 14. (W.) The morning went in a visit to the Bank & the Dvor.

We dined at the "Moscow Traktir" on a genuine Russian dinner, with Russian wine . . . Here is the bill of fare.

Супъ и пирошки	(soop ee pirashkée)
Поросенокъ	(parasainok)
Асетрина	(acetrina)
Котлеты	(kotletee)
Мороженое	(marojenoi)
Крымское	(krimskoe)
Кофе	(kofé)

The soup was clear, containing chopped vegetables & legs of chickens, & the "pirashkée," to eat with it, were patties consisting chiefly of hard-boiled eggs. The "parasaompl" was a piece of cold pork with a sauce made apparently of pounded horse-radish & cream. "Acetrina" is sturgeon: this was another cold dish—the "fixings" being crawfish, olives, capers, & a sort of thick gravy. The cutlets "Kotletee" were veal I think—"Marajensee" means "cream-ices"—these were delicious: one lemon, one black-currant, a kind new to me. The Crimean wine was also very pleasant, in fact the whole dinner (except perhaps the sturgeon concoction) was a very good one.

Spent the evening, as has now become very usual for us, with our hospitable friends, Mr. and Mrs. Penny. Before going there we paid a visit to the Strastny Monastery, containing a beautiful cemetery. Among the tombs, which universally showed great taste & artistic feeling, was one cross, which actually contained a burning lamp, protected by glass on each side.

AUG. 15. (TH.) We breakfasted about 6, in order to go off by the early train for the Monastery of "New Jerusalem." A Mr. Spier, a friend of Mr. Penny's, on his way to his house, beyond the Monastery, had kindly offered to go with us. We had thought it could easily be done in a day, but this proved to be entirely a delusion.

The railway part of the journey lasted till about 10. We then hired a "tarantas," (which is the form that an old barouche would assume if the body were made nearly twice as long & the springs taken away), & in this we jolted along over 14 miles of quite the worst road I have ever seen. It abounded in ruts & ditches & deep mud, & the bridges consisted of rough logs laid together anyhow.

Even with three horses, it took us nearly 3 hours to do the distance.

On the way we followed the suggestion made, I think, by Mr. Muri, of applying at a peasant's cottage for bread & milk, as a pretext for seeing the interior and their mode of life. The cottage we applied at contained two men, an old woman & 6 or 7 boys of various ages. The black bread, & the milk, were both very good, & it was very interesting to be able to realise for oneself the home of the Russian peasant. I tried 2 sketches, one of the interior, one of the exterior: for the latter we got 6 of the boys, & a little girl, to form a group: it would have been a capital scene for photography, but was rather beyond my powers of drawing.

We did not reach the village adjoining the Monastery till about 2, & we then discovered that, in order to reach Moscow that night, it would be necessary to leave again at 3. Accordingly we paid a hasty visit to the "Church of the Holy Sepulchre," & from thence sent a message to the post-house to harness the fresh horses which we had been told we should find there. At this point our plans broke down; when we returned to the post-house, we found no preparations for going—there were no fresh horses—nothing but the tired ones that had brought us, & the driver & all the bystanders agreed in declaring (in noisy Russian intelligible only to Mr. Spier) that the thing could not be done. So we yielded to fate, & got Mr. Spier to come to the hotel with us, & order us dinner, tea, beds, & breakfast at 3 in the morning. He assured us that there was no one in the whole place who knew a word of anything but Russ, and when he drove off, leaving us at the hotel-door, we certainly felt more desolate and Robinson-Crusoish than we have felt in all our tour as yet. We went off to the Monastery, guided by the hotel servant, who put us into the hands of a Russian monk—the genuine article, one who ignored all other languages. To him I exhibited a sentence in my Russian vocabulary, to the effect "is there any one here who speaks German, French or English?" That little sentence was the turning point of our fortunes—we were at once introduced to another monk, who talked wonderful, but fairly intelligible, French, & he most kindly devoted himself to our service—one might almost say for the rest of the day.

He showed us all over the "Church of the Holy Sepulchre," chiefly interesting from being exactly copied from the one at Jerusalem, as well as the library & sacristy, all very interesting, but not containing anything special or unique, unless it be an imitation ostrich-egg which we found in the sacristy. On looking through it at the light, through a hole in one end, one saw a coloured representation, which looked almost solid, of a female kneeling before a cross. It was now time to return to the hotel for dinner, which we did, after first arranging with our kind guide that we were to ask for him when we got back again.

On our return, the monk took us into his house, where, instead of a cell with skull, cross-bones, &c. we found a comfortable parlour with a little tea-party going on, consisting of 2 ladies, mother and daughter, & a gentleman who I think must have been the father. The elder lady spoke French fairly, & the younger English extremely well. She told us she was engaged in teaching French in one of the "Gymnases" of Moscow, & she was evidently well-educated & clever. It was a very pleasant scene to find oneself in, but so entirely sudden & unexpected that it felt almost like a dream. After tea, we were accompanied by the whole party through the monastery, and shown the rooms occupied by the imperial family when they visit the place, as they occasionally do. Among other things we saw the "Bethlehem," a cell imitated from the one on the spot where our Lord is said to have been born. The monk then took us out through the woods to see the "Hermitage" to which Nikon retreated during his voluntary banishment. On our way out, we bought at a sort of shop at the entrance, kept by the monks, small copies of the "Madonna of the three hands," a great Icon in one of the chapels, painted to commemorate a vision of the Virgin Mary, seen in the way represented in the Icon, with a third hand & arm coming in from below.

In the woods we saw the "Jordan," the "Pool of Bethesda," a little house with a real pool in the middle, and steps leading down to it, and another little house or shrine, called "The Well of Samaria"—but the Hermitage was more wonderful than all we had seen before. It looks but a small house from the outside, but contains a great many rooms, so miniature as hardly to deserve the name, connected by low narrow passages & winding stairs: the bedroom is about 6 feet long & wide: the bed, which is of stone, with a stone pillow, is only 5 ft. 9 in. long, and as it reaches right across the end of the room, with a place hollowed in the wall for the feet, the bishop, who was a tall man, must always have lain in a cramped position. The whole thing looks more like a toy-model of a house than a real one, & the bishop's life must have been one of continual mortification, only to be surpassed by that of his domestics, who lived in a tiny cellar entered by a door about 4 feet high, & with only a glimmer of daylight admitted.

The rest of the party joined us in the woods, & walked back with us, & soon afterwards, with many thanks for their kindness, we took leave of our new-found friends, & returned to the hotel in our former state of desolation, as we knew there was no one there who could speak anything but Russian.

But once more fortune favored us: at the door we found the landlord, who introduced to us with many bows & gesticulations, a Russian gentleman staying in the house, who talked French. He was most kind in transacting for us all we wanted, & sat with us, chatting till past 12. The landlord also, who seemed to be a little the worse for drink, and a good deal out of his mind, was constantly dropping in to shake hands with us & assure us of his friendship. He was, as the Russian gentleman informed us, a nobleman, though of the third order, & had lost a fortune of about a million rubles, a misfortune that had turned his brain. Our last interview with him was when he came in to make out our bill, which he begged us to pay over night, as we were going so early in the morning. He wrote it in pencil on a scrap of rough paper, shouting out the different items as he wrote them down, & then handed it over to me to be added up. This I did, putting in an additional item of "за труди" [3] "for service," & on receiving the money he rose, bowed to the Icon in the corner of the room, crossing himself as he did so, then seized Liddon by the hand, kissed him on both cheeks, & then kissed his hand: I had to submit to the same affectionate farewell, & at last left us to enjoy, as best we

[3] за труды.

might, a night of 3 1/2 hours long, which was further reduced to 2 1/2 hours by our Russian friend coming in for a final chat.

AUG. 16. (F.) We were called at 3, & after breakfasting, & waiting in vain for the prelodka, we set out to hunt it up: we met it coming out of the yard of the "post-house," & set out at 4 for another 3 hours of jolting—somewhat consoled by the spectacle of a beautiful sunrise, & by the music of the horse-bells belonging to a cart which followed close behind us nearly all the way.

At Moscow we found Mr. Penny waiting to carry off Liddon, & introduce him to the Abbé   , with whom we had a long talk.   Afterwards we paid another visit to the Dvor, & then to the foundling hospital.   The director was not there, so we could not see it all, & many of the elder children were in the country—so that we saw little else but a long series of gigantic corridors, full of beds, nurses, & an unlimited number of babies. The little children all seemed to be clean, well cared for, & happy.   In the evening we drove to the petrovski park, & staid a short time listening to a military band.

AUG. 17. (SAT.) The day of the jubilee at Troitsa, for which we had staid in Moscow, & had looked forward to as a great sight— a hope doomed to be disappointed.   Bishop Leonide had promised to take us into the church & into the side-room adjoining the chancel, where we had been before, but we entirely failed in finding him.   We made our way into the church, but could see little or nothing of what was going on, though we succeeded in getting into a room on the opposite side of the former one, so after a while I came out again, & went round alone to the other side. Here, simply by dint of taking every opportunity of moving on, I actually made my way into the very room to which the bishop had promised to take us.   Here I found myself in a most unique position, the only one in lay dress among a crowd of bishops & ecclesiastics.   It was pretty clear that I had not the smallest right to be there—however, as no notice was taken of me, I remained, & had a very good sight of the bishops themselves, & of some portions of the service—but Bishop Leonide never appeared: we afterwards found that he was performing the service in another place.

We did what we could to redeem the failure of the day by

visiting a monastery, & ascending the great tower of the Troitsa monastery, from which we had a splendid view, & made out, with my telescope, a group of towers on the horizon that I think must have been Moscow itself, 40 miles off.

AUG. 18. (SUN.) We went at 9 to the "Church of the Assumption" where Bishop Leonide was to take the principal part, & waited outside in the hope of his taking us in with him: however a gentleman took us in his name before he arrived, & placed us in the little room on the south side of the chancel. Liddon remained through the whole service, but I left in the middle in order to go to the English Church. We dined with the Pennys, & went in for tea after the evening service, & on our way home passed through the Kremlin, & so got our last impression of that most beautiful range of buildings, in perhaps, the most beautiful aspect of which it is capable—a flood of cold, clear moonlight, bringing out the pure white of the walls & towers, & the glittering points of light on the gilded domes, in a way that sunlight could never do—for it could not set them, as we saw them, in the midst of darkness.

AUG. 19. (M.) While breakfasting in the coffee-room, we had some talk with an American who was there with his wife & little boy, & found them very pleasant people. At parting he gave me his card—"R. M. Hunt, Membre du Jury International de l'Exposition Universelle de 1867—Studio B 8, 51 W. 10th St., New York." If I ever visit New York, I may possibly get this mysterious address interpreted. We did little else during the morning but prepare for our departure, & by 2 p.m. we were off for Petersburg —our friends from the vicarage crowning their many acts of kindness by coming to see us off, & to bring us a bottle of their delicious "Kimmel" to cheer us by the way.

We had sleeping-tickets, and there was only one other gentleman in the carriage, so that, with an open window we might have managed: but as our friend (who seemed to be a person of some distinction) had a cold & so objected to this—& as the third bed, which naturally fell to the lot of the youngest, the writer, was situated immovably crosswise, with the head under one bed, & the foot under the other—I preferred air & fatigue, on the platform at the end of the carriage, to rest & suffocation within. From 5 to 6 a. m. I came in & had a nap, but that was all. Before 10 we were once more in the "Gostinitsa Klee."

AUG. 20. (TU.) After a hearty breakfast, I left Liddon to rest & write letters, & went off shopping, &c. beginning with a call on Mr. Muir at No. 61, Galerne Ulitsa. I took a droshky to the house, having first bargained with the driver for 30 kopecks (he wanted 40 to begin with). When we got there we had a little scene, rather a novelty in my experience of droshky-driving. The driver began by saying "sorok" (40) as I got out: this was a warning of the coming storm, but I took no notice of it, but quietly handed over the 30. He received them with scorn & indignation, & holding them out in his open hand, delivered an eloquent discourse in Russian of which "sorok" was the leading idea. A woman who stood by with a look of amusement & curiosity, perhaps understood him. I didn't, but simply held out my hand for the 30, returned them to the purse, & counted out 25 instead. In doing this I felt something like a man pulling the string of a shower-bath— & the effect was like it—his fury boiled over directly, & quite eclipsed all the former row.

I told him in very bad Russian that I had offered 30 once, but wouldn't again: but this, oddly enough, did not pacify him. Mr. Muir's servant told him the same thing at length & finally Mr. Muir himself came out & gave him the substance of it sharply & shortly— but he failed to see it in a proper light. Some people are very hard to please.

We dined at a capital restaurant, Borrell's, in the Great Morskoy, where we got a first-rate dinner, including a bottle of Burgundy, for 5 roubles.

AUG. 21. (W.) Soon after breakfast Count Pontiatine called on Liddon, & hearing that we were thinking of trying to see the "Hermitage," he most kindly volunteered to take us in, & went with us not only through the gallery itself, but also through the winter palace, the suite of rooms assigned to the Prince of Wales, the chapel, &c., none of which are accessible to the ordinary visitor. This time we saw a section of the gallery, which we missed last time, and which has a special interest —"Ecóle Russe." It contains some really wonderful pictures—a gigantic one of "Moses lifting up the serpent in the wilderness" by *Bruni*, which, at a rough computation, was 27 feet wide & 18 high: the grandeur of the design, & the immense variety of expression in the crowd of Israelites, devotion, terror, despair—the wounded & the dying—make it quite an epic. The figure that dwells most in my memory is that of a strong man writhing in the agonies of death, in the centre of the foreground, with the gleaming coils of a serpent folded about his limbs. But perhaps the most striking of all the Russian pictures is a sea-piece, recently bought & not yet numbered: it represents a storm, the mast of a foundered ship, with a few survivors clinging to it, floats in front—behind, the waves are beaten up into mountains, & their crests shivered into driving showers of spray, by the fury of the wind—while the low sunlight shines through the higher waves with a pale green lustre that is perfectly deceptive in the way in which it seems to come *through* the water. I have seen the thing attempted in other pictures, but never so perfectly achieved.

In the afternoon we mounted to the top of the Isaac Church, and much enjoyed the view we got of this glorious city. The forest of white houses with green & red roofs had a marvellous effect in the clear sunlight. We dined at "Dominique's" in the Nevski, & afterwards took a drive through the islands, among the residences of the upper classes—beautiful little villas, with charming gardens tastefully laid out around them, every flower of which will have to be taken in at the approach of winter. The route we took was evidently the fashionable drive—a sort of Rotten Row.

AUG. 22. (TH.) At 9 we went over, by Mr. MacSwinney's kind invitation, to Cronstadt, where we had a most interesting day. He first took us through the dockyard & arsenal, & though we had not much time for examining details, we got a very good general idea of the great scale on which the works here are carried on, & the resources disposable in case of war: in the arsenal (through which the officer in command was kind enough to conduct us) we saw a rather unique trophy—a gun taken from the British: it belonged to the gunboat "Vulture," which drifted on shore & so became a prize of war—Then we visited the "magnetic observatory," & were introduced to the principal, Captain Вѣпавенецъ. He gave us an explanation, in a sort of English, of the theory & practice of his subject—which, so far as I was concerned, might as well have been in early Slavonic; the thing was entirely out of my depth—and at parting, he kindly presented us with his books on the same subject—books, alas, in Russian. We then took a boat & rowed through the harbour, landing once to inspect a colossal dock-yard in course of construction; the walls were being built of solid blocks of granite, with the outer face cut as smooth as if it were to decorate the interior of a building, & one of these blocks was in process of laying, in a bed of cement, under the direction of an officer, & not without much shouting & excitement. On a general view the place looked something like an ant-nest: hundreds of workmen swarming from end to end of the great hollow—and a constant tinkling of hammers sounding from all sides. It gave one an idea of what the scene must have been during the building of the Pyramids. The dock will probably cost about 3 1/2 millions of roubles.

We afterwards ascended the belfry to Mr. MacSwinney's church, & had a capital view of the place. We dined at his house, where he was obliged to leave us, as his boat left before ours. Liddon had surrendered his over-coat early in the day, & when going, we found it must be recovered from the waiting-maid, who only talked Russian, & as I had left the dictionary behind, & the little vocabulary did not contain "coat," we were in some difficulty. Liddon began by exhibiting his coat, with much gesticulation, including the taking it half off. To our delight, she appeared to understand at once—left the room, & returned in a minute with—a large clothes-brush. On this Liddon tried a further & more energetic demonstration—he took off his coat, & laid it at her feet, pointed downwards (to intimate that in the lower regions was the object of his desire) smiling with an expression of joy & gratitude with which he would receive it, & put the coat on again. Once more a gleam of intelligence lighted up the plain but expressive features of the young person: she was absent much longer this time, & when she brought, to our dismay, a large cushion and a pillow, & began to prepare the sofa for the nap that she now saw clearly was the thing the dumb gentleman wanted. A happy

thought occurred to me, & I hastily drew a sketch representing
Liddon, with one coat on, receiving a second & larger one from
the hands of a benignant Russian peasant. The language of hieroglyphics succeeded where all other means had failed, & we returned
to Petersburg with the humiliating knowledge that our standard
of civilisation was now reduced to the level of ancient Nineveh.

Instance of hieroglyphic writing of the date MDCCCLXVII.
Interpretation: "There is a coat here, left in the care of a
Russian peasant, which I should be glad to receive from him."

AUG. 23. (F.) We gave the day to miscellaneous occupation.
Called on the secretary of Count Tolstoy (the Count is away),
& visited the Troitsa Church & that of the Annunciation—both
very beautifully decorated. We also visited an Armenian church,
which differs from the Greek churches in having no screen concealing the altar—or rather, there *is* the screen, but the altar is
in front.

In our wanderings, I noticed a beautiful photograph of a child,
and bought a copy, small size, at the same time ordering a full
length to be printed, as they had none unmounted. Afterwards I
called to ask for the name of the original, & found they had already
printed the full length but were in great doubt what to do, as they
had asked the father of the child about it, & found he disapproved
of the sale. Of course there was nothing to do but return the carte
I had bought: at the same time I left a written statement that I
had done so, expressing a hope that I might still be allowed to
purchase it.

We also drove to the "Point" to see the sun set, & though it was just down when we arrived, we had a very beautiful picture to enjoy, in the clear sky, glowing with crimson & green—the bay as smooth almost as glass, reflecting the beds of rushes that rose out of it here & there—the dark line of the opposite shore, with the houses coming out nearly black against the sky—& one or two boats lazily splashing their way through the darkening bay, like some unknown waterfowl.

AUG. 24. (SAT.) If possible, a more miscellaneous day than yester-day. We made several calls in vain—visited a monastery & one or two churches, which call for no special record, except one church, the walls of which, inside, are all hung round with military trophies, while outside cannon are planted at regular intervals, & the very railing round the churchyard is an ingenious combination of cannons and chains. In the evening, we went to dine at Dus-seaux's restaurant, but after waiting a minute or two were informed that we could not have the dinner we had ordered for the very sufficient reason that the house was on fire! It may have been only a chimney, as it was all extinguished in about 1/2 an hour, but not till the event had assembled a large mob and about a score of fire-engines, which arrived in a leisurely & orderly manner, & were chiefly remarkable for their excessive smallness. Some of them seemed to have been made out of old water-carts. Mean-while we took our dinner at Borell's, opposite, & watched the scene from the window, while the entrance was crowded by the waiters, who looked on at their rival's misfortunes with interest, but I fear no very deep sympathy.

Afterwards we attended the evening-service at the Alexander-Nevski Monastery—one of the most beautiful services I have heard in a Greek church. The singing was quite delicious, & not so monotonous as it generally is. One piece in particular, which was repeated many times in the course of the service (that is, the *music* was: the words may have been different), was so lovely a piece of melody that I would gladly have listened to it many times more. There were two bishops present, & during the latter part of the service one of them stationed himself in the middle of the church, & with a small brush (dipped I suppose in consecrated oil) made the sign of the cross on the foreheads of the congregation, as they presented themselves one by one, each first kissing the books placed on the desk, then receiving the cross, & then (in many cases) kissing the bishop's hand.

AUG. 25. (SUN.) Count Pontiatine called for us according to promise, & took us in his carriage to the Greek Church. We went behind the screen with him, & were introduced to the Arcimandrite who officiated, &, as the service was in Greek, were able to follow it with the help of books, in spite of the pronunciation—and to join in it throughout, excepting one or two passages referring to the Virgin Mary. After the service, the Count took us on to the Alexander Nevski Monastery, & through the "Spiritual Academy" there, where about 80 youths are educated for the priesthood. We returned to this Monastery at 4 for the service, & spent the evening in strolling along the river-side, & saw the Nicholas bridge in all the glory of sunset, with its stream of human life set as black dots creeping along a line spanning a sea of crimson & green.

AUG. 26. (M.) We had little time for anything but to prepare for our departure. The photographer called ("Артистическая Фотографія," [4] at No. 4 Great Morskoi) to bring the pictures, as the father, Prince Golicen (?), had given them leave to sell them to me.

At 2 we entered the train for our weary journey to Warsaw, and found ourselves in the same carriage, though not the same compartment, with the Hunts, who were on their way to Berlin, so that our routes were the same to Wilna, which we reached 6 p. m. During the evening we visited each other, & my travelling chess-board proved of service. We had no sleeping accommodation, but as the carriage was nearly empty, we did very well.

AUG. 27. (TU.). We reached Warsaw at about 6 p. m. & drove off to the Hotel d'Angleterre, seemingly a very third-rate sort of place. Our passage is inhabited by a tall & very friendly greyhound, who walks in whenever the door is opened for a second or two, & who for some time threatened to make the labour of the servant, who was bringing water for a bath, of no effect, by drinking up the water as fast as it was brought.

AUG. 28. (W.) We spent the day in wandering about Warsaw,

---

[4] Artistic photographer.

& visited several churches, chiefly Roman Catholic, which contained the usual evidence of wealth & bad taste, in the profuse gilding, & the masses of marble carved into heaps (they can hardly be called groups) of ugly babies meant for cherubs. But there were some good Madonnas, &c., as altar pieces. The town, as a whole, is one of the noisiest and dirtiest I have yet visited.

AUG. 29. (TH.) The alarum woke us at 4—coffee & rolls were provided at 5—and by 1/2 past 6 we were on our way to Breslau, which we reached at 8 1/2 p. m. It was pleasant to see the country growing more & more inhabited & cultivated as we got further into Prussia—the fierce, coarse-looking Russian soldier replaced by the more gentle & intelligent Prussian—the very peasants seemed to be of a higher order, more individuality & independence: the Russian peasant, with his gentle, fine, often noble-looking face, always suggests to me a submissive animal, long used to bearing in silence harshness & injustice, rather than a man able & ready to defend himself.

We chose "the Golden Goose" as our hotel, & found it, if not a layer of golden eggs, certainly worthy of "golden opinions from all sorts of men."

AUG. 30. (F.) We gave the morning, one of clear sunlight & delicious balmy air, to wandering through the fine old city, & looking into churches, chiefly notable for their beautiful proportions, the great height giving to the brick towers & buttresses & the slender windows a beauty quite independent of all ornament. We looked at St. Mary Magdalene's—then St. Christopher's— then St. Dorothy's, one of enormous height: we tried to walk round it, but found there was no outlet from the court-yard behind, which was evidently the playground for the girls' school, & a very tempting field for a photographic camera: after the Russian children, whose type of face is ugly as a rule, & plain as an exception, it is quite a relief to get back among the Germans with their large eyes & delicate features.

After St. Dorothy's, we went through the "Ring" (a large square with a very picturesque town-hall & other buildings & statues in the middle, & a most charming series of quaint old gables, no two alike, all round it), to St. Elizabeth's, where we mounted, with much fatigue, the tallest tower in Prussia, & were repaid by a splendid view of the town and surrounding country with the windings of the Oder.

Liddon visited some churches alone in the afternoon, as I was not well enough for more walking, & in the evening we drove to the "winter-garden," & listened for a short while to the indispensable open-air concert which the German people love so well.

AUG. 31. (SAT.) We ascended the tower of the Kreutzkirch, from which we saw Breslau in one view—& also visited the new Roman Catholic church, S. Michael's, which is in process of building—& in the afternoon we went on to Dresden, & reached the "Hotel de Saxe" about 10 1/2 p. m.

SEP. 1. (SUN.) As the guide & the map give among them 3 churches, as "the English Church" two of which are no doubt dissenters, I went to none. Liddon attended the Roman Catholic Church, & I joined him there for a few minutes to hear the music. We visited some of the gardens, in which the principle of trying to drive people to enter the gardens of the cafes (where they pay for admission) seems to prevail throughout; the consequence being that the public grounds contain only a few backless benches.

SEP. 2. (M.) We visited the great picture-gallery in the morning. Two hours of gazing was enough for me: & it might all have been well given to the great "Sistine" Madonna. We strolled about the town in the afternoon, & afterwards, I went to the theatre in the "Royal Garden," from which I had to walk home about a mile (some of it country) in the dark, &, it is needless to say, lost my way. The performance (with the exception of the acting, which was commonplace) was a remarkable one. I entered during the second piece, & the first peculiarity I noticed was that the audience let the act drop descend without a symptom of applause: the chilling effect of this silence was not removed by the orchestra, who seemed to have a very easy time of it, with nothing to do but trim their very comfortable series of reading-lamps. When they *did* play, which was not till the piece was over & an awful silence had reigned for 5 or 10 minutes, one might well have wished them to return to their lamps, as the music was as dismal as any I ever heard in or out of a theatre. The evening ended with the "Wonder-Fountain," for the sake of which the house was reduced to total darkness (Qu.: Are there any pick-pockets in Dresden?) & we then saw a circle of jets with a fountain on the middle, lit by light which kept changing in colour, & produced a pretty effect, but one within the reach of magical lanterns & "chromatropes:" the fountain in the middle presently dies out, & there rose, in succession, Apollo, Time, & a group of figures supporting a smaller fountain. Each of these phenomena, after rising, performed one slow revolution as if under the influence of a kitchen-jack—& this last seemed to be *the* achievement of the evening: at least it roused the patient, not to say passive, audience, to the highest point of enthusiasm which they ever reached—there was almost as much applause as an English audience would bestow on a single speech.

SEP. 3. (TU.) We paid a hasty second visit to the picture gallery, to see Correggio's famous "La Notte"—of which I cannot say anything that would advance my character as a critic—& in the afternoon proceeded to Leipzig, which we reached in time to make an evening stroll, making the circuit of the old town through a series of gardens, well planted with trees. Our Hotel was "de Prussie."

SEP. 4. (W.) There was only time for a stroll in the town, not externally remarkable, & a visit to the castle tower from which the "Castellan" pointed out to us the various points noted on account of battles—& in particular the building where the great theological battle took place between Luther & Ecke.

And then we moved on to Giessen & put up at the "Rappe Hotel," for the night, & ordered an early breakfast of an obliging waiter who talked English. "Coffee!" he exclaimed delightedly, catching at the word as if it were a really original idea, "ah, coffee—very nice. And eggs. Ham with your eggs? Very nice"—"If we can have it broiled" I said. "Boiled?" the waiter repeated with an incredulous smile. "No, not *boiled*," I explained, "*broiled*." The waiter put aside the distinction as trivial, "yes, yes, ham" he repeated, reverting to his favourite idea. "Yes, ham," I said, "but how cooked?" "Yes, yes, how cooked," the waiter replied, with the careless air of one who assents to a proposition more from good nature than from a real conviction of its truth.

SEP. 5. (TH.) At midday we reached Ems, after a journey eventless, but through a very interesting country—valleys winding away in all directions among hills, clothed with trees to the very top, & white villages nestling away wherever there was a comfortable corner to hide in. The trees were so small, so uniform in colour, & so continuous, that they gave to the more distant hills something of the effect of banks covered with moss. The really unique feature of the scenery was the way in which the old castles seemed to grow, rather than to have been built, on the tops of the rocky promontories that showed their heads here & there among the trees. I have never seen architecture that seemed so entirely in harmony with the spirit of the place. By some subtle instinct the old architects seem to have chosen both form & colour, the grouping of the towers with their pointed spires, & the two neutral tints, light grey & brown, for the walls & roof, so as to produce buildings which look as naturally fitted to the spot as the heath or the harebells. And like the flowers & the rocks, they seemed instinct with no other meaning than rest & silence.

We went to the "Hotel d'Angleterre" & spent the rest of the day in strolls about this delightful place—where people have nothing to do, & all day to do it in. It is certainly the place for thoroughly enjoying idleness.

We visited the evening concert, & found play (rouge-et-noir, &c.) going on in an adjoining room, & it was a very interesting sight for novices to watch. There was but little feeling to detect in the faces of the gamblers, even when they lost heavily: what was to be seen was only momentary, & all the more intense for being suppressed. The women were a more interesting, & so a sadder, spectacle than the men: some old, some quite young, & all absorbed & with a fascinated look like helpless creatures magnetised by the gaze of a beast of prey.

SEP. 6. (F.) We set forth from Ems, all too soon, at about 10 a. m. & took the steamer, up the Rhine, as far as Bingen. The weather was quite perfect, & though we had tickets for the after-part of the vessel, (supposed, by a theory I never could quite understand, to be the most luxurious), I spent the whole time, (4 or 5 hours), in the bow, watching the series of pictures that opened out as we wound our way among the hills. There was of course great uniformity, not to say monotony, & the crowds of steep pointed hills, thinly covered with vineyards or small trees, with here & there a village at the foot, or a castle perched on a crag, of a most peculiar build, generally suggested by the shape of the crag (what the Paris shopkeepers would call "extraordinaire, forcé" architecture), but nevertheless it was a sight one would not soon tire of. We went to the "Hotel Victoria" at Bingen, & left early in the morning for our final run, to Paris, which we did not reach till nearly 10 p. m.

SEP. 8. (SUN.) I went to Mr. Archer Gurney's church, & heard an eccentric but very interesting sermon. On my way thither I fell in with Throley of Wadham & arranged to walk with him & the afternoon, when we went through the Tuileries Gardens & the Champs Elysées out into the Bois Boulogne, by which one got a fair idea of the amount of country beauty, in the way of parks, gardens, water, &c., this beautiful city manages to include. Seeing it, I wonder no more that Parisians call London "triste." In the evening we all 3 dined at the "Dinèr Européen" & then attended Mr. Gurney's church.

SEP. 9. (M.) We spent the day in the Exhibition, of which I saw little else but the pictures, a rare treat in modern art—so large a collection with hardly any inferior pictures or statues. I will not attempt the impossibility of describing any, but will merely record the name of Caroni, of Florence, whose works struck me as exceptionally beautiful: they are called "L'Amour vainquer de la Force" (a child playing with a lion), "Esclave au marche," and "Ophelia"—all in marble. The last is from the mad scene where she scatters flowers about her. The French pictures were of course most numerous, but they were also (what was by no means a thing of course) the best. *Our* artists seem to have almost vied with each other in sending second-rate pictures. The small collection of American pictures contains some that are quite exquisite.

Thorley & I visited the "Theatre Vaudeville" in the evening to see "La Famille Benviton," a capitally-acted play—every part without exception being well & carefully played. "Fanfan" was played by one of the cleverest children I ever saw (Mdlle. Camille as the bills called her) who could not have been more than 6 years old.

SEP. 10. (TU.) Quite a miscellaneous day. I fell in with Chandler & Page, & strolled about, first with them, & afterwards alone buying photographs till it was too late to go to the Exhibition. Liddon & I dined at the usual place & then went to an open-air military concert in the Champs Elysées.

SEP. 11. (W.) As the Louvre is far too large an hotel for comfort, Page & I made a tour of inspection among a number of others, ending with one recommended by Mrs. Hunt—the "Hotel des Deux Mondes"—which seemed best of all, & where we engaged a couple of rooms. In the afternoon I paid another visit to the Exhibition, & returned to dine in my new quarters, the dining-room of which is a restaurant as well, & a very good one.

SEP. 12. (TH.) Shopping, & then the Exhibition again. We wandered through the grounds outside, & passed a pavilion where Chinese music was going on, & paid half a franc to go in & listen to it nearer: & certainly the difference between being outside & inside was worth the half-franc—only the outside was the pleasantest of the two. It was just the kind of music which, once heard, one desires never to hear again . . . We made up for it in the evening by going to the "Opera Comique" to hear "Mignon"— a very pretty spectacle, with charming music & singing—the heroine, Mdme. Galli-Marie, contributing a very large share to both departments of beauty.

SEP. 13. (F.) Wandering about, and shopping: in the afternoon I went to the Convent of S. Thomas, Rue de Sevres, to try & procure some of the salve for the tic-doloreux which is made by the nuns there. I had interviews with two of the Sisters, & the elder, who appeared to have most authority, assured me in very fluent French, much of which was lost on me, that they never sold it, & only gave it to their own poor. As this appeared to be an exhaustive division of the category "modes of distribution of ointment" I was very nearly giving up the quest in despair—but there was an indication of some other process for obtaining it being practicable, & after much beating about the bush I said "then you cannot *sell* it me, but you will *give* me some, and permit me to give something, for your poor?" "Oui'. Certainment!" was the eager reply, & so the delicately-veiled bargain was at last concluded. At 7 p. m. I quitted the "Hotel des Deux Mondes," on my way to Calais, which I reached, after a peaceful & slumbrous journey, at about 2 a. m. We had a beautifully smooth passage, & a clear moonlight night to enjoy it in—the moon shining out with all its splendour, as if to make up for the time lost during the eclipse it had suffered four hours earlier—I remained in the bow most of the time of our passage, sometimes chatting with the sailor on the look-out, & sometimes watching, through the last hour of my first foreign tour, the lights of Dover, as they slowly broadened on the horizon, as if the old land were opening its arms to receive its homeward bound children—till they finally stood out clear and bold as the two light-houses on the cliff—till that which had long been merely a glimmering line on the dark water, like a reflection of the Milky Way, took form & substance as the lights of the shoreward houses—till the faint white line behind them, that looked at first like a mist creeping along the horizon, was visible at last in the grey twilight as the white cliffs of old England.

OXFORD PAPERS

THE DYNAMICS

OF A

PARTI-CLE.

" 'Tis strange the mind, that very fiery particle,
Should let itself be snuff'd out by an article."

FIRST PRINTED IN 1865.

Oxford:

JAMES PARKER AND CO.

1874.

THE DYNAMICS OF A PARTI-CLE [1]

INTRODUCTION

'It was a lovely Autumn evening, and the glorious effects of chromatic aberration were beginning to show themselves in the atmosphere as the earth revolved away from the great western luminary, when two lines might have been observed wending their weary way across a plain superficies. The elder of the two had by long practice acquired the art, so painful to young and impulsive loci, of lying evenly between her extreme points; but the younger, in her girlish impetuosity, was ever longing to diverge and become an hyperbola or some such romantic and boundless curve. They had lived and loved: fate and the intervening superficies had hitherto kept them asunder, but this was no longer to be: *a line had intersected them, making the two interior angles together less than two right angles.* It was a moment never to be forgotten, and, as they journeyed on, a whisper thrilled along the superficies in isochronous waves of sound, "Yes! We shall at length meet if continually produced!"' (Jacobi's Course of Mathematics, Chap. I.)

We have commenced with the above quotation as a striking illustration of the advantage of introducing the human element into the hitherto barren region of Mathematics. Who shall say what germs of romance, hitherto unobserved, may not underlie the subject? Who can tell whether the parallelogram, which in our ignorance we have defined and drawn, and the whole of whose properties we profess to know, may not be all the while panting

---

[1] Collingwood, in *The Lewis Carroll Picture Book*, page 58, supplies an explanatory note by Lewis Sergeant: ". . . In 1865 Mr. Gladstone was defeated at Oxford, after having represented his University in the House of Commons for eighteen years. The candidates, who appear in the following pages by their initials, were Sir W. Heathcote, Mr. Gathorne Hardy, and Mr. Gladstone. The polling extended over a week. On the third day Mr. Hardy led Mr. Gladstone by 230; but, after a strong appeal and rally on behalf of the Liberals, the final majority was no more than 180. The total number of voters was nearly twice as large as on any previous occasion—'whereby, the entry of the Convocation House being blocked up, men could pass neither in nor out'." [McD.]

for exterior angles, sympathetic with the interior, or sullenly repining at the fact that it cannot be inscribed in a circle? What mathematician has ever pondered over an hyperbola, mangling the unfortunate curve with lines of intersection here and there, in his efforts to prove some property that perhaps after all is a mere calumny, who has not fancied at last that the ill-used locus was spreading out its asymptotes as a silent rebuke, or winking one focus at him in contemptuous pity?

In some such spirit as this we have compiled the following pages. Crude and hasty as they are, they yet exhibit some of the phenomena of light, or "enlightenment," considered as a force, more fully than has hitherto been attempted by other writers.

June, 1865

CONTENTS.

CHAPTER I.

CHAPTER II.

CHAPTER I

General Considerations

DEFINITIONS

I

PLAIN SUPERFICIALITY is the character of a speech, in which any two points being taken, the speaker is found to lie wholly with regard to those two points.

II

PLAIN ANGER is the inclination of two voters to one another, who meet together, but whose views are not in the same direction.

III

When a Proctor, meeting another Proctor, makes the votes on one side equal to those on the other, the feeling entertained by each side is called RIGHT ANGER.

IV

When two parties, coming together, feel a RIGHT ANGER, each is *said* to be COMPLEMENTARY to the other (though, strictly speaking, this is very seldom the case).

V

OBTUSE ANGER is that which is greater than RIGHT ANGER.

POSTULATES

I

Let it be granted, that a speaker may digress from any one point to any other point.

II

That a finite argument (*i.e.*, one finished and disposed of) may be produced to any extent in subsequent debates.

III

That a controversy may be raised about any question, and at any distance from that question.

AXIOMS

I

Men who go halves in the same (quart) are (generally) equal to another.

II

Men who take a double in the same (term) are equal to anything.

ON VOTING

The different methods of voting are as follows:

I

ALTERNANDO, as in the case of Mr. ——, who voted for and against Mr. Gladstone, alternate elections.

II

INVERTENDO, as was done by Mr. ——, who came all the way from Edinburgh to vote, handed in a blank voting paper, and so went home rejoicing.

III

COMPONENDO, as was done by Mr. ——, whose name appeared on both committees at once, whereby he got great praise from all men, by the space of one day.

IV

DIVIDENDO, as in Mr. ——'s case, who, being sorely perplexed in his choice of candidates, voted for neither.

V

CONVERTENDO, as was wonderfully exemplified by Messrs. —— and ——, who held a long and fierce argument on the election, in which at the end of two hours, each had vanquished and converted the other.

VI

EX AEQUALI IN PROPORTIONE PERTURBATÂ SUE INORDINATÂ, as in the election, when the result was for a long time equalised, and as it were held in the balance, by reason of those who had first voted on the one side seeking to pair off with those who were last to vote on the one side being kept out by those who had first arrived on the other side, whereby, the entry to the Convocation House being blocked up, men could pass neither in nor out.

ON REPRESENTATION

Magnitudes are algebraically represented by letters, men by men of letters, and so on. The following are the principal systems of representation:—

1. CARTESIAN: *i.e.*, by means of "cartes." This system represents *lines* well, sometimes too well; but fails in representing *points*, particularly good points.

2. POLAR: *i.e.*, by means of the 2 poles, "North and South." This is a very uncertain system of representation, and one that cannot safely be depended upon.

3. TRILINEAR: *i.e.*, by means of a line which takes 3 different courses. Such a line is usually expressed by three letters, as W. E. G.

That the principle of Representation was known to the ancients is abundantly exemplified by Thucydides, who tells us that the favourite cry of encouragement during a trireme race was that touching allusion to Polar Co-ordinates which is still heard during the races of our own time, "$\varrho5$, $\varrho6$, cos ϕ, they're gaining!"

CHAPTER II

Dynamics of a Particle

Particles are logically divided according to GENIUS and SPEECHES. GENIUS is the higher classification, and this, combined with DIFFERENTIA (*i.e.*, difference of opinion), produces SPEECHES. These again naturally divide themselves into three heads.

Particles belonging to the great order of GENIUS are called "able" or "enlightened."

DEFINITIONS

I

A SURD is a radical whose meaning cannot be exactly ascertained. This class comprises a very large number of particles.

II

INDEX indicates the degree, or power, to which a particle is raised. It consists of two letters, placed to the right of the symbol representing the particle. Thus, "A.A." signified the oth degree; "B.A." the 1st degree; and so on, till we reach "M.A." the 2nd degree (the intermediate letters indicating fractions of a degree); the last two usually employed being "R.A." (the reader need hardly be reminded of that beautiful line in *The Princess* "Go dress yourself, Dinah, like a gorgeous R.A.") and "S.A." This last indicates the 360th degree, and denotes that the particle in question (which is 1/7th part of the function $\overline{E + R}$ "Essays and Reviews") has effected a complete revolution, and that the result $= 0$.

III

Moment is the product of the mass into the velocity. To discuss this subject fully, would lead us too far into the subject Vis Viva, and we must content ourselves with mentioning the fact that *no moment is ever really lost, by fully enlightened* Particles. It is scarcely necessary to quote the well-known passage: "Every moment, that can be snatched from academical duties, is devoted to furthering the cause of the popular Chancellor of the Exchequer." (Clarendon, "History of the Great Rebellion.")

IV

A COUPLE consists of a moving particle, raised to the degree M.A., and combined with what is technically called a "better half." The following are the principal characteristics of a Couple: (1) It may be easily transferred from point to point. (2) Whatever *force of translation* was possessed by the uncombined particle (and this is often considerable), is wholly lost when the Couple is formed. (3) The two forces constituting the Couple habitually *act in opposite directions.*

ON DIFFERENTIATION

The effect of Differentiation on a Particle is very remarkable, the first Differential being frequently of a greater value than the original Particle, and the second of less enlightenment.

For example, let L = "Leader," S = "Saturday," and then L.S.= "Leader in the Saturday" (a particle of no assignable value). Differentiating once, we get L.S.D., a function of great value. Similarly it will be found that, by taking the second Differential of an enlightened Particle (*i.e.*, raising it to the degree D. D.), the enlightenment becomes rapidly less. The effect is much increased by the addition of a C: in this case the enlightenment often vanishes altogether, and the Particle becomes conservative.

It should be observed that, whenever the symbol L is used to denote "Leader," it must be affected with the sign $\pm$: this serves to indicate that its action is sometimes positive and sometimes negative—some particles of this class having the property of drawing others after them (as "a Leader of an army"), and others of repelling them (as "a Leader of the Times").

PROPOSITIONS

PROP. I. PR.

To find the value of a given Examiner.

Example.—A takes in ten books in the Final Examination, and gets a 3rd Class: B takes in the Examiners, and gets a 2nd. Find the value of the Examiners in terms of books. Find also their value in terms in which no Examination is held.

To estimate Profit and Loss.

Example.—Given a Derby Prophet, who has sent three different winners to three different betting men, and given that none of the three horses are placed. Find the total Loss incurred by the three men (a) in money, (b) in temper. Find also the Prophet. Is this latter generally possible?

PROP. III. PR.

To estimate the direction of a line.

Example.—Prove that the definition of a line, according to Walton, coincides with that of Salmon, only that they begin at opposite ends. If such a line be divided by Frost's method, find its value according to Price.

PROP. IV. TH.

The end (*i.e.*, "the product of the extremes,") justifies (*i.e.*, "is equal to"—see Latin "aequus,") the means.

No example is appended to this Proposition, for obvious reasons.

PROP. V. PR.

To continue a given series.

Example.—A and B, who are respectively addicted to Fours and Fives occupy the same set of rooms, which is always at Sixes and Sevens. Find the probable amount of reading done by A and B while the Eights are on.

We proceed to illustrate this hasty sketch of the Dynamics of a Parti-cle, by demonstrating the great Proposition on which the whole theory of Representation depends, namely, "To remove a given Tangent from a given Circle, and to bring another given Line into Contact with it."

To work the following problem algebraically, it is best to let the circle be represented as referred to its two tangents, *i.e.*, first to WEG, WH, and afterwards to WH, GH. When this is effected, it will be found most convenient to project WEG to infinity. The process is not given here in full, since it requires the introduction of many complicated determinants.

PROP. VI. PR.

To remove a given Tangent from a given Circle, and to bring another given Line into contact with it.

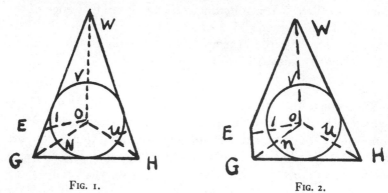

FIG. 1.   FIG. 2.

Let Univ be a Large Circle, whose centre is O (V being, of course, placed at the top), and let WGH be a triangle, two of whose sides, WEG and WH, are in contact with the circle, while GH (called "the base" by liberal mathematicians,) is not in contact with it. (See Fig. 1.) It is required to destroy the contact of WEG, and to bring GH into contact instead.

Let I be the point of maximum illumination of the circle, and therefore E the point of maximum enlightenment of the triangle. (E of course varying perversely as the square of the distance from O.)

Let WH be fixed absolutely, and remain always in contact with the circle, and let the direction of OI be also fixed.

Now, so long as WEG preserves a perfectly straight course, GH cannot possibly come into contact with the circle; but if the force of illumination, acting along OI, cause it to bend (as in Fig. 2), a partial revolution on the part of WEG and GH is effected, WEG ceases to touch the circle, and GH is immediately brought into contact with it. Q.E.F.

The theory involved in the foregoing Proposition is at present much controverted, and its supporters are called upon to show what is the fixed *point*, or "*locus standi*," on which they propose to effect the necessary revolution. To make this clear, we must go to the original Greek, and remind our readers that the true point or "locus standi" is in this case ἄρδις, (or ἄρδις according to modern usage), and therefore must not be assigned to WEG. In reply to this it is urged that, in a matter like the present, a single word cannot be considered a satisfactory explanation, such as ἀρδέως.

It should also be observed that the revolution here discussed is entirely the effect of enlightenment, since particles, when illuminated to such an extent as actually to become φώς, are always found to diverge more or less widely from each other; though undoubtedly the *radical* force of the word is "union" or "friendly feeling." The reader will find in "Liddell and Scott" a remarkable illustration of this, from which it appears to be an essential condition that the feeling should be entertained φοράδην, and that the particle entertaining it should belong to the genus σκότος, and should therefore be, nominally at least, unenlightened.

THE END

FACTS, FIGURES, AND FANCIES,

RELATING TO

THE ELECTIONS TO THE HEBDOMADAL COUNCIL,

THE OFFER OF THE CLARENDON TRUSTEES,

AND

THE PROPOSAL TO CONVERT THE PARKS INTO CRICKET-GROUNDS.

———

"Thrice the brinded cat hath mewed."

———

FIRST PRINTED IN 1866–1868.

Oxford:

JAMES PARKER AND CO.

1874.

FACTS, FIGURES, AND FANCIES
INTRODUCTORY
§ I. THE ELECTIONS TO THE HEBDOMADAL COUNCIL

In the year 1866, a Letter with the above title was published in Oxford, addressed to the Senior Censor of Christ Church, with the twofold object of revealing to the University a vast political misfortune which it had unwittingly encountered, and of suggesting a remedy which should at once alleviate the bitterness of the calamity and secure the suffers from its recurrence. The misfortune thus revealed was no less than the fact that, at a recent election of Members to the Hebdomadal Council, *two* Conservatives had been chosen, thus giving a Conservative majority in the Council; and the remedy suggested was a sufficiently sweeping one, embracing, as it did, the following details:—

1. "The exclusion" (from Congregation) "of the non-academical elements which form a main part of the strength of this party domination." These "elements" are afterwards enumerated as "the parish clergy and the professional men of the city, and the chaplains who are without any academical occupation."

2. The abolition of the Hebdomadal Council.

3. The abolition of the legislative functions of Convocation.

These are all the main features of this remarkable scheme of Reform, unless it be necessary to add

4. "To preside over a Congregation with full legislative powers, the Vice-Chancellor ought no doubt to be a man of real capacity."

But it would be invidious to suppose that there was any intention of suggesting this as a novelty.

The following rhythmical version of the Letter developes its principles to an extent which possibly the writer had never contemplated.

§ II. THE OFFER OF THE CLARENDON TRUSTEES
Letter from Mr. Gladstone to the Vice-Chancellor

DEAR MR. VICE-CHANCELLOR,—The Clarendon Trustees . . are ready, in concert with the University, to consider of the best

137

mode of applying the funds belonging to them for "adding to the New Museum Physical Laboratories and other accommodation requisite for the department of experimental Philosophy." . . .

I have the honour to remain,

Dear Mr. Vice-Chancellor,

Very faithfully yours,

W. E. Gladstone.

May 3, 1867.

The following passages are quoted from a paper which appeared on the subject.

"As Members of Convocation are called upon to consider the offer of the Clarendon Trustees, to employ the funds at their disposal in the erection of additional buildings to facilitate the study of Physics, they may perhaps find it useful to have a short statement of the circumstances which render additional buildings necessary, and of the nature of the accommodation required."

.   .   .   .

"Again, it is often impossible to carry on accurate Physical experiments in close contiguity to one another, owing to their mutual interference; and consequently different processes need different rooms, in which these delicate instruments, which are always required in a particular branch of science, have to be carefully and permanently fixed."

.   .   .   .

"It may be sufficient, in order to give an idea of the number of rooms required, to enumerate the chief branches of Physics which require special accommodation, owing to their mutual interference.

(1) Weighing and measuring.

(2) Heat.

(3) Radiant Heat.

(4) Dispersion of Light. Spectrum Analysis, &c.

(5) Statical electricity.

(6) General optics.

(7) Dynamical electricity.

(8) Magnetism.

(9) Acoustics.

Of these, (5) requires one large room or three smaller rooms, and these, together with those devoted to (3) and (4), should have a south aspect. Besides the fixed instruments, there is a large quantity of movable apparatus, which is either used with them or employed in illustrating lectures; and this must be carefully preserved from causes of deterioration when not in use; for this purpose a large room fitted with glass cases is required. A store-room for chemicals and other materials used is also necessary."

. . . .

"As Photography is now very much employed in multiplying results of observation, in constructing diagrams for lectures, &c., and as it is in fact a branch of Physics, a small Photographic room is necessary, both for general use and for studying the subject itself."

. . . .

§ III. The Proposal to Convert the Parks Into Cricket-Grounds

Notice from the Vice-Chancellor

"A form of Decree to the following effect will be proposed:—

"1. That the Curators of the Parks be authorized to receive applications from Members of the University for Cricket-grounds in the Parks, and that public notice be issued to that effect, a time being fixed within which applications are to be sent in.

"2. That at the expiration of such time the Curators be authorised to make Cricket-grounds, and allot them to Cricket-clubs or Colleges from which applications have been received, according to priority of application. . . .

"F. K. Leighton,
"*April* 29, 1867." "*Vice-Chancellor.*

THE ELECTIONS TO THE HEBDOMADAL COUNCIL

"Now is the winter of our discontent." [1]
"Heard ye the arrow hurtle in the sky?
Heard ye the dragon-monster's deathful cry?"—
Excuse this sudden burst of the Heroic;

[1] Dr. Wynter, President of St. John's, one of the recently elected Conservative members of Council.

The present state of things would vex a Stoic!
And just as Sairey Gamp, for pains within,
Administered a modicum of gin,
So does my mind, when vexed and ill at ease,
Console itself with soothing similes.
The "dragon-monster" (pestilential schism!)
I need not tell you is Conservatism;
The "hurtling arrow" (till we find a better)
Is represented by the present Letter.

    'Twas, I remember, but the other day,
Dear Senior Censor, that you chanced to say
You thought these party-combinations would
Be found, "though needful, no unmingled good."
Unmingled good? They are unmingled ill! [2]
I never took to them, and never will—— [3]
What am I saying? Heed it not, my friend:
On the next page I mean to recommend
The very dodges that I now condemn
In the Conservatives! Don't hint to them }
A word of this! (In confidence. Ahem!) }

    Need I rehearse the history of Jowett?
I need not, Senior Censor, for you know it. [4]
That was the Board Hebdomadal, and oh!
Who would be free, themselves must strike the blow!
Let each that wears a beard, and each that shaves,
Join in the cry "We never will be slaves!"
"But can the University afford
"To be a slave to any kind of board?
"A *slave?*" you shuddering ask. "Think you it can, Sir?"
"*Not at the present moment*,"—is my answer. [5]

[2] "In a letter on a point connected with the late elections to the Hebdo-madal Council you incidentally remarked to me that our combinations for these elections, 'though necessary were not an unmixed good.' They are an unmixed evil."

[3] "I never go to a *caucus* without reluctance: I never write a canvassing letter without a feeling of repugnance to my task."

[4] "I need not rehearse the history of the Regius Professor of Greek."

[5] "The University cannot afford at the present moment to be delivered over as a slave to any non-academical interest whatever."

I've thought the matter o'er and o'er again
And given to it all my powers of brain;
I've thought it out, and this is what I make it,
(And I don't care a Tory how you take it:)
It may be right to go ahead, I guess:
It may be right to stop, I do confess;
Also it may be right to retrogress.[6]
So says the oracle, and, for myself, I
Must say it beats to fits the one at Delphi!

    To save beloved Oxford from the yoke,
(For this majority's beyond a joke,)
We must combine,[7] aye! hold a *caucus*-meeting,[8]
Unless we want to get another beating.
That they should "bottle" us is nothing new—
But shall they bottle us and *caucus* too?
See the "fell unity of purpose" now
With which Obstructives plunge into the row! [9]
"Factious Minorities," we used to sigh—
"Factious Majorities!" is now the cry.
"Votes—ninety-two"—no combination here:
"Votes—ninety-three"—conspiracy, 'tis clear! [10]
You urge " 'Tis but a unit." I reply
That in that unit lurks their "unity."
Our voters often bolt, and often baulk us,
But then, they never, never go to *caucus!*
Our voters can't forget the maxim famous
"Semel electum semper eligamus";

[6] "It may be right to go on, it may be right to stand still, or it may be right to go back."

[7] "To save the University from going completely under the yoke . . . we shall still be obliged to combine."

[8] "Caucus-holding and wire-pulling would still be almost inevitably carried on to some extent."

[9] "But what are we to do? Here is a great political and theological party . . . labouring under perfect discipline and with fell unity of purpose, to hold the University in subjection, and fill her government with its nominees."

[10] At a recent election to Council, the Liberals mustered ninety-two votes, and the Conservatives ninety-three; whereupon the latter were charged with having obtained their victory by a conspiracy.

They never can be worked into a ferment
By visionary promise of preferment,
Nor taught, by hints of "Paradise" [11] beguiled,
To whisper "C for Chairman" like a child! [12]
And thus the friends that we have tempted down
Oft take the two-o'clock Express for town.[13]
    This is our danger: this the secret foe
That aims at Oxford such a deadly blow.
What champion can we find to save the State,
To crush the plot? We darkly whisper "Wait!" [14]
    My scheme is this: remove the votes of all
The residents that are not Liberal—[15]
Leave the young Tutors uncontrolled and free,
And Oxford then shall see—what it shall see.
What next? Why then, I say, let Convocation
Be shorn of all her powers of legislation.[16]
But why stop there? Let us go boldly on—
Sweep everything beginning with a "Con"
Into oblivion! Convocation first,
Conservatism next, and, last and worst,
"Concilium Hebdomadale" must,
Consumed and conquered, be consigned to dust! [17]

[11] "Not to mention that, as we cannot promise Paradise to our supporters they are very apt to take the train for London just before the election."

[12] It is not known to what the word "Paradise" was intended to allude, and therefore the hint, here thrown out, that the writer meant to recall the case of the late Chairman of Mr. Gladstone's committee, who had been recently collated to the See of Chester, is wholly wanton and gratuitous.

[13] A case of this kind had actually occurred on the occasion of the division just alluded to.

[14] Mr. Wayte, now President of Trinity, then put forward as the Liberal candidate for election to Council.

[15] "You and others suggest, as the only effective remedy, that the Constituency should be reformed, by the exclusion of the non-academical elements which form a main part of the strength of this party domination."

[16] "I confess that, having included all the really academical elements in Congregation, I would go boldly on, and put an end to the legislative functions of Convocation."

[17] "This conviction, that while we have Elections to Council we shall not entirely get rid of party organisation and its evils, leads me to venture a step further, and to raise the question whether it is really necessary that we should have an Elective Council for legislative purposes at all."

And here I must relate a little fable
I heard last Saturday at our high table:—
The cats, it seems, were masters of the house,
And held their own against the rat and mouse:
Of course the others couldn't stand it long,
So held a caucus, (not, in their case, wrong;)
And, when they were assembled to a man,
Uprose an aged rat, and thus began:—
    "Brothers in bondage! Shall we bear to be
For ever left in a minority?
With what 'fell unity of purpose' cats
Oppose the trusting innocence of rats!
So unsuspicious are we of disguise,
Their machinations take us by surprise—[18]
Insulting and tyrannical absurdities! [19]
It is too bad by half—upon my word it is!
For, now that these Con——, cats, I should say,
       (frizzle 'em!)
Are masters, they exterminate like Islam! [20]
How shall we deal with them? I'll tell you how:—
Let none but kittens be allowed to miaow!
The Liberal kittens seize us but in play,
And, while they frolic, we can run away:
But older cats are not so generous,
Their claws are too Conservative for us!
Then let *them* keep the stable and the oats,
While kittens, rats, and mice have all the votes.
    "Yes; banish cats! The kittens would not use
Their powers for blind obstruction,[21] nor refuse
To let us sip the cream and gnaw the cheese—

[18] "Sometimes, indeed, not being informed that the wires are at work, we are completely taken by surprise."

[19] "We are without protection against this most insulting and tyrannical absurdity."

[20] "It is as exterminating as Islam."

[21] "Their powers would scarcely be exercised for the purpose of fanaticism, or in a spirit of blind obstruction."

How glorious then would be our destinies! [22]
Kittens and rats would occupy the throne,
And rule the larder for itself alone!" [23]
    So rhymed my friend, and asked me what I thought
       of it
I told him that so much as I had caught of it
Appeared to me (as I need hardly mention)
Entirely undeserving of attention.
    But now, to guide the Congregation, when
It numbers none but really "able" men,
A *"Vice-Chancellarius"* will be needed
Of every kind of human weakness weeded!
Is such the president that we have got?
He ought no doubt to be; why should he not? [24]
I do not hint that Liberals should dare
To oust the present holder of the chair—
But surely he would not object to be
Gently examined by a Board of three?
Their duty being just to ascertain
That he's "all there" (I mean, of course, in brain,)
And that his mind, from "petty details" clear,
Is fitted for the duties of his sphere.
    All this is merely moonshine, till we get
The seal of Parliament upon it set.
A word then, Senior Censor, in your ear:
The Government is in a state of fear—
Like some old gentleman, abroad at night,
Seized with a sudden shiver of affright,
Who offers money, on his bended knees,

[22] "These narrow local bounds, within which our thoughts and schemes have hitherto been pent, will begin to disappear, and a far wider sphere of action will open on the view."

[23] "Those councils must be freely opened to all who can serve her well and who will serve her for herself."

[24] "To preside over a Congregation with full legislative powers, the Vice-Chancellor ought no doubt to be a man of real capacity; but why should he not? His mind ought also, for this as well as for his other high functions, to be clear of petty details, and devoted to the great matters of University business; but why should not this condition also be fulfilled?"

To the first skulking vagabond he sees—
Now is the lucky moment for our task;
They daren't refuse us anything we ask! [25]
And then our Fellowships shall open be
To Intellect, no meaner quality!
No moral excellence, no social fitness
Shall ever be admissible as witness.
"Avaunt, dull Virtue!" is Oxonia's cry:
"Come to my arms, ingenious Villainy!"
For Classic Fellowships, an honour high,
Simonides and Co. will then apply—
Our Mathematics will to Oxford bring
The 'cutest members of the betting-ring—
Law Fellowships will start upon their journeys
A myriad of unscrupulous attorneys—
While poisoners, doomed till now to toil unknown,
Shall mount the Physical Professor's throne!
And thus would Oxford educate, indeed,
Men far beyond a merely local need—
With no career before them, I may say,[26]
Unless they're wise enough to go away,
And seek far West, or in the distant East,
Another flock of pigeons to be fleeced.
I might go on, and trace the destiny
Of Oxford in an age which though it be
Thus breaking with tradition, owns a new
Allegiance to the intellectual few—
(I mean, of course, the —pshaw! no matter who!)
But, were I to pursue the boundless theme,
I fear that I should seem to you to dream.[27]

[25] "If you apply now to Parliament for this or any other University reform, you will find the House of Commons in a propitious mood. . . . Even the Conservative Government, as it looks for the support of moderate Liberals on the one great subject, is very unwilling to present itself in such an aspect that these men may not be able decently to give it their support."
[26] "With open Fellowships, Oxford will soon produce a supply of men fit for the work of high education far beyond her own local demands, and in fact with no career before them unless a career can be opened elsewhere."
[27] "I should seem to you to dream if I were to say what I think the

This to fulfil, or even—humbler far—
To shun Conservatism's noxious star
And all the evils that it brings behind,
These pestilential coils must be untwined—
The party-coils, that clog the march of Mind—
Choked in whose meshes Oxford, slowly wise,
Has lain for three disastrous centuries.[28]
Away with them! (It is for this I yearn!)
Each twist untwist, each Turner overturn!
Disfranchise each Conservative, and cancel
The votes of Michell, Liddon, Wall, and Mansel!
Then, then shall Oxford be herself again,
Neglect the heart, and cultivate the brain—
Then this shall be the burden of our song,
"All change is good—whatever is, is wrong—"
Then Intellect's proud flag shall be unfurled,
And Brain, and Brain alone, shall rule the world!

THE OFFER OF THE CLARENDON TRUSTEES

"Accommodated: that is, when a man is, as they say, accommodated; or when a man is—being—whereby—he may be thought to be accommodated; which is an excellent thing."

DEAR SENIOR CENSOR,—In a desultory conversation on a point connected with the dinner at our high table, you incidentally remarked to me that lobster-sauce, "though a necessary adjunct to turbot, was not entirely wholesome."

It is entirely unwholesome. I never ask for it without reluctance: I never take a second spoonful without a feeling of apprehension on the subject of possible nightmare.[29] This naturally brings me to the subject of Mathematics, and of the accommoda-

---

destiny of the University may be in an age which, though it is breaking with tradition, is, from the same causes, owning a new allegiance to intellectual authority."

[28] "But to fulfil this, or even a far humbler destiny—to escape the opposite lot—the pestilential coils of party, in which the University has lain for three disastrous centuries choked, must be untwined."

[29] See page 140, notes 2 and 3.

tion provided by the University for carrying on the calculations necessary in that important branch of Science.

As Members of Convocation are called upon (whether personally, or, as is less exasperating, by letter) to consider the offer of the Clarendon Trustees, as well as every other subject of human, or inhuman, interest, capable of consideration, it has occurred to me to suggest for your consideration how desirable roofed buildings are for carrying on mathematical calculations: in fact, the variable character of the weather in Oxford renders it highly inexpedient to attempt much occupation, of a sedentary nature, in the open air.

Again, it is often impossible for students to carry on accurate mathematical calculations in the close contiguity to one another, owing to their mutual interference, and a tendency to general conversation: consequently these processes require different rooms in which irrepressible conversationists, who are found to occur in every branch of Society, might be carefully and permanently fixed.

It may be sufficient for the present to enumerate the following requisites; others might be added as funds permitted.

A. A very large room for calculating Greatest Common Measure. To this a small one might be attached for Least Common Multiple: this, however, might be dispensed with.

B. A piece of open ground for keeping Roots and practising their extraction: it would be advisable to keep Square Roots by themselves, as their corners are apt to damage others.

C. A room for reducing Fractions to their Lowest Terms. This should be provided with a cellar for keeping the Lowest Terms when found, which might also be available to the general body of Undergraduates, for the purpose of "keeping Terms."

D. A large room, which might be darkened, and fitted up with a magic lantern for the purpose of exhibiting Circulating Decimals in the act of circulation. This might also contain cupboards, fitted with glass-doors, for keeping the various Scales of Notation.

E. A narrow strip of ground, railed off and carefully levelled, for investigating the properties of Asymptotes, and testing practically whether Parallel Lines meet or not: for this purpose it should reach, to use the expressive language of Euclid, "ever so far."

This last process, of "continually producing the Lines," may require centuries or more: but such a period, though long in the life of an individual, is as nothing in the life of the University.

As Photography is now very much employed in recording human expressions, and might possibly be adapted to Algebraical Expressions, a small photographic room would be desirable, both for general use and for representing the various phenomena of Gravity, Disturbance of Equilibrium, Resolution, &c., which affect the features during severe mathematical operations.

May I trust that you will give your immediate attention to this most important subject?

Believe me,
Sincerely yours,
MATHEMATICUS

Feb. 6, 1868.

THE DESERTED PARKS

"Solitudinum Faciunt: Parcum Appellant."

Museum! loveliest building of the plain
Where Cherwell winds towards the distant main;
How often have I loitered o'er thy green,
Where humble happiness endeared the scene!
How often have I paused on every charm,
The rustic couple walking arm in arm—
The groups of trees, with seats beneath the shade
For prattling babes and whisp'ring lovers made—
The never-failing brawl, the busy mill
Where tiny urchins vied in fistic skill—
(Two phrases only have that dusky race
Caught from the learned influence of the place;
Phrases in their simplicity sublime,
"Scramble a copper!" "Please, Sir, what's the time?")
These round thy walks their cheerful influence shed;
These were thy charms—but all these charms are fled.
　　Amidst thy bowers the tyrant's hand is seen,
And rude pavilions sadden all thy green;

One selfish pastime grasps the whole domain,
And half a faction swallows up the plain;
Adown thy glades, all sacrificed to cricket,
The hollow-sounding bat now guards the wicket;
Sunk are thy mounds in shapeless level all,
Lest aught impede the swiftly rolling ball;
And trembling, shrinking from the fatal blow,
Far, far away thy hapless children go.
    Ill fares the place, to luxury a prey,
Where wealth accumulates, and minds decay;
Athletic sports may flourish or may fade,
Fashion may make them, even as it has made;
But the broad Parks, the city's joy and pride,
When once destroyed can never be supplied!
      Ye friends to truth, ye statesmen, who survey
The rich man's joys increase, the poor's decay,
'Tis yours to judge, how wide the limits stand
Between a splendid and a happy land.
Proud swells go by with laugh of hollow joy,
And shouting Folly hails them with "Ahoy!"
Funds even beyond the miser's wish abound,
And rich men flock from all the world around.
Yet count our gains. This wealth is but a name,
That leaves our useful products still the same.
Not so the loss. The man of wealth and pride
Takes up a space that many poor supplied;
Space for the game, and all its instruments,
Space for pavilions and for scorers' tents;
The ball, that raps his shins in padding cased,
Has won the verdure to an arid waste;
His Park, where these exclusive sports are seen,
Indignant spurns the rustic from the green;
While through the plain, consigned to silence all,
In barren splendour flits the russet ball.
      In peaceful converse with his brother Don,
Here oft the calm Professor wandered on;
Strange words he used—men drank with wondering ears

The languages called "dead," the tongues of other years.
(Enough of Heber! Let me once again
Attune my verse to Goldsmith's liquid strain.)
A man he was to undergraduates dear,
And passing rich with forty pounds a year.
And so, I ween, he would have been till now,
Had not his friends ('twere long to tell you how)
Prevailed on him, Jack-Horner-like, to try
Some method to evaluate his pie,
And win from those dark depths, with skilful thumb,
Five times a hundredweight of luscious plum—
Yet for no thirst of wealth, no love of praise,
In learned labour he consumed his days!

    O Luxury! thou cursed by Heaven's decree,
How ill exchanged are things like these for thee!
How do thy potions, with insidious joy,
Diffuse their pleasures only to destroy;
Iced cobbler, Badminton, and shandy-gaff,
Rouse the loud jest and idiotic laugh;
Inspired by them, to tipsy greatness grown,
Men boast a florid vigour not their own;
At every draught more wild and wild they grow;
While pitying friends observe "I told you so!"
Till, summoned to their post, at the first ball,
A feeble under-hand, their wickets fall.

    Even now the devastation is begun,
And half the business of destruction done;
Even now, methinks while pondering here in pity,
I see the rural Virtues leave the city.
Contented Toil, and calm scholastic Care,
And frugal Moderation, all are there;
Resolute Industry that scorns the lure
Of careless mirth—that dwells apart secure—
To science gives her days, her midnight oil,
Cheered by the sympathy of others' toil—
Courtly Refinement, and that Taste in dress

That brooks no meanness, yet avoids excess—
All these I see, with slow reluctant pace
Desert the long-beloved and honoured place!
    While yet 'tis time, Oxonia, rise and fling
The spoiler from thee: grant no parleying!
Teach him that eloquence, against the wrong,
Though very poor, may still be very strong;
That party-interests we must forego,
When hostile to "pro bono publico";
That faction's empire hastens to its end,
When once mankind to common sense attend;
While independent votes may win the day
Even against the potent spell of "Play!"

May, 1867

THE END

THE NEW BELFRY

OF

CHRIST CHURCH, OXFORD.

A MONOGRAPH

BY

D. C. L.

"A thing of beauty is a joy for ever."

East view of the new Belfry, Ch. Ch., as seen from the Meadow.

SECOND THOUSAND

𝕺𝖝𝖋𝖔𝖗𝖉:

JAMES PARKER AND CO.

1872.

[Collingwood, in *The Lewis Carroll Picture Book*, pages 96-100, gives us this explanatory note by Lewis Sergeant: ". . . In or about the year 1871, one of the old canons' houses, which stood between the cathedral and the "Tom" Quadrangle, was vacated, and the authorities agreed that it should be demolished, in order to make space for a direct approach to the cathedral from the quadrangle. Dean Liddell called in the aid of Mr. Bodley, who constructed a double archway, running under the solid masonry, and of sufficient length to warrant the critics in describing it as the Tunnel. About the same time it was decided to remove the bells from the tower of the cathedral, and make a new belfry over the staircase of the Hall. The arcade of the tower was cut through for the purpose of liberating the bells, and the gap in the stonework is referred to by Mr. Dodgson as the Trench. From the lack of funds, or some other reason, Bodley's idea of a campanile of wood and copper was not proceeded with, and the bells were ensconced in a plain wooden case, of which the author of "The New Belfry"—first printed in 1872, and hurried by the Oxford public through five editions—made merciless fun. He likens it to a meat-safe, a box, a Greek Lexicon, a parallelopiped, a bathing-machine, a piece of bar-soap, a tea-caddy, a clothes-horse; but his favorite name for it is the Tea-chest. The Tunnel, the Trench, and the Tea-chest are the "three T's" immortalised in the "Monograph by D. C. L." and the "Threnody" published in 1873—of which there were three editions. Between these two skits, it may be mentioned, Mr. Dodgson printed for private circulation a four-page pamphlet in a more serious vein: "Objections submitted to the Governing Body of Christ Church, Oxford, against certain proposed alterations in the Great Quadrangle."

In justice to Mr. Bodley it should be stated that he lost no time in concealing his wooden case by a low tower with four corner turrets, at the northeast corner of the quadrangle. The Tea-chest, I need hardly say, is a thing of the past; only its memory survives in the "Notes by an Oxford Chiel."

. . . It may not be possible in all instances to explain an allusion, where it is evident that an allusion was made. One ought to know why the motto of the "Vision" is: "Call you this *baching* of your friends?" and why Venator, in the same piece, sings a "*Bach*analian Ode." Who was Bache, for instance? But attention may be called to a few of the allusions in these two "NOTES," at the risk of its being entirely superfluous for many readers.

The Treasurer, who (it is suggested) "strove to force" the belfry on an unwilling House, was Canon John Bull, a notable figure in his day, and a member of the Chapter of Christ Church. The Professor who, as some imagined, "designed this box, which, whether with a *lid on* or not, equally offends the eye," was the Ireland Professor of Exegesis, Mr. Dodgson's close friend Dr. Liddon. "The head of the House and the architect," who wished to embody their names among the alterations then in progress, and conceived the idea of representing in the belfry a gigantic copy of a Greek Lexicona, were Liddell and Scott—Sir George Gilbert Scott, who had originally undertaken the work, and then handed it over to his pupil, G. F. Bodley. "Jeeby," I am afraid, is Mr. George Bodley without any doubt. He is severely handled as the offender in chief. The apostrophe to the new feature of the "great educational establishment"—"Thou tea-chest"—is to be read in schoolboy fashion as "Tu doces."

References to passing events are frequent enough in these two pieces. The "bread and butter question," towards the end of "The New Belfry," was one of the recurring disputes on the quality of the battels, which every college periodically experiences. The "Indirect Claims" and the "anything but indirect Claimants" recall the Geneva Arbitration and the Tichborne case, both of which were the subject of much "prating" in 1872. The "shortcomings in the payment of the Greek Professor" takes us back to the story of the Jowett persecution.

"The Wandering Burgess," in "The Vision of the Three T's," is Mr. Gladstone, who had been defeated at Oxford in 1865, elected for South Lancashire in the same year, and for Greenwich in 1868. The reference in the ballad to Ayrton and Lowe, Odger and Beales, was natural enough to a satirist in 1873. Mr. Lowe's abortive match-tax is elsewhere commemorated. The Lunatic's speech in Chapter II ("Lo you, said our Rulers,") brings before us Gladstone and Cardwell by name, the proposal to make Oxford a military centre, and the disestablishment of the Irish Church in 1870. The professor with his *humerus*, and his gag on the necessity of German, reflects two controversies which ere now have counted for a good deal in the conversation of Oxford common rooms.]

CONTENTS.

———

THE NEW BELFRY

§ 1. *On the etymological significance of the new Belfry, Ch. Ch.*

The word "Belfry" is derived from the French *bel*, "beautiful, becoming, meet," and from the German frei, "free, unfettered, secure, safe." Thus the word is strictly equivalent to "meatsafe," to which the new belfry bears a resemblance so perfect as almost to amount to coincidence.

§ 2. *On the style of the new Belfry, Ch. Ch.*

The style is that which is usually known as "Early Debased": very early, and remarkably debased.

§ 3. *On the origin of the new Belfry, Ch. Ch.*

Outsiders have enquired, with a persistence verging on personality, and with a recklessness scarcely distinguishable from insanity, to *whom* we are to attribute the first grand conception of the work. Was it the Treasurer, say they, who thus strove to force it on an unwilling House? Was it a Professor who designed this bos, which, whether with a lid on or not, equally offends the eye? Or was it a Censor whose weird spells evoked the horrid thing, the bane of this and of succeeding generations? Until some reply is given to these and similar questions, they must and will remain—for ever—unanswered!

On this point Rumour has been unusually busy. Some say that the Governing Body evolved the idea in solemn conclave—the original motion being to adopt the Tower of St. Mark's at Venice as a model; and that by a series of amendments it was reduced at last to a simple cube. Others say that the Reader in Chemistry suggested it as a form of crystal. There are others who affirm that the Mathematical Lecturer found it in the Eleventh Book of Euclid. In fact, there is no end to the various myths afloat on the subject. Most fortunately, we are in possession of the real story.

The true origin of the design is as follows: we have it on the very best authority.

The head of the House, and the architect, feeling a natural wish that their names should be embodied, in some conspicuous way, among the alterations then in progress, conceived the beautiful and unique idea of representing, by means of the new Belfry, a gigantic copy of a Greek Lexicon.[1] But, before the idea had been reduced to a working form, business took them both to London for a few days, and during their absence, somehow (*this* part of the business has never been satisfactorily explained) the whole thing was put into the hands of a wandering architect, who gave the name of Jeeby. As the poor man is now incarcerated at Hanwell, we will not be too hard upon his memory, but will only say that he professed to have originated the idea in a moment of inspiration, when idly contemplating one of those high coloured, and mysteriously decorated chests which, filled with dried leaves from gooseberry bushes and quickset hedges, profess to supply the market with tea of genuine Chinese growth. Was there not something prophetic in the choice? What traveller is there, to whose lips, when first he enters that great educational establishment and gazes on this its newest decoration, the words do not rise unbidden—"Thou tea-chest"?

It is plain then that Scott, the great architect to whom the work of restoration has been entrusted, is not responsible for this. He is *said* to have pronounced it a "*casus belli*," which (with all deference to the Classical Tutors of the House, who insist that he meant merely "a case for a bell") we believe to have been intended as a term of reproach.

The following lines are attributed to Scott:—

> "If thou wouldst view the Belfry aright,
> Go visit it at the mirk midnight—
> For the least hint of open day
> Scares the beholder quite away.
> When wall and window are black as pitch,
> And there's no deciding which is which;
> When the dark Hall's uncertain roof
> In horror seems to stand aloof;

[1] The Editor confesses to a difficulty here. No sufficient reason has been adduced why a model of a Greek Lexicon should in any way "embody" the names of the above illustrious individuals.

> When corner and corner, alternately,
> Is wrought to an odious symmetry:
> When distant Thames is heard to sigh
> And shudder as he hurries by;
> Then go, if it be worth the while,
> Then view the Belfry's monstrous pile,
> And, home returning, soothly swear,
> ' 'Tis more than Job himself could bear!' "

§ 4. *On the chief architectural merit of the new Belfry, Ch. Ch.*

Its chief merit is its simplicity—a simplicity so pure, so profound, in a word, so *simple*, that no other word will fitly describe it. The meagre outline, and baldness of detail, of the present Chapter, are adopted in humble imitation of this great feature.

§ 5. *On the other architectural merits of the new Belfry, Ch. Ch.*

The Belfry has no other architectural merits.

§ 6. *On the means of obtaining the best views of the new Belfry, Ch. Ch.*

The visitor may place himself, in the first instance, at the opposite corner of the Great Quadrangle, and so combine, in one grand spectacle, the beauties of the North and West sides of the edifice. He will find that the converging lines forcibly suggest a vanishing point, and if that vanishing point should in its turn suggest the thought, "Would that *it* were on the point of vanishing!" he may perchance, like the soldier in the ballad, "lean upon his sword" (if he has one: they are not commonly worn by modern tourists), "and wipe away a tear."

He may then make the circuit of the Quadrangle, drinking in new visions of beauty at every step—

> "Ever charming, ever new,
> When will the Belfry tire the view?"

as Dyer sings in his well-known poem, "Grongar Hill"—and as he walks along from the Deanery towards the Hall staircase, and breathes more and more freely as the Belfry lessens on the view, the delicious sensation of relief, which he will experience when it has finally disappeared, will amply repay him for all he will have endured.

The *best* view of the Belfry is that selected by our artist for the admirable frontispiece which he has furnished for the first volume of the present work.[2] This view may be seen, in all its beauty, from the far end of Merton Meadow. From that point the imposing position (or, more briefly, the imposition) of the whole structure is thrillingly apparent. There the thoughtful passer-by, with four right angles on one side of him, and four anglers, who have no right to be there, on the other, may ponder on the mutability of human things, or recall the names of Euclid and Isaak Walton, or smoke, or ride a bicycle, or do anything that the local authorities will permit.

§ 7. *On the impetus given to Art in England by the new Belfry, Ch. Ch.*

The idea has spread far and wide, and is rapidly pervading all branches of manufacture. Already an enterprising maker of bonnet-boxes is advertising "the Belfry pattern": two builders of bathing machines at Ramsgate have followed his example: one of the great London houses is supplying "bar-soap" cut in the same striking and symmetrical form: and we are credibly informed that Borwick's Baking Powder and Thorley's Food for Cattle are now sold in no other shape.

§ 8. *On the feelings with which old Ch. Ch. men regard the new Belfry.*

Bitterly, bitterly do all old Ch. Ch. men lament this latest lowest development of native taste. "We see the Governing Body," say they: "where is the Governing *Mind?*" and Echo (exercising a judicious "natural selection," for which even Darwin would give her credit) answers "where?"

At the approaching "Gaudy," when a number of old Ch. Ch.

2 On further consideration, it was deemed inexpedient to extend this work beyond the compass of one Volume.

men will gather together, it is proposed, at the conclusion of the banquet, to present to each guest a portable model of the new Belfry, tastefully executed in cheese.

§ 9. *On the feelings with which resident Ch. Ch. men regard the new Belfry.*

Who that has seen a Ch. Ch. man conducting his troop of "lionesses" (so called from the savage and pitiless greed with which they devour the various sights of Oxford) through its ancient precincts, that has noticed the convulsive start and ghastly stare that always affect new-comers, when first they come into view of the new Belfry, that has heard the eager questions with which they assail their guide as to how, the why, the what for, and the how long, of this astounding phenomenon, can have failed to mark the manly glow which immediately suffuses the cheek of the hapless cicerone?

> "Is it the glow of conscious pride—
> Of pure ambition gratified—
> That seeks to read in other eye
> Something of its own ecstasy?
> Or wrath, that worldlings should make fun
> Of anything 'the House' has done?
> Or puzzlement, that seeks in vain
> The rigid mystery to explain?
> Or is it shame that, knowing not
> How to defend or cloak the blot—
> The foulest blot on fairest face
> That ever marred a noble place—
> Burns with the pangs it will not own,
> Pangs felt by loyal sons alone?"

§ 10. *On the logical treatment of the new Belfry, Ch. Ch.*

The subject has been reduced to three Syllogisms.
The first is in "Barbara." It is attributed to the enemies of the Belfry.

Wooden buildings in the midst of stone-work are barbarous;
Plain rectangular forms in the midst of arches and decorations are barbarous;
Ergo, the whole thing is ridiculous and revolting.

The second is in "Celarent," and has been most carefully composed by the friends of the Belfry.

> The Governing Body would conceal this appalling structure, if they could;
> The Governing Body would conceal the feelings of chagrin with which
> they now regard it, if they could;
> *Ergo,* . . . (MS. *unfinished*).

The third Syllogism is in "Festino," and is the joint composition of the friends and the enemies of the Belfry.

> To restore the character of Ch. Ch. a tower must be built;
> To build a tower, ten thousand pounds must be raised;
> *Ergo,* no time must be lost.

These three Syllogisms have been submitted to the criticism of the Professor of Logic, who writes that "he fancies he can detect some slight want of logical sequence in the Conclusion of the third." He adds that, according to *his* experience of life, when people thus commit a fatal blunder in child-like confidence that money will be forthcoming to enable them to set it right, in ten cases out of nine the money is *not* forthcoming. This is a large percentage.

§ 11. *On the dramatic treatment of the new Belfry, Ch. Ch. Curtain rises, discovering the DEAN, CANONS, and STU-DENTS seated round a table, on which the mad ARCHITECT, fantastically dressed, and wearing a Fool's cap and bells, is placing a square block of deal.*

DEAN (AS HAMLET). Methinks I see a Bell-tower!
CANONS (*Looking wildly in all directions*). Where, my good Sir?
DEAN. In my mind's eye————(*Knocking heard*) Who's there?
FOOL. A spirit, a spirit; he says his name's poor Tom.
(*Enter* THE GREAT BELL, *disguised as a mushroom.*)
GREAT BELL. Who gives anything to poor Tom, whom the foul fiend hath led through bricks and through mortar, through rope and windlass, through plank and scaffold; that hath torn down his balustrades, and torn up his terraces; that hath made him go as a common pedlar, with a wooden box upon his back. Do poor Tom some charity. Tom's a-cold.

> Rafters and planks, and such small deer,
> Shall be Tom's food for many a year.

CENSOR. I feared it would come to this.

DEAN (AS KING LEAR). The little Dons and all, Tutor, Reader, Lecturer—see, they bark at me!

CENSOR. His wits begin to unsettle.

DEAN (AS HAMLET). Do you see yonder box that's almost in shape of a tea-caddy?

CENSOR. By its mass, it is like a tea-caddy, indeed.

DEAN. Methinks it is like a clothes-horse.

CENSOR. It is backed by a clothes-horse.

DEAN. Or like a tub.

CENSOR. Very like a tub.

DEAN. They fool me to the top of my bent.

(*Enter from opposite sides* THE BELFRY *as* Box, *and* THE BODLEY LIBRARIAN *as* COX.)

LIBRARIAN. Who are you, Sir?

BELFRY. If it comes to that, Sir, who are you?

(*They exchange cards.*)

LIBRARIAN. I should feel obliged to you if you could accommodate me with a more protuberant Bell-tower, Mr. B. The one you have now seems to me to consist of corners only, with nothing whatever in the middle.

BELFRY. Anything to accommodate you, Mr. Cox. (*Places jauntily on his head a small model of the skeleton of an umbrella, upside down.*)

LIBRARIAN. Ah, tell me—in mercy tell me—have you such a thing as a redeeming feature, or the least mark of artistic design, about you?

BELFRY. No!

LIBRARIAN. Then you are my long-lost door scraper!

(*They rush into each other's arms.*)

(*Enter* TREASURER *as* ARIEL. *Solemn music.*)

SONG AND CHORUS

> Five fathom square the Belfry frowns;
> All its sides of timber made;
> Painted all in greys and browns;
> Nothing of it that will fade.

Christ Church may admire the change—
Oxford thinks it sad and strange.
Beauty's dead! Let's ring her knell.
Hark! now I hear them—ding-dong, bell.

§ 12. *On the Future of the new Belfry, Ch. Ch.*

The Belfry has a great Future before it—at least, if it has not, it has very little to do with Time at all, its Past being (fortunately for our ancestors) a nonentity, and its Present a blank. The advantage of having been born in the reign of Queen Anne, and of having died in that or the subsequent reign, has never been so painfully apparent as it is now.

Credible witnesses assert that, when the bells are rung, the Belfry must come down. In that case considerable damage (the process technically described as "pulverisation") must ensue to the beautiful pillar and roof which adorn the Hall staircase. But the architect is prepared even for this emergency. "On the first symptom of deflection" (he writes from Hanwell) "let the pillar be carefully removed and placed, with its superstruent superstructure" (we cannot forbear calling attention to this beautiful phrase), "in the center of 'Mercury.' *There* it will constitute a novel and most unique feature of the venerable House."

"Yes, and the Belfry shall serve to generations yet unborn as an ariel Ticket-office," so he cries with his eye in a fine frenzy rolling, "where the Oxford and London balloon shall call ere it launch forth on its celestial voyage—and where expectant passengers shall while away the time with the latest edition of *Bell's Life!*"

§ 13. *On the Moral of the new Belfry, Ch. Ch.*

The moral position of Christ Church is undoubtedly improved by it. "We have been attacked, and perhaps not without reason, on the Bread-and-Butter question," she remarks to an inattentive World (which heeds her not, but prates on of Indirect Claims and of anything but indirect Claimants), "we have been charged—and, it must be confessed, in a free and manly tone—with shortcomings in the payment of the Greek Professor, but who shall say that we are not all 'on the square' *now?*"

This, however, is not *the* Moral of the matter. Everything has a moral, if you choose to look for it. In Wordsworth, a good half of every poem is devoted to the Moral: in Byron, a smaller proportion: in Tupper, the whole. Perhaps the most graceful tribute we can pay to the genius of the last-named writer, is to entrust to him, as an old member of Christ Church, the conclusion of this Monograph.

"Look on the Quadrangle of Christ, squarely, for is it not a Square?
And a Square recalleth a Cube; and a Cube recalleth the Belfry;
And the Belfry recalleth a Die, shaken by the hand of the gambler;
Yet, once thrown, it may not be recalled, being, so to speak, irrevocable.
There it shall endure for ages, treading hard on the heels of the Sublime—
For it is but a step, saith the wise man, from the Sublime unto the Ridiculous:
And the Simple dwelleth midway between, and shareth the qualities of either."

FINIS.

THE VISION

OF

THE THREE T'S.

A THRENODY

BY

THE AUTHOR OF

"THE NEW BELFRY."

"Cal you this, baching of your friends?"

West view of the new Tunnel

SECOND EDITION

𝔒𝔵𝔣𝔬𝔯𝔡:
JAMES PARKER AND CO.
1873.

CONTENTS.

CHAPTER I.

A Conference (held on the Twentieth of March, 1873), betwixt an Angler, *a* Hunter, *and a* Professor; *concerning angling, and the beautifying of Thomas his Quadrangle. The Ballad of "The Wandering Burgess."*

CHAPTER II.

A Conference with one distraught: who discourseth strangely of many things.

CHAPTER III.

A Conference of the Hunter *with a* Tutor, *whilom the* Angler *his eyes be closed in sleep. The* Angler *awaking relateth his Vision. The* Hunter *chaunteth "A Bachanalian Ode."*

THE VISION OF THE THREE T'S [1]

CHAPTER I

A Conference betwixt an Angler, *a* Hunter, *and a* Professor *concerning angling, and the beautifying of Thomas his Quadrangle. The Ballad of "The Wandering Burgess."*

PISCATOR, VENATOR

PISCATOR. My honest Scholar, we are now arrived at the place whereof I spake, and trust me, we shall have good sport. How say you? Is not this a noble Quadrangle we see around us? And be not these lawns trimly kept, and this lake marvellous clear?

VENATOR. So marvellous clear, good Master, and withal so brief in compass, that methinks, if any fish of a reasonable bigness were therein, we must perforce espy it. Come, let's sit down, and while we unpack the fishing gear, I'll deliver a few remarks, both as to the fish to be met with hereabouts, and the properest method of fishing.

But you are to note first (for, as you are pleased to be my Scholar, it is but fitting you should imitate my habits of close observation) that the margin of this lake is so deftly fashioned that each portion thereof is at one and the same distance from that tumulus which rises in the centre.

VEN. O' my word 'tis so! You have indeed a quick eye, dear Master, and a wondrous readiness of observing.

PISC. Both may be yours in time, my Scholar, if with humility and patience you follow me as your model.

VEN. I thank you for that hope, great Master! But ere you begin your discourse, let me enquire of you one thing touching this noble Quadrangle—Is all we see of a like antiquity? To be brief, think you that those two tall archways, that excavation in the parapet,

---

[1] An explanation of *The Vision of the Three T's* may be found in the note accompanying *The New Belfry*. See pages 153-154. [*McD.*]

167

and that quaint wooden box, belong to the ancient design of the building, or have men of our day thus sadly disfigured the place?

PISC. I doubt not they are new, dear Scholar. For indeed I was here but a few years since, and saw naught of these things. But what book is that I see lying by the water's edge?

VEN. A book of ancient ballads, and truly I am glad to see it, as we may herewith beguile the tediousness of the day, if our sport be poor, or if we grow aweary.

PISC. This is well thought of. But now to business. And first I'll tell you somewhat of the fish proper to these waters. The Commoner kinds we may let pass: for though some of them be easily Plucked forth from the water, yet are they so slow, and withal have so little in them, that they are good for nothing, unless they be crammed up to the very eyes with such stuffing as comes readiest to hand. Of these the Stickleback, a mighty slow fish, is chiefest, and along with him you may reckon the Fluke, and divers others: all these belong to the "Mullet" genus, and be good to play, though scarcely worth examination.

I will say somewhat of the Nobler kinds, and chiefly of the Gold-fish, which is a species highly thought of, and much sought after in these parts, not only by men, but by divers birds, as for example the King-fishers: and note that wheresoever you shall see those birds assemble, and but few insects about, there shall you ever find the Gold-fish most lively and richest in flavour; but wheresoever you perceive swarms of a certain gray fly, called the Dun-fly, there the Gold-fish are ever poorer in quality, and the King-fishers seldom seen.

A good Perch may sometimes be found hereabouts: but for a good fat Plaice (which is indeed but a magnified Perch) you may search these waters in vain. They that love such dainties must needs betake them to some distant Sea.

But for the manner of fishing, I would have you note first that your line be not thicker than an ordinary bell-rope; for look you, to flog the water, as though you laid on with a flail, is most preposterous, and will surely scare the fish. And note further, that your rod must by no means exceed ten, or at the most twenty, pounds in weight, for—

Ven. Pardon me, my Master, that I thus break in on so excellent a discourse, but there now approaches us a Collegian, as I guess him to be, from whom we may haply learn the cause of these novelties we see around us. Is not that a bone which, ever as he goes, he so cautiously waves before him?

Enter Professor

Pisc. By his reverend aspect and white hair, I guess him to be some learned Professor. I give you good day, reverend Sir! If it be not ill manners to ask it, what bone is that you bear about with you? It is, methinks, a humerous whimsy to chuse so strange a companion.

Prof. Your observation, Sir, is both anthropolitically and ambidexterously opportune: for this is indeed a *Humerus* I carry with me. You are, I doubt not, strangers in these parts, for else you would surely know that a Professor doth ever carry that which most aptly sets forth his Profession. Thus, the Professor of Uniform Rotation carries with him a wheelbarrow—the Professor of Graduated Scansion a ladder—and so of the rest.

Ven. It is an inconvenient and, methinks, an ill-advised custom.

Prof. Trust me, Sir, you are absolutely and amorphologically mistaken: yet time would fail me to show you wherein lies your error, for indeed I must now leave you, being bound for this great performance of music, which even at this distance salutes your ears.

Pisc. Yet, I pray you, do us one courtesy before you go; and that shall be to resolve a question, whereby my friend and I are sorely exercised.

Prof. Say on, Sir, and I will e'en answer you to the best of my poor ability.

Pisc. Briefly, then, we would ask the cause for piercing the very heart of this fair building with that uncomely tunnel, which is at once so ill-shaped, so ill-sized, and so ill-lighted.

Prof. Sir, do you know German?

Pisc. It is my grief, Sir, that I know no other tongue than mine own.

Prof. Then, Sir, my answer is this, *Warum nicht?*

Pisc. Alas, Sir, I understand you not.

PROF. The more the pity. For now-a-days all that is good comes from the German. Ask our men of science: they will tell you that any German book must needs surpass an English one. Aye, and even an English book, worth naught in this its native dress, shall become, when rendered into German, a valuable contribution to Science.

VEN. Sir, you much amaze me.

PROF. Nay, Sir, I'll amaze you yet more. No learned man doth now talk, or even so much as cough, save only in German. The time has been, I doubt not, when an honest English "Hem!" was held enough, both to clear the voice and rouse the attention of the company, but now-a-days no man of Science, that setteth any store by his good name, will cough otherwise than thus, *Ach! Euch! Auch!*

VEN. 'Tis wondrous. But, not to stay you further, wherefore do we see that ghastly gash above us, hacked, as though by some wanton schoolboy, in the parapet adjoining the Hall?

PROF. *Sir*, do you know German?

VEN. Believe me, No.

PROF. Then, Sir, I need but ask you this, *Wie befinden Sie Sich?*

VEN. I doubt not, Sir, but you are in the right on't.

PISC. But, Sir, I will by your favour ask you one other thing, as to that unseemly box that blots the fair heavens above. Wherefore, in this grand old City, and in so conspicuous a place, do men set so hideous a thing?

PROF. Be you mad, Sir? Why this is the very climacteric and coronal of all our architectural aspirations! In all Oxford there is naught like it!

PISC. It joys me much to hear you say so.

PROF. And, trust me, to an earnest mind, the categorical evolution of the Abstract, ideologically considered, must infallibly develope itself in the parallelopipedisation of the Concrete! And so Farewell.

Exit PROFESSOR.

PISC. He is a learned man, and methinks there is much that is sound in his reasoning.

VEN. It is *all* sound, as it seems to me. But how say you? Shall

I read you one of these ballads? Here is one called "The Wandering Burgess," which (being forsooth a dumpish ditty) may well suit the ears of us whose eyes are oppressed with so dire a spectacle.

PISC. Read on, good Scholar, and I will bait our hooks the while.

VENATOR readeth.

THE WANDERING BURGESS

Our Willie had been sae lang awa',
  Frae bonnie Oxford toon,
The townsfolk they were greeting a'
  As they went up and doon.

He hadna been gane a year, a year,
  A year but barely ten,
When word cam unto Oxford toon
  Our Willie wad come agen.

Willie he stude at Thomas his Gate,
  And made a lustie din;
And who so blithe as the gate-porter
  To rise and let him in?

"Now enter Willie, now enter Willie,
  And look around the place,
And see the pain that we have ta'en
  Thomas his Quad to grace."

The first look that our Willie cast,
  He leuch loud laughters three,
The neist look that our Willie cast,
  The tear blindit his e'e.

Sae square and stark the Tea-chest frowned
  Athwart the upper air,
But when the Trench our Willie saw,
  He thoucht the Tea-chest fair.

Sae murderous-deep the Trench did gape
  The parapet aboon,
But when the Tunnel Willie saw,
  He loved the Trench eftsoon.

'Twas mirk beneath the tane archway,
  'Twas mirk beneath the tither;
Ye wadna ken a man therein,
  Though it were your ain dear brither.

He turned him round and round about,
  And looked upon the Three;
And dismal grew his countenance,
  And drumlie grew his e'e.

"What cheer, what cheer, my gallant knight?"
  The gate-porter 'gan say.
"Saw ever ye sae fair a sight
  As ye have seen this day?"

"Now haud your tongue of your prating, man:
  Of your prating now let me be.
For, as I'm true knight, a fouler sight
  I'll never live to see.

"Before I'd be the ruffian dark
  Who planned this ghastly show,
I'd serve as secretary's clerk
  To Ayrton or to Lowe.

"Before I'd own the loathly thing
  That Christ Church Quad reveals,
I'd serve as shoeblack's underling
  To Odger and to Beales!"

CHAPTER II

A Conference with one distraught: who discourseth strangely of many things.

PISCATOR. 'Tis a marvellous pleasant ballad. But look you, another Collegian draws near. I wot not of what station he is, for indeed his apparel is new to me.

VENATOR. It is compounded, as I take it, of the diverse dresses of a jockey, a judge, and a North American Indian.

Enter LUNATIC

PISC. Sir, may I make bold to ask your name?

LUN. With all my heart. It is Jeeby, at your service.

PISC. And wherefore (if I may further trouble you, being, as you see, a stranger) do you wear so gaudy, but withal so ill-assorted, a garb?

LUN. Why, Sir, I'll tell you. Do you read the *Morning Post?*

PISC. Alas, Sir, I do not.

LUN. 'Tis pity of your life you do not. For, look you, not to read the *Post*, and not to know the newest and most commended fashions, are but one and the same thing. And yet this raiment, that I wear, is *not* the newest fashion. No, nor has it ever been, nor will it ever be, the fashion.

VEN. I can well believe it.

LUN. And therefore 'tis, Sir, that I wear it. 'Tis but a badge of greatness. My deeds you see around you. *Si monumentum quaeris, circumspice!* You know Latin?

VEN. Not I, Sir! It shames me to say it.

LUN. You are then (let me roundly tell you) *monstrum horrendum, informe, ingens, cui lumen ademptum!*

VEN. Sir, you may tell it me roundly—or, if you list squarely—or again, triangularly. But if, as you affirm, I see your deeds around me, I would fain know which they be.

LUN. Aloft, Sir, stands the first and chiefest! That soaring minaret! That gorgeous cupola! That dreamlike effulgence of—

VEN. That wooden box?

LUN. The same, Sir! 'Tis mine!

VEN. (*After a pause*). Sir, it is worthy of you.

LUN. Lower now your eyes by a hairsbreadth, and straight you light upon my *second* deed. Oh, Sir, what toil of brain, what cudgelling of forehead, what rending of locks, went to the fashioning of it!

VEN. Mean you that newly-made gap?

LUN. I do, Sir. 'Tis mine!

VEN. (*After a long pause*). What else, Sir? I would fain know the worst.

LUN. (*Wildly*). It comes, it comes. My *third* great deed! Lend, lend your ears—your nose—any feature you can least conveniently spare! See you those twin doorways? Tall and narrow they loom upon you—severely simple their outline—massive the masonry between—black as midnight the darkness within! Sir, of what do they mind you?

VEN. Of vaults, Sir, and of charnel-houses.

LUN. This is a goodly fancy, and yet they are not vaults. No, Sir, you see before you a Railway Tunnel!

VEN. 'Tis very strange.

LUN. But no less true than strange. Mark me. 'Tis love, 'tis love, that makes the world go round! Society goes round of itself. In circles. Military society in military circles. Circles must needs have centres. Military circles military centres.

VEN. Sir, I fail to see—

LUN. Lo you, said our Rulers, Oxford shall be a military centre! Then the chiefest of them (glad in countenance, yet stony, I wot, in heart) so ordered it by his underling (I remember me not his name, yet is he one that can play a card well, and so serveth meetly the behests of that mighty one, who played of late in Ireland a game of cribbage such as no man, who saw it, may lightly forget); and then, Sir, this great College, ever loyal and generous, gave this Quadrangle as a Railway Terminus, whereby the troops might come and go. By that Tunnel, Sir, the line will enter.

PISC. But, Sir, I see no rails.

LUN. Patience, good Sir! For railing we look to the Public. The College doth but furnish sleepers.

PISC. And the design of that Tunnel is—

LUN. Is mine, Sir! Oh, the fancy! Oh, the wit! Oh, the rich vein of humour! When came the idea? I' the mirk midnight. Whence came the idea? From a cheese-scoop! How came the idea? In a wild dream. Hearken, and I will tell. Form square, and prepare to receive a canonry! All the evening long I had seen lobsters marching around the table in unbroken order. Something sputtered in the candle—something hopped among the tea-things— something pulsated, with an ineffable yearning, beneath the enraptured hearthrug! My heart told me something was coming—and something came. A voice cried "Cheese-scoop!" and the Great Thought of my life flashed upon me! Placing an ancient Stilton cheese, to represent this venerable Quadrangle, on the chimney-piece, I retired to the further end of the room, armed only with a cheese-scoop, and with a dauntless courage awaited the word of command. Charge, Cheesetaster, charge! On, Stilton, on! With a yell and a bound I crossed the room, and plunged my scoop into the very heart of the foe! Once more! Another yell—another bound— another cavity scooped out! The deed was done!

VEN. And yet, Sir, if a cheese-scoop were your guide, these cavities must needs be circular.

LUN. They were so at the first—but, like the fickle Moon, my guardian satellite, I change as I go on. Oh, the rapture, Sir, of that wild moment! And did I reveal the Mighty Secret! Never, never! Day by day, week by week, behind a wooden screen, I wrought out that vision of beauty. The world came and went, and knew not of it. Oh, the ecstasy, when yesterday the Screen was swept away, and the Vision was a Reality! I stood by Tom-Gate, in that triumphal hour, and watched the passers-by. They stopped! They stared!! They started!!! A thrill of envy paled their cheeks! Hoarse inarticulate words of delirious rapture rose to their lips. What withheld me—what, I ask you candidly, withheld me from leaping upon them, holding them in a frantic clutch, and yelling in their ears " 'Tis mine, 'tis mine!"

PISC. Perchance, the thought that—

LUN. You are right, Sir. The thought that there is a lunatic asylum in the neighborhood, and that two medical certificates— but I will be calm. The deed is done. Let us change the subject. Even now a great musical performance is going on within. Wilt hear it? The Chapter give it—ha, ha! They give it!

PISC. Sir, I will very gladly be their guest.

LUN. Then, guest, you have not guessed all! You shall be bled, Sir, ere you go! 'Tis love, 'tis love, that makes the hat go round! Stand and deliver! Vivat Regina! No money returned!

PISC. How mean you, Sir?

LUN. I said, Sir, "No money returned!"

PISC. And I said, Sir, "How mean——"

LUN. Sir, I am with you. You have heard of Bishops' Charges. Sir, what are Bishops to Chapters? Oh, it goes to my heart to see these quaint devices! First, sixpence for use of a door-scraper. Then, fivepence for right of choosing by which archway to approach the door. Then, a poor threepence for turning of the handle. Then, a shilling a head for admission, and half-a-crown for every two-headed man. Now this, Sir, is manifestly unjust, for you are to note that the double of a shilling—

PISC. I do surmise, Sir, that the case is rare.

LUN. And then, Sir, five shillings each for care of your umbrella! Hence comes in that each visitor of ready wit hides his umbrella, ere he enter, either by swallowing it (which is perilous to the health of the inner man), or by running it down within his coat, even from the nape of the neck, which indeed is the cause of that which you may have observed in me, namely, a certain stiffness in mine outward demeanour. Farewell, gentlemen, I go to hear the music.

Exit LUNATIC

CHAPTER III

A Conference of the Hunter with a Tutor, whilom the Angler his eyes be closed in sleep. The Angler awaking relateth his Vision. The Hunter chaunteth "A Bachanalian Ode."

PISCATOR, VENATOR, TUTOR

VENATOR. He has left us, but methinks we are not to lack company, for look you, another is even now at hand, gravely apparelled, and bearing upon his head Hoffmann's Lexicon in four volumes folio.

PISCATOR. Trust me, this doth symbolise his craft. Good morrow, Sir. If I rightly interpret these that you bear with you, you are a teacher in this learncd place.

TUTOR. I am, Sir, a Tutor, and profess the teaching of divers unknown tongues.

PISC. Sir, we are happy to have your company, and, if it trouble you not too much, we would gladly ask (as indeed we did ask another of your learned body, but understood not his reply) the cause of these new things we see around us, which indeed are as strange as they are new, and as unsightly as they are strange.

TUTOR. Sir, I will tell you with all my heart. You must know then (for herein lies the pith of the matter) that the motto of the Governing Body is this:—

"Diruit, aedificat, mutat quadrata rotundis"; which I thus briefly expound.

Diruit. "It teareth down." Witness that fair opening which, like a glade in an ancient forest, we have made in the parapet at the sinistral extremity of the Hall. Even as a tree is the more admirable when the hewer's axe hath all but severed its trunk—or as a row of pearly teeth, enshrined in ruby lips, are yet the more lovely for the loss of one—so, believe me, this our fair Quadrangle is but enhanced by that which foolish men in mockery call the "Trench."

Aedificat. "It buildeth up." Witness that beauteous Belfry which, in its ethereal grace, seems ready to soar away even as we gaze upon it! Even as a railway porter moves with an unwonted majesty when bearing a portmanteau on his head—or as I myself (to speak modestly) gain a new beauty from these massive tomes— or as ocean charms us most when the rectangular bathing-machine breaks the monotony of its curving marge—so are we blessed by the presence of that which an envious world hath dubbed "the Tea-chest."

Mutat quadrata rotundis. "*It exchangeth square things for round.*" Witness that series of square-headed doors and windows, so beautifully broken in upon by that double archway! For indeed, though simple ("*simplex munditiis*," as the poet saith), it is matchless in its beauty. Had those twin archways been greater, they would but have matched those at the corners of the Quadrangle— had they been less, they would but have copied, with an abject servility, the doorways around them. In such things, it is only a vulgar mind that thinks of a *match*. The subject is lowe. *We* seek the Unique, the Eccentric! *We* glory in this twofold excavation, which scoffers speak of as "the Tunnel."

VEN. Come, Sir, let me ask you a pleasant question. Why doth the Governing Body chuse for motto so trite a saying? It is, if I remember me aright, an example of a rule in the Latin Grammar.

TUTOR. Sir, if we are not grammatical, we are nothing!

VEN. But for the Belfry, Sir. Sure none can look on it without an inward shudder?

TUTOR. I will not gainsay it. But you are to note that it is not permanent. This shall serve its time, and a fairer edifice shall succeed it.

VEN. In good sooth I hope it. Yet for the time being it doth not, in that it is not permanent, the less disgrace the place. Drunkenness, Sir, is not permanent, and yet is held in no good esteem.

TUTOR. 'Tis an apt simile.

VEN. And for these matchless arches, as you do most truly call them, would it not savour of more wholesome Art, had they matched the doorways, or the gateways?

TUTOR. Sir, do you study the Mathematics?

VEN. I trust, Sir, I can do the Rule of Three as well as another; and for Long Division—

Tutor. You must know, then, that there be three Means treated of in Mathematics. For there is the Arithmetic Mean, the Geometric, and the Harmonic. And note further that a Mean is that which falleth between two magnitudes. Thus it is, that the entrance you here behold falleth between the magnitudes of the doorways and the gateways, and is in truth the Non-harmonic Mean, the Mean Absolute. But that the Mean, or Middle, is ever the safer course, we have a notable ensample in Egyptian history, in which land (as travellers tell us) the Ibis standeth ever in the midst of the river Nile, so best to avoid the onslaught of the ravenous alligators, which infest the banks on either side; from which habit of that wise bird is derived the ancient maxim, "*Medio tutissimus Ibis.*"

Ven. But wherefore be they *two?* Surely *one* arch were at once more comely and more convenient?

Tutor. Sir, so long as public approval be won, what matter for the arch? But that they are two, take this as sufficient explication—that they are too tall for doorways, too narrow for gateways; too light without, too dark within; too plain to be ornamental, and withal too fantastic to be useful. And if this be not enough, you are to note further that, were it all one arch, it must needs cut short one of those shafts which grace the Quadrangle on all sides—and that were a monstrous and unheard-of thing, in good sooth, look you.

Ven. In good sooth, Sir, if I look I cannot miss seeing that there be three such shafts already cut short by doorways: so that it hath fair ensample to follow.

Tutor. Then will I take other ground, Sir, and affirm (for I trust I have not learned Logic in vain) that to cut short the shaft were a common and vulgar thing to do. But indeed a single arch, where folk might smoothly enter in, were wholly adverse to Nature, who formeth never a mouth without setting a tongue as an obstacle in the midst thereof.

Ven. Sir, do you tell me that the block of masonry, between the gateways, was left there of set purpose, to hinder those that would enter in?

Tutor. Trust me, it was even so; for firstly, we may thereby more easily control the entering crowds (*"divide et impera,"* say the Ancients), and secondly, in this matter a wise man will ever follow Nature. Thus, in the centre of a hall-door we usually place an umbrella stand—in the midst of a wicket-gate, a milestone, what place so suited for a watchbox as the centre of a narrow bridge?— Yea, and in the most crowded thoroughfare, where the living tide flows thickest, there, in the midst of all, the true *ideal* architect doth ever plant an obelisk! You may have observed this?

VEN. (*Much bewildered*). I *may* have done so, worthy Sir; and yet, methinks—

TUTOR. I must now bid you farewell; for the music, which I would fain hear, is even now beginning.

VEN. Trust me, Sir, your discourse hath interested me hugely.

TUTOR. Yet it hath, I fear me, somewhat wearied your friend, who is, as I perceive, in a deep slumber.

VEN. I had partly guessed it, by his loud and continuous snoring.

TUTOR. You had best let him sleep on. He hath, I take it, a dull fancy, that cannot grasp the Great and the Sublime. And so farewell: I am bound for the music.

Exit TUTOR.

VEN. I give you good day, good Sir. Awake, my Master! For the day weareth on, and we have catched no fish.

PISC. Think not of fish, dear Scholar, but hearken! Trust me, I have seen such things in my dreams as words may hardly compass! Come, Sir, sit down, and I'll unfold to you, in such poor language as may best suit both my capacity and the briefness of our time.

THE VISION OF THE THREE T'S

Methought that, in some bygone Age, I stood beside the waters of Mercury, and saw, reflected on its placid face, the grand old buildings of the Great Quadrangle: near me stood one of portly form and courtly mien, with scarlet gown, and broad-brimmed hat whose strings, wide-fluttering in the breezeless air, at once defied the laws of gravity and marked the reverend Cardinal! 'Twas Wolsey's self! I would have spoken, but he raised his hand and pointed to the cloudless sky, from whence deep-muttering thunders now began to roll. I listened in wild terror.

Darkness gathered overhead, and through the gloom sobbingly down-floated a gigantic Box! With a fearful crash it settled upon the ancient Col-

*lege, which groaned beneath it, while a mocking voice cried, "Ha! Ha!"
I looked for Wolsey: he was gone. Down in those glassy depths lay the
stalwart form, with scarlet mantle grandly wrapped around it: the broad-
brimmed hat floated, boatlike, on the lake, while the strings with their complex
tassels, still defying the laws of gravity, quivered in the air, and seemed to
point a hundred fingers at the horrid Belfry! Around, on every side, spirits
howled in the howling blast, blatant, stridulous!*

*A darker vision yet! A black gash appeared in the shuddering parapet!
Spirits flitted hither and thither with face, and warning finger pressed to
quivering lips!*

*Then a wild shriek rang through the air, as, with volcanic roar, two murky
chasms burst upon the view, and the ancient College reeled giddily around me!*

*Spirits in patent-leather boots stole by on tiptoe, with hushed breath and
eyes of ghastly terror! Spirits with cheap umbrellas, and unnecessary go-
loshes, hovered over me, sublimely pendant! Spirits with carpet bags, dressed
in complete suits of dittos, sped by me, shrieking "Away! Away! To the
arrowy Rhine! To the rushing Guadalquiver! To Bath! To Jericho!
To anywhere!"*

*Stand here with me and gaze. From this thrice-favoured spot, in one
rapturous glance gather in, and brand for ever on the tablets of memory,
the Vision of the Three T's! To your left frowns the abysmal blackness of
the tenebrous Tunnel. To your right yawns the terrible Trench. While
far above, away from the sordid aims of Earth and the petty criticisms of
Art, soars, tetragonal and tremendous, the tintinnabulatory Tea-chest!
Scholar, the Vision is complete!*

VEN. I am glad on't; for in good sooth I am a-hungered. How
say you, my Master? Shall we not leave fishing, and fall to eating
presently? And look you, here is a song, which I have chanced
on in this book of ballads, and which methinks suits well the present
time and this most ancient place.

PISC. Nay, then, let's sit down. We shall, I warrant you, make
a good, honest, wholesome, hungry nuncheon with a piece of
powdered beef and a radish or two that I have in my fish-bag.
And you shall sing us this same song as we eat.

VEN. Well, then, I will sing; and I trust it may content you
as well as your excellent discourse hath oft profited me.

VENATOR *chaunteth*

A BACHANALIAN ODE

Here's to the Freshman of bashful eighteen!
Here's to the Senior of twenty!

Here's to the youth whose moustache can't be seen!
  And here's to the man who has plenty!
      Let the men Pass!
      Out of the mass
I'll warrant we'll find you some fit for a Class!

Here's to the Censors, who symbolise Sense,
  Just as Mitres incorporate Might, Sir!
To the Bursar, who never expands the expense
  And the Readers, who always do right, Sir
      Tutor and Don,
      Let them jog on!
I warrant they'll rival the centuries gone!

Here's to the Chapter, melodious crew!
  Whose harmony surely *intends* well:
For, though it commences with "harm," it is true
  Yet its motto is "All's well that ends well!"
      'Tis love, I'll be bound,
      That makes it go round!
For "In for a penny is in for a pound!"

Here's to the Governing Body, whose Art
  (For they're Masters of Arts to a man, Sir!)
Seeks to beautify Christ Church in every part,
  Though the method seems hardly to answer!
      With three T's it is graced—
      Which letters are placed
To stand for the names of Tact, Talent, and Taste!

Pisc. I thank you, good Scholar, for this piece of merriment, and this Song, which was well humoured by the maker, and well rendered by you.

Ven. Oh, me! Look you, Master! A fish! a fish!

Pisc. Then let us hook it.

They hook it.

FINIS

THE BLANK CHEQUE,

A FABLE.

BY

THE AUTHOR OF

"THE NEW BELFRY"

AND

"THE VISION OF THE THREE T'S.'

"Vell, perhaps," said Sam, "you bought houses, vich is delicate English for
goin' mad; or took to buildin', vich is a medical term for being incurable."

Oxford:
JAMES PARKER AND CO.
1874.

THE BLANK CHEQUE [1]

"Five o'clock tea" is a phrase that our "rude forefathers," even of the last generation, would scarcely have understood, so completely is it a thing of to-day; and yet, so rapid is the March of Mind, it has already risen into a national institution, and rivals, in its universal application to all ranks and ages, and as a specific for "all the ills that flesh is heir to," the glorious Magna Charta.

Thus it came to pass that, one chilly day in March, which only made the shelter indoors seem by contrast the more delicious, I found myself in the cosy little parlour of my old friend, kind, hospitable Mrs. Nivers. Her broad, good-humoured face wreathed itself into a sunny smile as I entered, and we were soon embarked on that wayward smooth-flowing current of chat about nothing in particular, which is perhaps the most enjoyable of all forms of conversation. John (I beg his pardon, "Mr. Nivers," I should say: but he was so constantly talked *of*, and *at*, by his better half, as "John," that his friends were apt to forget he had a surname at all) sat in a distant corner with his feet tucked well under his chair, in an attitude rather too upright for comfort, and rather

[1] Collingwood, in *The Lewis Carroll Picture Book*, pages 147-8, supplies an explanatory note by Lewis Sergeant: The explanation of this skit is conveyed in the "Moral" at the end. It was a fact that the building of the New Schools was decided on in principle, and that the arrangements were made for putting the work in hand, without precisely counting the cost. "Mrs. Nivers" is the U-nivers-ity. The name which the author gives himself, "Mr. De Ciel," is an easy cryptogram for "D. C. L.," that is for C. L. D., and would not for a moment puzzle the Oxford man of 1874. "Mr. Prior Burgess" and his "three courses" and the "next boarder," who had to be more "hardy" in his notions, is a reflection from 1865. "Susan," who was entrusted with the blank cheque, and empowered to find "a New School for Angela," was the committee appointed to select a plan and submit an estimate. The "boys" are not difficult to recognize: "Harry-Parry" (Liddon) who had been trying to make "Pussy" stand on one leg; "a Chase in the Hall" (Dr. Chase of St. Mary's); "Sam," the heavy-"weight" (Dr. Wayte of Trinity); "Freddy . . . something of a Bully at times" (Dr. Bulley of Magdalen); "Benjy . . . oh the work we had with that boy till we raised his allowance" (Dr. Jowett, recently elected Master of Balliol); and "Arthur," who had gone to Westminster (Dean Stanley), "a set of dear good boys on the whole: they've only one real Vice among them."—*McD.*

too suggestive of general collapse for anything like dignity, and sipped his tea in silence. From some distant region came a sound like the roar of the sea, rising and falling, suggesting the presence of many boys; and indeed I knew that the house was full to over-flowing of noisy urchins, overflowing with high spirits and mis-chief, but on the whole a very creditable set of little folk.

"And where are you going for your sea-side trip this summer, Mrs. Nivers?"

My old friend pursed up her lips with a mysterious smile and nodded.

"Can't understand you," I said.

"You understand me, Mr. De Ciel, just as well as I understand myself, and *that's* not saying much. I don't know where we're going: *John* doesn't know where we're going—but we're certainly going *somewhere;* and we shan't even know the name of the place till we find ourselves there! *Now* are you satisfied?"

I was more hopelessly bewildered than ever. "One of us is dreaming, no doubt," I faltered; "or—or perhaps I'm going mad, or—"

The good lady laughed merrily at my discomfiture.

"Well, well! It's a shame to puzzle you so," she said. "I'll tell you all about it. You see, last year we *couldn't* settle it, do what we would. *John* said 'Herne Bay,' and I said 'Brighton,' and the *boys* said 'somewhere where there's a circus,' not that we gave much weight to *that*, you know; well, and Angela (she's a growing girl, and we've got to find a new school for her this year); *she* said 'Portsmouth, because of the soldiers'; and Susan (she's my maid, you know), *she* said 'Ramsgate.' Well, with all those contrary opinions, somehow it ended in our going *nowhere;* and John and I put our heads together last week, and we settled that it should never happen again. And now, how do you think we've man-aged it?"

"Quite impossible to guess," I said dreamily, as I handed back my empty cup.

"In the first place," said the good lady, "we need change sadly. Housekeeping worries me more every year, particularly with boarders—and John *will* have a couple of gentlemen-boarders always on hand; he says it looks respectable, and that they talk so well, they make the House quite lively. As if *I* couldn't talk enough for him!"

"It isn't that!" muttered John. "It's——"

"They're well enough sometimes," the lady went on (she never seemed to hear her husband's remarks), "but I'm sure when Mr. Prior Burgess was here, it was enough to turn one's hair grey! He was an open-handed gentleman enough—as liberal as could be—but *far* too particular about his meals. Why, if you'll believe me, he wouldn't sit down to dinner without there were three courses. We couldn't go on in *that* style, you know. I had to tell the next boarder he must be more hardy in his notions, or I could warrant him we shouldn't suit each other."

"Quite right," I said. "Might I trouble you for another half cup?"

"Seaside air we *must* have, you see," Mrs. Nivers went on, mechanically taking up the teapot, but too much engrossed in the subject to do more, "and as we can't agree where to go, and yet we must go *somewhere*—did you say half a cup?"

"Thanks," said I. "You were going to tell me what it was you settled."

"We settled," said the good lady, pouring out the tea without a moment's pause in her flow of talk, "that the only course was (cream I think you take, but no sugar? Just so) was to put the whole matter—but stop, John shall read it all out to you. We've drawn up the agreement in writing—quite ship-shape, isn't it, John? Here's the document: John shall read it you—and mind your stops, there's a dear!"

John put on his spectacles, and in a tone of gloomy satisfaction (it was evidently his own composition) read the following:--

"*Be it hereby enacted and decreed,*

"*That Susan be appointed for the business of choosing a watering-place for this season, and finding a New School for Angela.*

"*That Susan be empowered not only to procure plans, but to select a plan, to submit the estimate for the execution of such plan to the Housekeeper, and, if the Housekeeper sanction the proposed expenditure, to proceed with the execution of such plan, and to fill up the Blank Cheque for the whole expense incurred.*"

Before I could say another word the door burst open, and a whole army of boys tumbled into the room, headed by little Harry, the pet of the family, who hugged in his arms the much-enduring parlour cat, which, as he eagerly explained in his broken English, he had been trying to teach to stand on one leg.

"Harry-Parry Ridy Pidy Coachy-Poachy!" said the fond mother, as she lifted the little fellow to her knee and treated him to a jog-trot. "Harry's very fond of Pussy, he is, but he mustn't tease it, he mustn't! Now go and play on the stairs, there's dear children. Mr. De Ciel and I want to have a quiet talk." And the boys tumbled out of the room again, as eagerly as they had tumbled in, shouting, "Let's have a Chase in the Hall!"

"A good set of heads, are they not, Mr. De Ciel?" my friend continued, with a wave of her fat hand towards the retreating army. "Phrenologists admire them much. Look at little Sam, there. He's one of the latest arrivals, you know, but he grows—mercy on us, how that boy does grow! You've no idea what a Weight he is! Then there's Freddy, that tall boy in the corner: he's rather too big for the others, that's a fact—and he's something of a Bully at times, but the boy has a tender heart, too; give him a bit of poetry, now, and he's as maudlin as a girl! Then there's Benjy, again: a nice boy, but I daren't tell you what he costs us in pocket money! Oh, the work we had with that boy till we raised his allowance! Hadn't we, John?" ("John" grunted in acquiescence). "It was Arthur took up his cause so much, and worried poor John and me nearly into our graves. Arthur was a very nice boy, Mr. De Ciel, and as great a favourite with the other boys as Harry is now, before he went to Westminster. He used to tell them stories, and draw them the prettiest pictures you ever saw! Houses that were all windows and chimnies—what they call 'High Art,' I believe. We tried a conservatory once on the High-Art principle, and (would you believe it?) the man stuck the roof up on a lot of rods like so many knitting needles! Of course it soon came down about our ears, and we had to do it all over again. As I said to John at the time, 'If this is High Art, give me a little more of the Art next time, and a little less of the High!' He's doing very well at Westminster, I hear, but his tutor writes that he's very asthmatic, poor fellow——"

"Æsthetic, my dear, aesthetic!" remonstrated John.

"Ah, well, my love," said the good lady, "all those long medical words are one and the same thing to *me*. And they come to the same thing in the Christmas bills, too; they both mean 'Draught as before'! Well, well! They're a set of dear good boys on the whole: they've only one real Vice among them—but I shall tire you, talking about the boys so much. What do you think of that agreement of ours?"

I had been turning the paper over and over in my hands, quite at a loss to know what to say to so strange a scheme. "Surely I've misunderstood you?" I said. "You don't mean to say that you've left the whole thing to your maid to settle for you?"

"But that's exactly what I *do* mean, Mr. De Ciel," the lady replied a little testily. "She's a very sensible young person, I can assure you. So now, wherever Susan chooses to take us, *there* we go!" ("There we go! There we go!" echoed her husband in a dismal sort of chant, rocking himself backwards and forwards in his chair.) "You've no idea what a comfort it is to feel that the whole thing's in Susan's hands!"

"Go where Susan takes thee," I remarked, with a vague idea that I was quoting an old song. "Well, no doubt Susan has very correct taste, and all that—but still, if I might advise, I wouldn't leave all to her. She may need a little check—"

"That's the very word, dear Mr. De Ciel!" cried my old friend, clapping her hands. "And that's the very thing we've done, isn't it, John?" ("The very thing we've done," echoed John). "I made him do it only this morning. He has signed her a Blank Cheque, so that she can go to any cost she likes. It's such a comfort to get things settled and off one's hands, you know! John's been grumbling about it ever since, but now that I can tell him it's *your* advice——"

"But, my dear Madame," I exclaimed, "I don't mean cheque with a 'Q'!"

"——your advice," repeated Mrs. N., not heeding my interruption, "why, of course he'll see the reasonableness of it, like a sensible creature as he is!" Here she looked approvingly at her husband, who tried to smile a "slow wise smile," like Tennyson's "wealthy miller," but I fear the result was more remarkable for slowness than for wisdom.

I saw that it would be waste of words to argue the matter further, so took my leave, and did not see my old friends again before their departure for the sea-side. I quote the following from a letter which I received yesterday from Mrs. Nivers:—

"Margate, April 1.

"DEAR FRIEND,—*You know the old story of the dinner-party, where there was nothing hot but the ices, and nothing cold but the soup? Of this place I may safely say that there is nothing high but the prices, the staircases, and the eggs; nothing low but the sea and the company; nothing strong but the butter, and nothing weak but the tea!*"

From the general tenour of her letter I gather that they are not enjoying it.

MORAL

It is really seriously proposed—in the University of Oxford, and towards the close of the nineteenth century (never yet reckoned by historians as part of the Dark Ages)—to sign a Blank Cheque for the expenses of building New Schools, before any plan has been laid before the University, from which such an estimate could be made—before any architect has been found to design such a plan—before any Committee has been elected to find such an architect?

FINIS

ALICE ON THE STAGE [1]

"Look here; here's all this Judy's clothes falling to pieces again." Such were the pensive words of Mr. Thomas Codlin; and they may fitly serve as a motto for a writer who has set himself the unusual task of passing in review a set of puppets that are virtually his own—the stage embodiments of his own dream-children.

Not that the play itself is in any sense mine. The arrangements, in dramatic form, of a story written without the slightest idea that it would be so adapted, was a task that demanded powers denied to me, but possessed in an eminent degree, so far as I can judge, by Mr. Savile Clarke. I do not feel myself qualified to criticise his play, as a play; nor shall I venture on any criticism of the players as players.

What is it, then, I have set myself to do? And what possible claim have I to be heard? My answer must be that, as the writer of the two stories thus adapted, and the originator (as I believe, for at least I have not *consciously* borrowed them) of the "airy nothings" for which Mr. Savile Clarke has so skilfully provided, if not a name, at least a "local habitation," I may without boastfulness claim to have a special knowledge of what it was I meant them to be, and so a special understanding of how far that intention has been realised. And I fancied there might be some readers of *The Theatre* who would be interested in sharing that knowledge and that understanding.

Many a day had we rowed together on that quiet stream—the three little maidens and I—and many a fairy tale had been extemporised for their benefit—whether it were at times when the narrator was "i' the vein," and fancies unsought came crowding thick upon him, or at times when the jaded Muse was goaded into action, and plodded meekly on, more because she had to say something than that she had something to say—yet none of these many tales got written down: they lived and died, like summer midges, each in its own golden afternoon until there came a day when, as it

[1] From *The Theatre*, April, 1887.—*McD.*

chanced, one of my little listeners petitioned that the tale might be written out for her. That was many a year ago, but I distinctly remember, now as I write, how, in a desperate attempt to strike out some new line of fairy-lore, I had sent my heroine straight down a rabbit-hole, to begin with, without the least idea what was to happen afterwards. And so, to please a child I loved (I don't remember any other motive), I printed in manuscript, and illustrated with my own crude designs—designs that rebelled against every law of Anatomy or Art (for I had never had a lesson in drawing)—the book which I have just had published in facsimile. In writing it out, I added many fresh ideas, which seemed to grow of themselves upon the original stock; and many more added themselves when, years afterwards, I wrote it all over again for publication: but (this may interest some readers of "Alice" to know) every such idea and nearly every word of the dialogue, *came of itself*. Sometimes an idea comes at night, when I have had to get up and strike a light to note it down—sometimes when out on a lonely winter walk, when I have had to stop, and with half-frozen fingers jot down a few words which should keep the new-born idea from perishing—but whenever or however it comes, *it comes of itself*. I cannot set invention going like a clock, by any voluntary winding up: nor do I believe that any *original* writing (and what other writing is worth preserving?) was ever so produced. If you sit down, unimpassioned and uninspired, and *tell* yourself to write for so many hours, you will merely produce (at least I am sure I should merely produce) some of that article which fills, so far as I can judge, two-thirds of most magazines— most easy to write, most weary to read—men call it "padding," and it is to my mind one of the most detestable things in modern litera- ture. "Alice" and the "Looking-Glass" are made up almost wholly of bits and scraps, single ideas which came of themselves. Poor they may have been; but at least they were the best I had to offer: and I can desire no higher praise to be written of me than the words of a Poet, written of a Poet,

> "He gave the people of his best:
> The worst he kept, the best he gave."

I have wandered from my subject, I know: yet grant me another minute to relate a little incident of my own experience. I was walking on a hill-side, alone, one bright summer day, when suddenly there came into my head one line of verse—one solitary line—"For the *Snark* was a Boojum, you see." I knew not what it meant, then: I know not what it means, now; but I wrote it down: and, some time afterwards, the rest of the stanza occurred to me, that being its last line: and so by degrees, at odd moments during the next year or two, the rest of the poem pieced itself together, that being its last stanza. And since then, periodically I have received courteous letters from strangers, begging to know whether "The Hunting of the Snark" is an allegory, or contains some hidden moral, or is a political satire: and for all such questions I have but one answer, "*I don't know!*" And now I return to my text, and will wander no more.

Stand forth, then, from the shadowy past, "Alice," the child of my dreams. Full many a year has slipped away, since that "golden afternoon" that gave thee birth, but I can call it up almost as clearly as if it were yesterday—the cloudless blue above, the watery mirror below, the boat drifting idly on its way, the tinkle of the drops that fell from the oars, as they waved so sleepily to and fro, and (the one bright gleam of life in all the slumberous scene) the three eager faces, hungry for news of fairyland, and who would not be said "nay" to: from whose lips "Tell us a story, please," had all the stern immutability of Fate!

What wert thou, dream-Alice, in thy foster-father's eyes? How shall he picture thee? Loving, first, loving and gentle: loving as a dog (forgive the prosaic simile, but I know no earthly love so pure and perfect), and gentle as a fawn: then courteous—courteous to *all*, high or low, grand or grotesque, King or Caterpillar, even as though she were herself a King's daughter, and her clothing wrought gold: then trustful, ready to accept the wildest impossibilities with all that utter trust that only dreamers know; and lastly, curious—wildly curious, and with the eager enjoyment of Life that comes only in the happy hours of childhood, when all is new and fair, and when Sin and Sorrow are but names—empty words signifying nothing!

And the White Rabbit, what of *him?* Was *he* framed on the "Alice" lines, or meant as a contrast? As a contrast, distinctly. For *her* "youth," "audacity," "vigour," and "swift directness of purpose," read "elderly," "timid," "feeble," and "nervously shilly-shallying," and you will get *something* of what I meant him to be. I *think* the White Rabbit should wear spectacles. I am sure his voice should quaver, and his knees quiver, and his whole air suggest a total inability to say "Bo" to a goose!

But I cannot hope to be allowed, even by the courteous Editor of *The Theatre,* half the space I should need (even if my *reader's* patience would hole out) to discuss each of my puppets one by one. Let me cull from the two books a Royal Trio—the Queen of Hearts, the Red Queen, and the White Queen. It was certainly hard on my Muse, to expect her to sing of *three* Queens, within such brief compass, and yet to give to each her own individuality. Each, of course, had to preserve, through all her eccentricities, a certain queenly *dignity.* *That* was essential. And for distinguishing traits, I pictured to myself the Queen of Hearts as a sort of embodiment of ungovernable passion—a blind and aimless Fury. The Red Queen I pictured as a Fury, but of another type; *her* passion must be cold and calm; she must be formal and strict, yet not unkindly; pedantic to the tenth degree, the concentrated essence of all governesses! Lastly, the White Queen seemed, to my dreaming fancy, gentle, stupid, fat and pale; helpless as an infant; and her just *suggesting* imbecility, but never quite passing into it; that would be, I think, fatal to any comic effect she might otherwise produce. There is a character strangely like her in Wilkie Collins' novel "No Name": by two different converging paths we have somehow reached the same ideal, and Mrs. Wragg and the White Queen might have been twin-sisters.

As it is no part of my present purpose to find fault with any of those who have striven so zealously to make this "dream-play" a waking success, I shall but name two or three who seemed to me specially successful in realising the characters of the story.

None, I think, was better realised than the two undertaken by Mr. Sydney Harcourt, "the Hatter" and "Tweedledum." To see him enact the Hatter was a weird and uncanny thing, as though some grotesque monster, seen last night in a dream, should walk into the room in broad daylight, and quietly say "Good morning!" I need not try to describe what I meant the Hatter to be, since, so far as I can now remember, it was exactly what Mr. Harcourt has made him: and I may say nearly the same of Tweedledum: but the Hatter surprised me most—perhaps only because it came first in the play.

There were others who realised my ideas nearly as well; but I am not attempting a complete review: I will conclude with a few words about the two children who played "Alice" and "the Dormouse."

Of Miss Phoebe Carlo's performance it would be difficult to speak too highly. As a mere effort of memory, it was surely a marvellous feat for so young a child, to learn no less than two hundred and fifteen speeches—nearly three times as many as Beatrice in "Much Ado About Nothing." But what I admired most, as realising most nearly my ideal heroine, was her perfect assumption of the high spirits, and readiness to enjoy *everything*, of a child out for a holiday. I doubt if any grown actress, however experienced, could have worn this air so perfectly; *we* look before and after, and sigh for what is not; a child never does *this:* and it is only a child that can utter from her heart the words poor Margaret Fuller Ossoli so longed to make her own, "I am all happy *now!*"

And last (I may for once omit the time-honoured addition "not least," for surely no tinier maiden ever yet achieved so genuine a theatrical success?) comes our dainty Dormouse. "Dainty" is the only epithet that seems to me exactly to suit her: with her beaming baby-face, the delicious crispness of her speech, and the perfect realism with which she makes herself the embodied essence of Sleep, she is surely the daintiest Dormouse that ever yet told us "I sleep when I breathe!" With the first words of that her opening speech, a sudden silence falls upon the house (at least it has been so every time I have been there), and the baby tones sound strangely clear in the stillness. And yet I doubt if the charm is due only to the incisive clearness of her articulation; to me there was an even greater charm in the utter self-abandonment and conscientious *thoroughness* of her acting. If Dorothy ever adopts a motto, it ought to be "thorough." I hope the time may soon come when she will have a better part than "Dormouse" to play—when some enterprising manager will revive the "Midsummer Night's Dream" and do his obvious duty to the public by securing Miss Dorothy d'Alcourt as "Puck"!

It would be well indeed for our churches if some of the clergy could take a lesson in enunciation from this little child; and better still, for "our noble selves," if *we* would lay to heart some things that she could teach us, and would learn by her example to realise, rather more than we do, the spirit of a maxim I once came across in an old book, "Whatsoever thy hand findeth to do, *do it with thy might*."

PUZZLES

A LOGICAL PARADOX

"What, *nothing* to do?" said Uncle Jim. "Then come along with me down to Allen's. And you can just take a turn while I get myself shaved."

"All right," said Uncle Joe. "And the Cub had better come too, I suppose?"

The "Cub" was *me*, as the reader will perhaps have guessed for himself. I'm turned *fifteen*—more than three months ago, but there's no sort of use in mentioning *that* to Uncle Joe; he'd only say, "Go to your cubbicle, little boy!" or, "Then I suppose you can do cubbic equations?" or some equally vile pun. He asked me yesterday to give him an instance of a PROPOSITION in A. And I said, "All uncles make vile puns." And I don't think he liked it. However, that's neither here nor there. I was glad enough to go. I *do* love hearing those uncles of mine "chop logic," as they call it; and they're desperate hands at it, I can tell you!

"That is not a logical inference from my remark," said Uncle Jim.

"Never said it was," said Uncle Joe; "it's a *Reductio ad Absurdum*."

"*An Illicit Process of the Minor!*" chuckled Uncle Jim. That's the sort of way they always go on, whenever *I'm* with them. As if there was any fun in calling me a Minor!"

After a bit, Uncle Jim began again, just as we came in sight of the barber's. "I only hope *Carr* will be at home," he said. "Brown's so clumsy. And Allen's hand has been shaky ever since he had that fever."

"Carr's *certain* to be in," said Uncle Joe.

"I'll bet you sixpence he *isn't!*" said I.

"Keep your bets for your betters," said Uncle Joe. "I mean"—he hurried on, seeing by the grin on my face what a slip he'd made—"I mean that I can *prove* it logically. It isn't a matter of *chance*."

"Prove it *logically!*" sneered Uncle Jim. "Fire away, then! I defy you to do it!"

"For the sake of argument," Uncle Joe began, "let us assume

Carr to be *out*. And let us see what the assumption would lead to. I'm going to do this by *Reductio ad Absurdum*."

"Of course you are!" growled Uncle Jim. "Never knew any argument of *yours* that didn't end in some absurdity or other!"

"Unprovoked by your unmanly taunts," said Uncle Joe in a lofty tone, "I proceed. Carr being out, you will grant that, if Allen is *also* out, *Brown* must be at home?"

"What's the good of *his* being at home?" said Uncle Jim. "I don't want *Brown* to shave me! He's too clumsy."

"Patience is one of those inestimable qualities—" Uncle Joe was beginning; but Uncle Jim cut him off short.

"*Argue!*" he said. "Don't *moralise!*"

"Well, but do you grant it?" Uncle Joe persisted. "Do you grant me that, if Carr is out, it follows that if Allen is out Brown *must* be in?"

"Of course he must," said Uncle Jim; "or there'd be nobody to mind the shop."

"We see, then, that the absence of Carr brings into play a certain Hypothetical, whose *protasis* is 'Allen is out,' and whose *apodosis* is 'Brown is in.' And we see that, so long as Carr remains out, this Hypothetical remains in force?"

"Well, suppose it does. What then?" said Uncle Jim.

"You will also grant me that the truth of a Hypothetical—I mean its *validity* as a logical *sequence*—does not in the least depend on its *protasis* being actually *true*, nor even on its being *possible*. The Hypothetical 'If you were to run from here to London in five minutes you would surprise people,' remains true as a sequence, whether you can do it or not."

"I can't do *it*," said Uncle Jim.

"We have now to consider *another* Hypothetical. What was that you told me yesterday about Allen?"

"I told you," said Uncle Jim, "that ever since he had that fever he's been so nervous about going out alone, he always takes Brown with him."

"Just so," said Uncle Joe. "Then the Hypothetical 'If Allen is out Brown is out' is *always* in force, isn't it?"

"I suppose so," said Uncle Jim. (He seemed to be getting a little nervous himself now.)

"Then, if Carr is out, we have *two* Hypotheticals, 'if Allen is out Brown is *in*,' and 'if Allen is out Brown is *out*,' in force at once. And two *incompatible* Hypotheticals, mark you! They can't *possibly* be true together!"

"*Can't* they?" said Uncle Jim.

"How *can* they?" said Uncle Joe. "How *can* one and the same *protasis* prove two contradictory *apodoses*? You grant that the two *apodoses*, 'Brown is *in*' and 'Brown is *out*,' *are* contradictory, I suppose?"

"Yes, I grant *that*," said Uncle Jim.

"Then I may sum up," said Uncle Jim. "If Carr is out, these two Hypotheticals are true together. And we know that they *cannot* be true together. Which is absurd. Therefore Carr *cannot* be out. There's a nice *Reductio ad Absurdum* for you!"

Uncle Jim looked thoroughly puzzled; but after a bit he plucked up courage, and began again. "I don't feel at all clear about that *incompatibility*. Why shouldn't those two Hypotheticals be true together? It seems to me that would simply prove '*Allen* is in.' Of course it's clear that the *apodoses* of those two Hypotheticals are incompatible—'Brown is in' and 'Brown is out.' But why shouldn't we put it like this? If Allen is out Brown is *out*. If Carr and Allen are *both* out, Brown is *in*. Which is absurd. Therefore Carr and Allen can't be *both* of them out. But, so long as Allen is *in*, I don't see what's to hinder Carr from going out."

"My dear, but most illogical brother!" said Uncle Joe. (Whenever Uncle Joe begins to "dear" you, you may make pretty sure he's got you in a cleft stick!) "Don't you see that you are wrongly dividing the *protasis* and the *apodosis* of that Hypothetical? Its *protasis* is simply 'Carr is out'; and its *apodosis* is a sort of sub-Hypothetical, 'If Allen is out, Brown is *in*.' And a most absurd apodosis it is, being hopelessly incompatible with that other Hypothetical, that we know is *always* true, 'If Allen is out, Brown is *out*.' And it's simply the assumption 'Carr is *out*' that has caused this absurdity. So there's only *one* possible conclusion—*Carr is in!*"

How long this argument *might* have lasted I haven't the least idea. I believe *either* of them could argue for six hours at a stretch. But just at this moment we arrived at the barber's shop; and, on going inside, we found—

THREE PUZZLES

I

THE MONKEY AND WEIGHT PROBLEM

A rope is supposed to be hung over a wheel fixed to the roof of a building; at one end of the rope a weight is fixed, which exactly counterbalances a monkey which is hanging on to the other end. Suppose that the monkey begins to climb the rope, what will be the result?

II

CROSSING THE RIVER

Four gentlemen and their wives wanted to cross the river in a boat that would not hold more than two at a time.

The conditions were, that no gentleman must leave his wife on the bank unless with only women or by herself, and also that some-one must always bring the boat back.

How did they do it?

III

THE CAPTIVE QUEEN

A captive Queen and her son and daughter were shut up in the top room of a very high tower. Outside their window was a pulley with a rope round it, and a basket fastened at each end of the rope of equal weight. They managed to escape with the help of this and a weight they found in the room, quite safely. It would have been dangerous for any of them to come down if they weighed more than 15 lbs. more than the contents of the lower basket, for they would do so too quick, and they also managed not to weigh less either.

The one basket coming down would naturally of course draw the other up.

How did they do it?

The Queen weighed 195 lbs., daughter 165, son, 90, and the weight 75.

This is an addition to the puzzle—

The Queen had with her in the room, besides her son and daughter and the weight, a pig weighing 60 lbs., a dog 45 lbs., and a cat 30. These have to be brought down safely, too, with the same restriction. The weight can come down any way, of course.

The additional puzzle consists in this—there must be some one at each end to put the animals into and out of the baskets.

SELECTIONS FROM
SYLVIE AND BRUNO
AND FROM
SYLVIE AND BRUNO CONCLUDED

THE MONEY ACT [1]

. . . The Professor brightened up again. "The Emperor started the thing," he said. "He wanted to make everybody in Outland twice as rich as he was before—just to make the new Government popular. Only there wasn't nearly enough money in the Treasury to do it. So *I* suggested that he might do it by doubling the value of every coin and banknote in Outland. It's the simplest thing possible. I wonder nobody ever thought of it before! And you never saw such universal joy. The shops are full from morning to night. Everybody's buying everything." . . .

[1] From *Sylvie and Bruno*, 312.—*McD.*

A NEW WAY TO PAY OLD DEBTS [2]

"Come in!" [called the Professor]

"Only the tailor, Sir, with your little bill," said a meek voice outside the door.

"Ah, well, I can soon settle *his* business," the Professor said to the children, "if you'll just wait a minute. How much is it, this year, my man?" The tailor had come in while he was speaking.

"Well, it's been a doubling so many years, you see," the tailor replied, a little gruffly, "and I think I'd like the money now. It's two thousand pound, it is!"

"Oh, that's nothing!" the Professor carelessly remarked, feeling in his pocket, as if he always carried at least *that* amount about with him. "But wouldn't you like to wait just another year, and make it *four* thousand? Just think how rich you'd be! Why, you might be a *King*, if you liked!"

"I don't know as I'd care about being a King," the man said thoughtfully. "But it *dew* sound a powerful sight o' money! Well, I think I'll wait—"

"Of course, you will," said the Professor. "There's good sense in *you*, I see. Good day to you, my man!"

"Will you ever have to pay him that four thousand pounds?" Sylvie asked as the door closed on the departing creditor.

"*Never*, my child!" the Professor replied emphatically. "He'll go on doubling it, till he dies. You see, it's always worth while waiting another year, to get twice as much money!"

2 From *Sylvie and Bruno*, 130-132.—*McD.*

THE ACTIVE TOURIST'S PORTABLE BATH [3]

"And you actually got a plunge-bath every morning?" said the Sub-Warden, seemingly in continuation of a conversation with the Professor. "Even at the little road-side inns?"

"Oh, certainly, certainly!" the Professor replied with a smile on his jolly face. "Allow me to explain. It is, in fact, a very simple problem in Hydrodynamics. (That means a combination of Water and Strength.) If we take a plunge-bath, and a man of great strength (such as myself) about to plunge into it, we have a perfect example of this science. I am bound to admit," the Professor continued, in a lower tone and with downcast eyes, "that we need a man of remarkable strength. He must be able to spring from the floor to about twice his own height, gradually turning over as he rises, so as to come down again head first."

"Why, you need a flea, not a man!" exclaimed the Sub-Warden.

"Pardon me," said the Professor. "This particular kind of bath is not adapted for a flea. Let us suppose," he continued, folding his table-napkin into a graceful festoon, "that this represents what is perhaps the necessity of this Age—the Active Tourist's Portable Bath. You may describe it briefly, if you like," looking at the Chancellor, "by the letters A.T.P.B."

The Chancellor much disconcerted at finding everybody looking at him, could only murmur, in a shy whisper, "Precisely so!"

"One great advantage of this plunge-bath," continued the Professor, "is that it requires only half-a-gallon of water—"

"I don't call it a plunge-bath," His Sub-Excellency remarked, "unless your Active Tourist goes right under!"

"But he does go right under," the old man gently replied. "The A.T. hangs up the P.B. on a nail—thus. He then empties the water-jug into it—places the empty jug below the bag—leaps into the air—descends head-first into the bag—the water rises round him to the top of the bag—and there you are!" he triumphantly concluded.

[3] From *Sylvie and Bruno*, 25-28.—*McD.*

"The A.T. is as much under water as if he'd gone a mile or two down into the Atlantic!"

"And he's drowned, let us say, in about four minutes—"

"By no means!" the Professor answered with a proud smile. "After about a minute, he quietly turns a tap at the lower end of the P.B.—all the water runs back into the jug—and there you are again!"

"But how in the world is he to get out of the bag again?"

"That, I take it," said the Professor, "is the most beautiful part of the whole invention. All the way up the P.B., inside, are loops for the thumbs; so it's something like going up-stairs, only perhaps less comfortable; and, by the time the A.T. has risen out of the bag, all but his head, he's sure to topple over, one way or the other— the Law of Gravity secures that. And there he is on the floor again!"

"A little bruised, perhaps?"

"Well, yes, a little bruised; but having had his plunge-bath: that's the great thing."

"Wonderful! It's almost beyond belief!" murmured the Sub-Warden. The Professor took it as a compliment, and bowed with a gratified smile.

"Quite beyond belief!" my Lady added—meaning, no doubt, to be more complimentary still. The Professor bowed, but he didn't smile this time.

"I can assure you," he said earnestly, "that, provided the bath was made, I used it every morning. I certainly ordered it—that I am clear about—my only doubt is, whether the man ever finished making it. It's difficult to remember, after so many years—"

At this moment the door, very slowly and creakingly, began to open, and Sylvie and Bruno jumped up, and ran to meet the well-known footstep.

L. C.'S EXPLANATION OF "CA'N'T," ETC.[4]

Other critics have objected to certain innovations in spelling, such as "ca'n't," "wo'n't," "traveler." In reply, I can only plead my firm conviction that the popular usage is *wrong*. As to "ca'n't," it will not be disputed that, in all *other* words ending in "n't," these letters are an abbreviation of "not"; and it is surely absurd to suppose that, in this solitary instance, "not" is represented by " 't"! In fact "can't" is the *proper* abbreviation for "can it," just as "is't" is for "is it." Again, in "wo'n't," the first apostrophe is needed, because the word "would" is here *abridged* into "wo": but I hold it proper to spell "don't" with only *one* apostrophe, because the word "do" is here *complete*. As to such words as "traveler," I hold the correct principle to be, to *double* the consonant when the accent falls on that syllable; otherwise to leave it *single*. This rule is observed in most cases (e.g., we double the "r" in "preferred," but leave it single in "offered"), so that I am only extending, to other cases, an existing rule. I admit, however, that I do not spell "parallel," as the rule would have it; but here we are constrained, by the etymology, to insert the double "l".

[4] From the *Preface* to *Sylvie and Bruno Concluded*.

THE OUTLANDISH WATCH [5]

I was passing a pretty little villa, which stood rather far back from the road in its own grounds, with bright flowerbeds in front,— an easy chair forgotten on the lawn, with a newspaper lying near it—a small pug-dog "couchant" before it, resolved to guard the treasure even at the sacrifice of life—and a front door standing invitingly open. "Here is my chance," I thought, "for testing the reverse action of the Magic Watch!" I pressed the 'reversal-peg' and walked in. In *another* house the entrance of a stranger might cause surprise but *here* I knew nothing of the sort could happen. The *ordinary* course of events—first, to think nothing about me; then, hearing my footsteps to look up and see me; and then to wonder what business I had there—, would be reversed by the action of my Watch. They would *first* wonder who I was, *then* see me, then look down, and think no more about me. And as to being expelled with violence, *that* event would necessarily come first in this case. "So, if I can once get *in*," I said to myself, "all risk of expulsion is over!"

The pug-dog sat up, as a precautionary measure, as I passed; but as I took no notice of the treasure he was guarding, he let me go by without even one remonstrant bark. "He that takes my life," he seemed to be saying, wheezily, to himself, "takes trash: But he that takes the *Daily Telegraph*—!" But this awful contingency I did not face.

The party in the drawing-room—I had walked straight in, you understand, without ringing the bell, or giving any notice of my approach—consisted of four laughing rosy children, of ages from about fourteen about down to ten, who were, apparently, coming toward the door (I found they were really walking *backwards*), while their mother, seated by the fire with some needlework in her lap, was saying, just as I entered the room, "Now, girls, you may get your things on for a walk."

[5] From *Sylvie and Bruno*, 350-356.—McD.

211

To my utter astonishment—for I was not yet accustomed to the action of the Watch—"all smiles ceased" (as Browning says) on the four pretty faces, and they all got out pieces of needlework, and sat down. No one noticed *me* in the least, as I quietly took a chair and sat down to watch them.

When the needlework had been unfolded, and they were all ready to begin, their mother said "Come, *that's* done, at last! You may fold up your work, girls." But the children took no notice whatever of the remark; on the contrary, they set to work at once sewing—if that is the proper word to describe an operation such as *I* had never before witnessed. Each of them threaded her needle with a short end of thread attached to the work, which was instantly pulled by an invisible force through the stuff, dragging the needle after it: the nimble fingers of the little sempstress caught it at the other side, but only to lose it the next moment. And so the work went on, steadily undoing itself, and the neatly stitched little dresses, or whatever they were, steadily falling to pieces. Now and then one of the children would pause, as the recovered thread became inconveniently long, wind it on a bobbin, and start again with another short end.

At last all the work was picked to pieces and put away, and the lady led the way into the next room, walking backwards, and making the insane remark "Not yet, dear: we *must* get the sewing done first." After which, I was not surprised to see the children skipping backwards after her, exclaiming, "Oh, mother, it *is* such a lovely day for a walk!"

In the dining-room, the table had only dirty plates and empty dishes upon it. However, the party—with the addition of a gentleman—seated themselves at it very contentedly.

You have seen people eating cherry-tart and every now and then cautiously conveying a cherry-stone from their lips to their plates? Well, something like that went on all through this ghastly—or shall we say 'ghostly'—banquet. An empty fork is raised to the lips: there it receives a neatly-cut piece of mutton, and swiftly conveys it to the plate, where it instantly attaches itself to the mutton already there. Soon one of the plates, furnished with a complete slice of mutton and two potatoes, was handed up to the presiding gentleman, who quietly replaced the slice on the joint, and the potatoes in the dish.

Their conversation was, if possible, more bewildering than their mode of dining. It began by the youngest girl suddenly, and without provocation, addressing her eldest sister. "Oh, you *wicked* story-teller!" she said.

I expected a sharp reply from the sister; but, instead of this, she turned laughingly to her father, and said, in a very loud stage-whisper, "To be a bride!"

The father, in order to do *his* part in a conversation that seemed only fit for lunatics, replied "Whisper it to me, dear."

But she *didn't* whisper (these children never did anything they were told): she said, quite loud, "Of course not! Everybody knows what *Dolly* wants!"

And little Dolly shrugged her shoulders, and said, with a pretty pettishness, "Now, Father, you're not to tease! You know I don't want to be bride's-maid to *anybody!*"

"And Dolly's to be the fourth," was her father's idiotic reply.

Here Number Three put in her oar. "Oh, it *is* settled, Mother dear, really and truly! Mary told us all about it. It's to be next Tuesday four weeks—and three of her cousins are coming to be bride's-maids—and—"

"*She* doesn't forget it, Minnie!" the Mother laughingly replied. "I do wish they get it settled! I don't like long engagements."

And Minnie wound up the conversation—if so chaotic a series of remarks deserves the name—with "Only think! We passed the Cedars this morning, just exactly as Mary Davenant was standing at the gate, saying good-bye to Mister—I forget his name. Of course we looked the other way."

By this time I was so hopelessly confused that I gave up listening, and followed the dinner down into the kitchen.

But to you, O hypercritical reader, resolute to believe no item of this weird adventure, what need to tell how the mutton was placed on the spit, and slowly unroasted—how the potatoes were wrapped in their skins, and handed over to the gardener to be buried—how, when the mutton had at length attained to rawness, the fire, which had gradually changed from red-heat to a mere blaze, died down so suddenly that the cook had only just time to catch its last flicker on the end of a match—or how the maid, having taken the mutton off the spit, carried it (backwards, of course,) out of the house, to meet the butcher, who was coming (also backwards) down the road? . . . .

TEETOTALING [6]

The red-faced man scowled, but evidently considered Arthur beneath his notice. So Lady Muriel took up the cudgels. "Do you hold the theory," she enquired, "that people can preach teetotalism more effectually by being teetotalers themselves?"

"Certainly I do!" replied the red-faced man. "Now, here is a case in point," unfolding a newspaper-cutting: "let me read you this letter from a teetotaler. *To the Editor. Sir, I was once a moderate drinker, and knew a man who drank to excess. I went to him. 'Give up this drink,' I said. 'It will ruin your health!' 'You drink,' he said: 'why shouldn't I?' 'Yes,' I said, 'but I know when to leave off.' He turned away from me. 'You drink in your way,' he said: 'let me drink in mine. Be off!' Then I saw that, to do any good with him, I must forswear drink. From that hour I haven't touched a drop!*"

"There! What do you say to *that?*" He looked round triumphantly, while the cutting was handed round for inspection.

"How very curious!" exclaimed Arthur, when it had reached him. "Did you happen to see a letter, last week, about early rising? It was strangely like this one."

The red-faced man's curiosity was roused. "Where did it appear?" he asked.

"Let me read it to you," said Arthur. He took some papers from his pocket, opened one of them, and read as follows. *To the Editor. Sir, I was once a moderate sleeper, and knew a man who slept to excess. I pleaded with him. 'Give up this lying in bed,' I said, 'It will ruin your health!' 'You go to bed,' he said: 'why shouldn't I?' 'Yes,' I said, 'but I know when to get up in the morning.' He turned away from me. 'You sleep in your way,' he said: 'let me sleep in mine. Be off!' Then I saw that to do any good with him, I must forswear sleep. From that hour I haven't been to bed!*"

[6] From *Sylvie and Bruno Concluded*, 140-141.—McD.

METHODS FOR STIMULATING
DINNER-TABLE CONVERSATION [7]

"But it needs many other things to make a *perfect* dinner!" said Lady Muriel, evidently anxious to change the subject. "Mein Herr! What is *your* idea of a perfect dinner-party?"

The old man looked round smilingly, and his gigantic spectacles seemed more gigantic than ever. "A *perfect* dinner-party?" he repeated. "First, it must be presided over by our present hostess!"

"That, of *course!*" she gaily interposed. "But what *else*, Mein Herr?"

"I can but tell you what I have seen," said Mein Herr, "in mine own—in the country I have traveled in."

He paused for a full minute, and gazed steadily at the ceiling— with so dreamy an expression on his face, that I feared he was going off into a reverie, which seemed to be his normal state. However, after a minute, he suddenly began again.

"That which chiefly causes the failure of a dinner-party, is the running-short—not of meat, nor yet of drink, but of *conversation*."

"In an *English* dinner-party," I remarked, "I have never known *small-talk* run short!"

"Pardon me," Mein Herr respectfully replied, "I did not say 'small-talk.' I said 'conversation.' All such topics as the weather, or politics, or local gossip, are unknown among us. They are either vapid or controversial. What we need for *conversation* is a topic of *interest* and of *novelty*. To secure these things we have tried various plans—Moving-Pictures, Wild-Creatures, Moving-Guests, and a Revolving-Humorist. But this last is only adapted to *small* parties."

"Let us have it in four separate Chapters, please!" said Lady Muriel, who was evidently deeply interested—as, indeed, most of the party were, by this time: and, all down the table, talk had ceased, and heads were leaning forwards, eager to catch fragments of Mein Herr's oration.

[7] From *Sylvie and Bruno Concluded*, 142-146.—*McD.*

"Chapter One! Moving-Pictures!" was proclaimed in the silvery voice of our hostess.

"The dining-table is shaped like a circular ring," Mein Herr began, in low dreamy tones, which, however, were perfectly audible in the silence. "The guests are seated at the inner side as well as the outer, having ascended to their places by a winding-staircase, from the room below. Along the middle of the table runs a little railway; and there is an endless train of trucks, worked round by machinery; and on each truck there are two pictures, leaning back to back. The train makes two circuits during dinner; and, when it has been *once* round, the waiters turn the pictures round in each truck, making them face the other way. Thus *every* guest sees *every* picture!"

He paused, and the silence seemed deader than ever. Lady Muriel looked aghast. "Really, if this goes on," she exclaimed, "I shall have to drop a pin! Oh, it's *my* fault, is it?" (In answer to an appealing look from Mein Herr.) "I was forgetting my duty. Chapter Two! Wild-Creatures!"

"We found the Moving-Pictures a *little* monotonous," said Mein Herr. "People didn't care to talk Art through a whole dinner; so we tried Wild-Creatures. Among the flowers, which we laid (just as *you* do) about the table, were to be seen, here a mouse, there a beetle; here a spider," (Lady Muriel shuddered) "there a wasp; here a toad, there a snake"; ("Father!" said Lady Muriel, plaintively. "Did you hear *that?*") "so we had plenty to talk about!"

"And when you got stung—" the old lady began.

"They were all chained-up, dear Madam!"

And the old lady gave a satisfied nod.

There was no silence to follow, *this* time. "Third Chapter!" Lady Muriel proclaimed at once, "Moving-Guests!"

"Even the Wild-Creatures proved monotonous," the orator proceeded. "So we left the guests to choose their own subjects; and, to avoid monotony, we changed *them*. We made the table of *two* rings; and the inner ring moved slowly round, all the time, along with the floor in the middle and the inner row of guests.

Thus *every* inner guest was brought face-to-face with *every* outer guest. It was a little confusing, sometimes, to have to *begin* a story to one friend and *finish* it to another; but *every* plan has its faults, you know."

"Fourth Chapter!" Lady Muriel hastened to announce. "The Revolving-Humorist!"

"For a *small* party we found it an excellent plan to have a round table, with a hole cut in the middle large enough to hold *one* guest. Here were placed our *best* talker. He revolved slowly, facing every other guest in turn: and he told lively anecdotes the whole time!"

"I shouldn't like it!" murmured the pompous man. "It would make me giddy, revolving like that! I should decline to—" here it appeared to dawn upon him that perhaps the assumption he was making was not warranted by the circumstances: he took a hasty gulp of wine, and choked himself.

But Mein Herr had relapsed into reverie, and made no further remark. Lady Muriel gave the signal, and the ladies left the room.

SOME MATTERS OF LOGIC [8]

The children came willingly. With one of them on each side of me, I approached the corner occupied by 'Mein Herr.' "You don't object to *children,* I hope?" I began.

"*Crabbed age and youth cannot live together!*" the old man cheerfully replied, with a most genial smile. "Now take a good look at me, my children! You would guess me to be an *old* man, wouldn't you?"

At first sight, though his face had reminded me so mysteriously of "the Professor," he had seemed to be decidedly a *younger* man: but, when I came to look into the wonderful depth of those large dreamy eyes, I felt, with a strange sense of awe, that he was incalculably *older:* he seemed to gaze at us out of some bygone age, centuries away.

"I don't know if oo're an *old man,*" Bruno answered, as the children, won over by the gentle voice, crept a little closer to him. "I thinks oo're *eighty-three.*"

"He is very exact!" said Mein Herr.

"Is he anything like right?" I said.

"There are reasons," Mein Herr gently replied, "reasons which I am not at liberty to explain, for not mentioning *definitely* any Persons, Places, or Dates. One remark only I will permit myself to make—that the period of life, between the ages of a hundred-and-sixty-five and a hundred-and-seventy-five, is a specially *safe* one."

"How do you make that out?" I said.

"Thus. You would consider swimming to be a very safe amusement, if you scarcely ever heard of any one dying of it. Am I not right in thinking that you never heard of any one dying between those two ages?"

"I see what you mean," I said: "but I'm afraid you ca'n't prove *swimming* to be safe, on the same principle. It is no uncommon thing to hear of some one being *drowned.*"

[8] From *Sylvie and Bruno Concluded*, 162-172.—McD.

"In *my* country," said Mein Herr, "no one is *ever* drowned."

"Is there no water deep enough?"

"Plenty! But we ca'n't *sink*. We are all *lighter than water*. Let me explain," he added, seeing my look of surprise. "Suppose you desire a race of *pigeons* of a particular shape or colour, do you not select, from year to year, those that are nearest to the shape or colour you want, and keep those, and part with the others?"

"We do," I replied. "We call it 'Artificial Selection.'"

"Exactly so," said Mein Herr. "Well, *we* have practised that for some centuries—constantly selecting the *lightest* people: so that, now, *everybody* is lighter than water."

"Then you never can be drowned at *sea?*"

"Never! It is only on the *land*—for instance, when attending a play in a theatre—that we are in such a danger."

"How can that happen at a *theatre?*"

"Our theatres are all *underground*. Large tanks of water are placed above. If a fire breaks out, the taps are turned, and in one minute the theatre is flooded, up to the very roof! Thus the fire is extinguished."

"*And* the audience, I presume?"

"That is a minor matter," Mein Herr carelessly replied. "But they have the comfort of knowing that, whether drowned or not, they are all *lighter than water*. We have not yet reached the standard of making people lighter than *air:* but we are *aiming* at it; and, in another thousand years or so—"

"What doos oo do wiz the peoples that's too heavy?" Bruno solemnly enquired.

"We have applied the same process," Mein Herr continued, not noticing Bruno's question, "to many other purposes. We have gone on selecting *walking-sticks*—always keeping those that walked *best*—till we have obtained some, that can walk by themselves! We have gone on selecting *cotton-wool*, till we have got some lighter than air! You've no idea what a useful material it is! We call it 'Imponderal.'"

"What do you use it for?"

"Well, chiefly for *packing* articles, to go by Parcel-Post. It makes them weigh *less than nothing*, you know."

"And how do the Post-Office people know what you have to pay?"

"That's the beauty of the new system!" Mein Herr cried exultingly. "They pay *us:* we don't pay *them!* I've often got as much as five shillings for sending a parcel."

"But doesn't your Government object?"

"Well, they *do* object, a little. They say it comes so expensive, in the long run. But the thing's as clear as daylight, by their own rules. If I send a parcel, that weighs a pound *more* than nothing, I *pay* three-pence: so, of course, if it weighs a pound *less* than nothing, I ought to *receive* three-pence."

"It is *indeed* a useful article!" I said.

"Yet even 'Imponderal' has its disadvantages," he resumed. "I bought some, a few days ago, and put it into my *hat*, to carry it home, and the hat simply floated away!"

*   *   *   *   *   *   *   *   *

Mein Herr looked so thoroughly bewildered that I thought it best to change the subject. "What a useful thing a pocket-map is!" I remarked.

"That's another thing we've learned from *your* Nation," said Mein Herr, "map-making. But we've carried it much further than *you.* What do you consider the *largest* map that would be really useful?"

"About six inches to the mile."

"Only *six inches!*" exclaimed Mein Herr. "We very soon got to six *yards* to the mile. Then we tried a *hundred* yards to the mile. And then came the grandest idea of all! We actually made a map of the country, on the scale of a *mile to the mile!*"

"Have you used it much?" I enquired.

"It has never been spread out, yet," said Mein Herr: "the farmers objected: they said it would cover the whole country, and shut out the sunlight! So we now use the country itself, as its own map, and I assure you it does nearly as well. Now let me ask you *another* question. What is the smallest *world* you would care to inhabit?"

"*I* know!" cried Bruno, who was listening intently. "I'd like a little teeny-tiny world, just big enough for Sylvie and me!"

"Then you would have to stand on opposite sides of it," said Mein Herr. "And so you would never see your sister *at all!*"

"And I'd have no *lessons*," said Bruno.

"You don't mean to say you've been trying experiments in *that* direction!" I said.

"Well, not *experiments* exactly. We do not profess to *construct* planets. But a scientific friend of mine, who has made several balloon-voyages, assures me he has visited a planet so small that he could walk right round in it twenty minutes! There had been a great battle, just before his visit, which had ended rather oddly: the vanquished army ran away at full speed, and in a very few minutes found themselves face-to-face with the victorious army, who were marching home again, and who were so frightened at finding themselves between *two* armies, that they surrendered at once! Of course that lost them the battle, though, as a matter of fact, they had killed *all* the soldiers on the other side."

"Killed soldiers *ca'n't* run away," Bruno thoughtfully remarked.

" 'Killed' is a technical word," replied Mein Herr. "In the little planet I speak of, the bullets were made of soft black stuff, which marked everything it touched. So, after a battle, all you had to do was to count how many soldiers on each side were 'killed'—that means 'marked on the *back*,' for marks in *front* didn't count."

"Then you couldn't 'kill' any, unless they ran away?" I said.

"My scientific friend found out a better plan than *that*. He pointed out that, if only the bullets were sent *the other way round the world*, they would hit the enemy in the *back*. After that, the *worst* marksmen were considered the *best* soldiers; and *the very worst of all* always got First Prize."

"And how did you decide which was *the very worst of all?*"

"Easily. The *best* possible shooting is, you know, to hit what is exactly in *front* of you: so of course the *worst* possible is to hit what is exactly *behind* you."

"They were strange people in that little planet!" I said.

"They were indeed! Perhaps their method of *government* was the strangest of all. In *this* planet, I am told, a Nation consists of a number of Subjects, and one King: but, in the little planet I speak of, it consisted of a number of *Kings* and one *Subject!*"

"You say you are 'told' what happens in *this* planet," I said. "May I venture to guess that you yourself are a visitor from some *other* planet?"

Bruno clapped his hands in his excitement. "Is oo the Man-in-the-Moon?" he cried.

Mein Herr looked uneasy. "I am *not* in the Moon, my child," he said evasively. "To return to what I was saying. I think *that* method of government ought to answer *well*. You see, the Kings would be sure to make Laws contradicting each other: so the Subject could never be punished, because, *whatever* he did, he'd be obeying *some* Law."

"And, whatever he did, he'd be *dis*obeying *some* Law!" cried Bruno. "So he'd *always* be punished!"

OF THE HIGHER LEARNING:

*The qualifications of teachers—rewards of genius—Cub-Hunting—
the Theory of Accelerated Velocity—degree examinations—*[9]

The old man sighed. "Ah, well! We're old folk *now;* and yet I was a child myself, once—at least I fancy so."

It *did* seem a rather unlikely fancy, I could not help owning to myself—looking at the shaggy white hair, and the long beard—that he could *ever* have been a child. "You are fond of young people?" I said.

"Young *men,*" he replied. "Not of *children* exactly. I used to teach young men—many a year ago—in my dear old University!"

"I didn't quite catch its *name?*" I hinted.

"I did not name it," the old man replied mildly. "Nor would you know the name if I did. Strange tales I could tell you of all the changes I have witnessed there! But it would weary you, I fear."

"No, *indeed!*" I said. "Pray go on. What kind of changes?"

But the old man seemed to be more in a humour for questions than for answers. "Tell me," he said, laying his hand impressively on my arm, "tell me something. For I am a stranger in your land, and I know little of *your* modes of education; yet something tells me *we* are further on than *you* in the eternal cycle of change—and that many a theory *we* have tried and found to fail, *you* also will try, with a wilder enthusiasm: you also will find to fail, with a bitterer despair!"

*   *   *   *   *   *   *   *   *

He paused a moment, and passed his hand uneasily across his brow. "One forgets," he murmured. "What was I saying? Oh! Something you were to tell me. Yes. Which of your teachers do you value the most highly, those whose words are easily understood, or those who puzzle you at every turn?"

I felt obliged to admit that we generally admired most the teachers we couldn't quite understand.

[9] From *Sylvie and Bruno Concluded,* 173-211.—McD.

"Just so," said Mein Herr. "That's the way it begins. Well, *we* were at that stage some eighty years ago—or was it ninety? Our favourite teacher got more obscure every year; and every year we admired him more—just as *your* Art-fanciers call *mist* the fairest feature in a landscape, and admire a view with frantic delight when they can see nothing! Now I'll tell you how it ended. It was Moral Philosophy that our idol lectured on. Well, his pupils couldn't make head or tail of it, but they got it all by heart; and, when Examination-time came, they wrote it down; and the Examiners said 'Beautiful! What depth!' "

"But what good was it to the young men *afterwards?*"

"Why, don't you see?" replied Mein Herr. "*They* became teachers in their turn, and *they* said all these things over again; and *their* pupils wrote it all down; and the Examiners accepted it; and nobody had the ghost of an idea what it all meant!"

"And how did it end?"

"It ended this way. We woke up one fine day, and found there was no one in the place that knew *anything* about Moral Philosophy. So we abolished it, teachers, classes, examiners, and all. And if any one wanted to learn anything about it, he had to make it out for himself; and after another twenty years or so there were several men that really knew something about it! Now tell me another thing. How long do you teach a youth before you examine him, in your Universities?"

I told him, three or four years.

"Just so, just what *we* did!" he exclaimed. "We taught 'em a bit, and, just as they were beginning to take it in, we took it all out again! We pumped our wells dry before they were a quarter full—we stripped our orchards while the apples were still in blossom—we applied the severe logic of arithmetic to our chickens, while peacefully slumbering in their shells! Doubtless it's the early bird that picks up the worm—but if the bird gets up so outrageously early that the worm is still deep underground, what *then* is its chance of a breakfast?"

Not much, I admitted.

"Now see how that works!" he went on eagerly. "If you want

to pump your wells so soon—and I suppose you tell me that is what you *must* do?"

"We must," I said. "In an over-crowded country like this, nothing but Competitive Examinations—"

Mein Herr threw up his hands wildly. "What, *again?*" he cried. "I thought it was dead, fifty years ago! Oh this Upas-tree of Competitive Examinations! Beneath whose deadly shade all the original genius, all the exhaustive research, all the untiring life-long diligence by which our forefathers have so advanced human knowledge, must slowly but surely wither away, and give place to a system of Cookery, in which the human mind is a sausage, and all we ask is, how much indigestible stuff can be crammed into it!"

Always, after these bursts of eloquence, he seemed to forget himself for a moment, and only to hold on to the thread of thought by some single word. "Yes, *crammed*," he repeated. "We went through all that stage of the disease—had it bad, I warrant you! Of course, as the Examination was all in all, we tried to put in just what was wanted—and the *great* thing to aim at was, that the Candidate should know absolutely *nothing* beyond the needs of the Examination! I don't say it was ever *quite* achieved: but one of my own pupils (pardon an old man's egotism) came very near it. After the Examination, he mentioned to me the few facts which he knew but had *not* been able to bring in, and I can assure you they were trivial, Sir, absolutely trivial!"

I feebly expressed my surprise and delight.

The old man bowed, with a gratified smile, and proceeded. "At that time, no one had hit on the much more rational plan of watching for the individual scintillations of genius, and rewarding them as they occurred. As it was, we made our unfortunate pupil into a Leyden-jar, charged him up to the eyelids—then applied the knob of a Competitive Examination, and drew off one magnificent spark, which very often cracked the jar! What mattered *that?* We labeled it 'First Class Spark,' and put it away on the shelf."

"But the more rational system—?" I suggested.

"Ah, yes! *that* came next. Instead of giving the whole reward of learning in one lump, we used to pay for every good answer as it occurred. How well I remember lecturing in those days, with a heap of small coins at my elbow! It was 'A *very* good answer, Mr. Jones!' (that meant a shilling, mostly). 'Bravo, Mr. Robinson!' (that meant half-a-crown). Now I'll tell you how *that* worked. Not one single fact would any of them take in, without a fee! And when a clever boy came up from school, he got paid more for learning than we got paid for teaching him! Then came the wildest craze of all."

"What, *another* craze?" I said.

"It's the last one," said the old man. "I must have tired you out with my long story. Each College wanted to get the clever boys: so we adopted a system which we had heard was very popular in England: the Colleges competed against each other, and the boys let themselves out to the highest bidder! What geese we were! Why, they were bound to come to the University *some-how*. We needn't have paid 'em! And all our money went in getting clever boys to come to one College rather than another! The competition was so keen, that at last mere money-payments were not enough. Any College, that wished to secure some specially clever young man, had to waylay him at the Station, and hunt him through the streets. The first who touched him was allowed to have him."

"That hunting-down of the scholars, as they arrived, must have been a curious business," I said. "Could you give me some idea of what it was like?"

"Willingly!" said the old man. "I will describe to you the very last Hunt that took place, before that form of Sport (for it was actually reckoned among the *Sports* of the day: we called it 'Cub-Hunting') was finally abandoned. I witnessed it myself, as I happened to be passing by at the moment, and was what we called 'in at the death.' I can see it now!" he went on in an excited tone, gazing into vacancy with those large dreamy eyes of his. "It seems like yesterday; and yet it happened—" He checked himself hastily, and the remaining words died away into a whisper.

"*How* many years ago did you say?" I asked, much interested in the prospect of at last learning *some* definite fact in his history.

"*Many* years ago," he replied. "The scene at the Railway-Station had been (so they told me) one of wild excitement. Eight or nine Heads of Colleges had assembled at the gates (no one was allowed inside), and the Station-Master had drawn a line on the pavement, and insisted on their all standing behind it.

The gates were flung open! The young man darted through them, and fled like lightning down the street, while the Heads of Colleges actually *yelled* with excitement on catching sight of him! The Proctor gave the word, in the old statutory form, '*Semel! Bis! Ter! Currite!*', and the Hunt began! Oh, it was a fine sight, believe me! At the first corner he dropped his Greek Lexicon: further on, his railway-rug: then various small articles: then his umbrella: lastly, what I suppose he prized most, his hand-bag: but the game was up: the spherical Principal of—of—"

"Of *which* College?" I said.

"—of *one* of the Colleges," he resumed, "had put into operation the Theory—his own discovery—of Accelerated Velocity, and captured him just opposite to where I stood. I shall never forget that wild breathless struggle! But it was soon over. Once in those great bony hands, escape was impossible!"

"May I ask why you speak of him as the '*spherical*' Principal?" I said.

"The epithet referred to his *shape*, which was a perfect *sphere*. You are aware that a bullet, another instance of a perfect sphere, when falling in a perfectly straight line, moves with Accelerated Velocity?"

I bowed assent.

"Well, my spherical friend (as I am proud to call him) set himself to investigate the *causes* of this. He found them to be *three*. One; that it is a perfect *sphere*. Two; that it moves in a *straight line*. Three; that its direction is *not upwards*. When these three conditions are fulfilled, you get Accelerated Velocity."

"Hardly," I said: "if you will excuse my differing from you. Suppose we apply the theory to *horizontal* motion. If a bullet is fired *horizontally*, it—"

"—it does *not* move in a *straight line*," he quietly finished my sentence for me.

"I yield the point," I said. "What did your friend do next?"

"The next thing was to apply the theory, as you rightly suggest, to *horizontal* motion. But the moving body, ever tending to *fall*, needs *constant support*, if it is to move in a true horizontal line. 'What, then,' he asked himself, 'will give *constant support to a moving body?'* And his answer was *'Human legs!' That* was the discovery that immortalised his name!"

"His name being—?" I suggested.

"I had not mentioned it," was the gentle reply of my most unsatisfactory informant. "His next step was an obvious one. He took to a diet of suet-dumplings, until his body had become a perfect sphere. *Then* he went out for his first experimental run— which nearly cost him his life!"

"How was *that?*"

"Well, you see, he had no idea of the *tremendous* new Force in Nature that he was calling into play. He began too fast. In a very few minutes he found himself moving at a hundred miles an hour! And, if he had not had the presence of mind to charge into the middle of a haystack (which he scattered to the four winds) there can be no doubt that he would have left the Planet he belonged to, and gone right away into Space!"

"And how came that to be the *last* of the Cub-Hunts?" I enquired.

"Well, you see, it led to a rather scandalous dispute between two of the Colleges. *Another* Principal had laid his hand on the young man, so nearly at the same moment as the *spherical* one, that there was no knowing which had touched him first. The dispute got into print, and did us no credit, and, in short, Cub-Hunts came to an end. Now I'll tell you what cured us of that wild craze of ours, the bidding against each other, for the clever scholars, just as if they were articles to be sold by auction! Just when the craze had reached its highest point, and when one of the Colleges had actually advertised a Scholarship of one thousand pounds *per annum*, one of our tourists brought us the manuscript of an old African legend—I happen to have a copy of it in my pocket. Shall I translate it for you?"

"Pray go on," I said.

*   *   *   *   *   *   *   *   *

"In a city that stands in the very centre of Africa, and is rarely visited by the casual tourist, the people had always bought eggs— a daily necessary in a climate where egg-flip was the usual diet—

from a Merchant who came to their gates once a week. And the people always bid wildly against each other: so there was quite a lively auction every time the Merchant came, and the last egg in his basket used to fetch the value of two or three camels, or thereabouts. And eggs got dearer every week. And still they drank their egg-flip, and wondered where all their money went to.

"And there came a day when they put their heads together. And they understood what donkeys they had been.

"And next day, when the Merchant came, only *one* Man went forth. And he said 'Oh, thou of the hook-nose and the goggle-eyes, thou of the measureless beard, how much for that lot of eggs?'

"And the Merchant answered him 'I *could* let thee have that lot at ten thousand piastres the dozen.'

"And the Man chuckled inwardly, and said '*Ten* piastres the dozen I offer thee, and no more, oh descendant of a distinguished grandfather!'

"And the Merchant stroked his beard, and said 'Hum! I will await the coming of thy friends.' So he waited. And the Man waited with him. And they waited both together."

"The manuscript breaks off here," said Mein Herr, as he rolled it up again; "but it was enough to open our eyes. We saw what simpletons we had been—buying our Scholars much as those ignorant savages bought their eggs—and the ruinous system was abandoned. If only we could have abandoned, along with it, all the *other* fashions we had borrowed from you, instead of carrying them to their logical results! But it was not to be. What ruined my country, and drove me from my home, was the introduction—into the *Army*, of all places—of your theory of Political Dichotomy!" [10]

*   *   *   *   *   *   *   *   *

"Now tell me one thing more," he said. "Am I right in thinking that in *your* Universities, though a man may reside some thirty or forty years, you examine him, once for all, at the end of the first three or four?"

"That is so, undoubtedly," I admitted.

"Practically, then, you examine a man at the *beginning* of his career!" the old man said to himself rather than to me. "And what guarantee have you that he *retains* the knowledge for which you have rewarded him—beforehand, as *we* should say?"

"None," I admitted, feeling a little puzzled at the drift of his remarks. "How do *you* secure that object?"

"By examining him at the *end* of his thirty or forty years—not at the beginning," he gently replied. "On an average, the knowledge then found is about one-fifth of what it was at first—the process of forgetting going on at a very steady uniform rate—and he, who forgets *least*, gets *most* honour, and most rewards."

"Then you give him the money when he needs it no longer? And you make him live most of his life on *nothing!*"

"Hardly that. He gives his orders to the tradesmen: they supply him, for forty, sometimes fifty, years, at their own risk: then he gets his Fellowship—which pays him in *one* year as much as *your*

[10] For explanation of theory, see following selection.

Fellowships pay in fifty—and then he can easily pay all his bills, with interest."

"But suppose he fails to get his Fellowship? That must occasionally happen."

"That occasionally happens." It was Mein Herr's turn, now, to make admissions.

"And what becomes of the tradesmen?"

"They calculate accordingly. When a man appears to be getting alarmingly ignorant, or stupid, they will sometimes refuse to supply him any longer. You have no idea with what enthusiasm a man will begin to rub up his forgotten sciences or languages, when his butcher has cut off the supply of beef and mutton!"

"And who are the Examiners?"

"The young men who have just come, brimming over with knowledge. You would think it a curious sight," he went on, "to see mere boys examining such old men. I have known a man set to examine his own grandfather. It was a little painful for both of them, no doubt. The old gentleman was as bald as a coot—"

"How bald would that be?" I've no idea why I asked this question. I felt I was getting foolish. . . . . . .

THE THEORY OF POLITICAL DICHOTOMY:

And Its Further Application to Agriculture, Commerce, and War [11]

"Shall I trouble you too much," I said, "if I ask you to explain what you mean by 'the Theory of Political Dichotomy'?"

"No trouble at all!" was Mein Herr's most courteous reply. "I quite enjoy talking, when I get so good a listener. What started the thing, with us, was the report brought to us, by one of our most eminent statesmen, who had stayed some time in England, of the way affairs were managed there. It was a political necessity (so he assured us, and we believed him, though we had never discovered it till that moment) that there should be *two* Parties, in every affair and on every subject. In *Politics*, the two Parties, which you had found it necessary to institute, were called, he told us, 'Whigs' and 'Tories'."

"That must have been some time ago?" I remarked.

"It *was* some time ago," he admitted. "And this was the way the affairs of the British Nation were managed. (You will correct me if I misrepresent it. I do but repeat what our traveler told us.) These two Parties—which were in chronic hostility to each other— took turns in conducting the Government; and the Party, that happened *not* to be in power, was called the 'Opposition', I believe?"

"That is the right name," I said. "There have always been, so long as we have had a Parliament at all, *two* Parties, one 'in', and one 'out'."

"Well, the function of the 'Ins' (if I may so call them) was to do the best they could for the national welfare—in such things as making war or peace, commercial treaties, and so forth?"

"Undoubtedly," I said.

"And the function of the 'Outs' was (so our traveller assured us, though we were very incredulous at first) to *prevent* the 'Ins' from succeeding in any of these things?"

[11] From *Sylvie and Bruno Concluded*, 199-208.—*McD.*

"To *criticize* and to *amend* their proceedings," I corrected him. "It would be *unpatriotic* to *hinder* the Government in doing what was for the good of the Nation! We have always held a *Patriot* to be the greatest of heroes, and an *unpatriotic* spirit to be one of the worst of human ills!"

"Excuse me for a moment," the old gentleman courteously replied, taking out his pocketbook. "I have a few memoranda here, of a correspondence I had with our tourist, and, if you will allow me, I'll just refresh my memory—although I quite agree with you—it is, as you say, one of the worst of human ills—"

*   *   *   *   *   *   *   *   *

"It is exactly what my friend told me," he resumed, after conning over various papers. " '*Unpatriotic*' is the very word I had used, in writing to him, and '*hinder*' is the very word he used in his reply! Allow me to read you a portion of his letter:—

" '*I can assure you,*' he writes, '*that, unpatriotic as you may think it, the recognised function of the 'Opposition' is to hinder, in every manner not forbidden by the Law, the action of the Government. This process is called 'Legitimate Obstruction': and the greatest triumph the 'Opposition' can ever enjoy, is when they are able to point out that, owing to their 'Obstruction', the Government have failed in everything they have tried to do for the good of the Nation!*' "

"Your friend has not put it *quite* correctly," I said. "The Opposition would no doubt be glad to point out that the Government had failed *through their own fault;* but *not* that they had failed on account of *Obstruction!*"

"You think so?" he gently replied. "Allow me now to read to you this newspaper-cutting, which my friend enclosed in his letter. It is part of the report of a public speech, made by a Statesman who was at the time a member of the 'Opposition':—

" '*At the close of the Session, he thought they had no reason to be discontented with the fortunes of the campaign. They had routed the enemy at every point. But the pursuit must be continued. They had only to follow up a disordered and dispirited foe.*' "

"Now to what portion of your national history would you guess that the speaker was referring?"

"Really, the number of *successful* wars we have waged during the last century," I replied, with a glow of British pride, "is *far* too great for me to guess, with any chance of success, *which* it was we were then engaged in. However, I will name '*India*' as the most probable. The Mutiny was no doubt, all but crushed, at the time that speech was made. What a fine, manly, *patriotic* speech it must have been!" I exclàimed in an outburst of enthusiasm.

"You think so?" he replied, in a tone of gentle pity. "Yet my friend tells me that the '*disordered and dispirited foe*' simply meant the Statesmen who happened to be in power at the moment; that the '*pursuit*' simply meant 'Obstruction'; and that the words '*they had routed the enemy*' simply meant that the 'Opposition' had succeeded in hindering the Government from doing any of the work which the Nation had empowered them to do!"

I thought it best to say nothing.

"It seemed queer to *us*, just at first," he resumed, after courteously waiting a minute for me to speak: "but, when once we had mastered the idea, our respect for your Nation was so great that we carried it into every department of life! It was '*the beginning of the end*' with us. My country never held up its head again!" And the poor old gentleman sighed deeply.

"Let us change the subject," I said. "Do not distress yourself, I beg!"

"No, no!" he said, with an effort to recover himself. "I had rather finish my story! The next step (after reducing our Government to impotence, and putting a stop to all useful legislation, which did not take us long to do) was to introduce what we called 'the glorious British Principle of Dichotomy' into *Agriculture*. We persuaded many of the well-to-do farmers to divide their staff of labourers into two Parties, and to set them one against the other. They were called, like our political Parties, the 'Ins' and the 'Outs': the business of the 'Ins' was to do as much of ploughing, sowing, or whatever might be needed, as they could manage in a day, and at night they were paid according to the amount they had *done:* the business of the 'Outs' was to hinder them, and *they* were paid for the amount they had *hindered*. The farmers found they had to pay only *half* as much wages as they did before, and they didn't observe that the amount of work done was only a *quarter* as much as was done before: so they took it up quite enthusiastically, *at first*."

"And *afterwards—*?" I enquired.

"Well, *afterwards* they didn't like it quite so well. In a very short time, things settled down into a regular routine. No work *at all* was done. So the 'Ins' got no wages, and the 'Outs' got full pay. And the farmers never discovered, till most of them were ruined, that the rascals had agreed to manage it so, and had shared the pay between them! While the thing lasted, there were funny sights to be seen! Why, I've often watched a ploughman, with two horses harnessed to the plough, doing his best to get it *forwards*; while the opposition-ploughman, with three donkeys harnessed at the *other* end, was doing *his* best to get it *backwards!* And the plough never moving an inch, *either* way!"

"But *we* never did anything like *that!*" I exclaimed.

"Simply because you were less *logical* than we were," replied Mein Herr. "There is *sometimes* an advantage in being a donk— Excuse me! No *personal* allusion intended. All this happened *long ago*, you know!"

"Did the Dichotomy-Principle succeed in *any* direction?" I enquired.

"In *none*," Mein Herr candidly confessed. "It had a *very* short trial in *Commerce*. The shop-keepers *wouldn't* take it up, after once trying the plan of having half the attendants busy in folding up and carrying away the goods which the other half were trying to spread out upon the counters. They said the Public didn't like it!"

"I don't wonder at it," I remarked.

"Well, we tried 'the British Principle' for some years. And the end of it all was—" His voice suddenly dropped, almost to a whisper; and large tears began to roll down his cheeks. "—the end was that we got involved in a war; and there was a great battle, in which we far out-numbered the enemy. But what could one expect, when only *half* of our soldiers were fighting, and the other half pulling them back? It ended in a crushing defeat—an utter rout. This caused a Revolution; and most of the Government were banished. I myself was accused of Treason, for having so strongly advocated 'the British Principle.' My property was all forfeited, and—and—I was driven into exile! 'Now the mischief's done,' they said, 'perhaps you'll kindly leave the country?' It nearly broke my heart, but I had to go!"

APPENDIX

A NOTE ON THE VERSE IN THIS VOLUME

(Since in this book of prose selections there is embedded a good deal of verse, a note about it will not be out of place. None of the verse here included appears in *The Collected Verse of Lewis Carroll:* either it was not available at the time that volume was made or else it was deemed too much tied up in context or too fragmentary to bear unsupported appearance. For the convenience of the reader I have placed in the front matter a list of all pieces, fragmentary or otherwise, that are to be found in this book.)

In the main body of Lewis Carroll's verse one can observe his interest in pure nonsense, his delight in parody, and his use of both nonsense-form and parody as satire. On reading some of his prose—*Alice*, for instance—one notices also that he uses verse to make more emphatic the presentation of his ideas. These characteristics are all present in the poems and fragments presented in this book.

If we look first at those stanzas in "Photography Extraordinary" we see such use. As everyone knows, photography, at that time still unusual, was Carroll's principal hobby; in this paper he turns an idea suggested by photography into the basis for a criticism of certain types of popular novel. Under his skillful hand the characteristics of the Milk-and-Water, of the Matter-of-Fact, and of the Spasmodic Schools are reduced to their essence by illustration in the pair of stanzas to which we are repeatedly treated; his skill in parody is as evident here as in any of the completed works in the *Collected Verse*.

The central character of "Novelty and Romancement" is Leopold Edgar Stubbs whose passion is "for poetry untrammelled by the laws of sense, rhyme, or rhythm, soaring through the universe, and echoing the music of the spheres." Though the main incident is not concerned with his poetry, Stubbs is a picture of the romantic aesthete, of the poetaster whose heavy, unhappy, and insistent use of that "dignified" form, the sonnet, is taken off in the meaningless jumble of impressive phrases which make up the sonnet that we see. The "Letter" to Carroll's brother and sister is an amusing bit of rhyming describing the necessity of dignity on the part of the teacher and the difficulty that arises in teaching under such circumstances. It assures us once more that there is a very human quality about this Don. The fragments which we find in "The Legend of 'Scotland' " are obviously burlesque of the sort of verse quoted in the sort of ghost fiction he is here imitating rather harshly:

> Lorenzo dwelt at Heighington
>   (Hys cote was made of Dimity)
> Leastways if not exactly there,
>   Yet yn its close proximity.
> Hee called on mee—hee stayed to tea—
>   Yet not a word hee ut-tered,
> Untyl I sayd "D'ye lyke your bread
> Dry?" and he answered "But-tered."

This and some other pieces of Carroll's verse would be more effective if he had not felt obliged to strain himself in what was made to seem old-fashioned spelling; yet even here he was mocking a standing tradition. The "spell" recited by the lady ghost and the Auckland castle song at the end of the story continue this amusing mockery in a vein thoroughly in accord with the absurdity maintained in the whole piece.

Three of the Oxford Papers make use of verse. The situation in the first of these, *Facts, Figures, and Fancies,* is carefully explained in the introductory remarks. "The Elections to the Hebdomadal Council" (which the present-day reader might unadvisedly assume to be of little interest to himself) is concerned with party difficulties in the administrative system of Oxford. In his denunciation of the situation Carroll takes for his medium the heroic couplet which he employs with a great deal of Byronic freedom and anticlimax—probably the most effective vehicle for satire ever worked out in English. He demands:

> Heard ye the arrow hurtle in the sky?
> Heard ye the dragon-monster's deathful cry?—
> Excuse this sudden burst of the Heroic;
> The present state of things would vex a Stoic!
> And just as Sairey Gamp, for pains within,
> Administered a modicum of gin,

> So does my mind, when vexed and ill at ease,
> Console itself with soothing similes.
> The "dragon-monster" (pestilential schism!)
> I need not tell you is Conservatism;
> The "hurtling arrow" (till we find a better)
> Is represented by the present Letter.

Though the matters concerned here be local in time and place and so of no direct interest to us now, the method Lewis Carroll uses in presenting his ideas shows the flexibility of his mind and the skill of his dialectic. He is, of course, ironic in his whole presentation. The footnotes are principally direct quotation from the Letter of great wisdom to which he refers in his Introductory remarks—his whole poem in fact is a rhythmical variation (!) of that letter. Many of the lashes are of universal application:

> *It may be right to go ahead, I guess:*
> *It may be right to stop, I do confess:*
> *Also it may be right to retrogress.*
> So says the oracle, and, for myself, I
> Must say it beats to fits the one at Delphi!

The fable of the cat and the rats is another reduction to absurdity of the heroic method and of the immediate situation. Like Pope and other classicists who made effective use of the couplet in satire, Carroll is a conservative; like them, he is excellent in the flaying of his opponents.

The other piece of verse from this paper is called "The Deserted Parks." In form it is a parody on "The Deserted Village." In content it is a spirited denunciation of or attack upon a proposal to establish cricket-grounds in the parks—a good piece of Carroll satire. In *The New Belfry* he again makes use of fragments of verse to make more pointed the arguments he advances. Here, however, the verse is not so successful as the brilliant prose mockery which distinguishes this paper. In *The Vision of the Three T's* we find two complete poems. The first is about the wanderings of Gladstone, for years the member from Oxford but defeated as the note to *The Dynamics of a Parti-cle* explains. In form this is a parody of the Scottish ballads, but the point is not to ridicule the ballad so much as to permit Carroll to ridicule the "tea-chest."

The other is a rollicking "Bachanalian" ode modeled on Sheridan's "Here's to the maiden."

> Here's to the Censors who symbolise Sense,
> Just as Mitres incorporate Might, Sir. . . .

We are come then to the pieces I have placed in the appendix. The first of these, "Lays of Sorrow, No. 1," dates from *The Rectory Umbrella;* its content is evidently some happening in the family which the seventeen-year-old versifier amused himself by turning into the stilted and grandiloquent ode form so favored in the eighteenth century, complete with mock-heroic figure and all. "The Two Brothers" was written at Croft in 1853 and appeared in *Misch-Masch.* It is a parody of the old ballad of "The Twa Sisters," with apparently another ballad mixed in, and overflowing all is the author's delight in puns, an example approaching that of Tom Hood in his "Faithless Nelly Gray." "She's All My Fancy Painted Him" is, of course, the first stage of that poem later appearing in *Alice* as the evidence of the White Rabbit—an example of Carroll approaching close to pure nonsense. It is apparently a parody of a poem entitled "Alice Gray" written by one William Mee. "The Palace of Humbug," written at Croft in 1855, is a pleasing parody of that Bunn-*bouche,* "I dreamt I dwelt in marble halls."

> I dreamt I dwelt in marble halls,
> And each damp thing that creeps and crawls
> Went wobble-wobble on the walls. . . .

In all four of these appended poems we can see readily the hand of Lewis Carroll, but the high skill of that writer has become completely and satisfyingly evident in the last two, which I present here for what will be for most Americans the first time.

LAYS OF SORROW [1]

No. 1

> The day was wet, the rain fell souse
> Like jars of strawberry jam,[2] a
> Sound was heard in the old henhouse,
> A beating of a hammer.

[1] From *The Rectory Umbrella.—McD.*
[2] *i.e.,* the jam without the jars observe the beauty of this rhyme.

Of stalwart form, and visage warm,
  Two youths were seen within it,
Splitting up an old tree into perches for their poultry,
  At a hundred strokes [3] a minute.

The work is done, the hen has taken
Possession of her nest and eggs,
Without a thought of eggs and bacon,[4]
(Or I am very much mistaken:)
    She turns over each shell,
    To be sure that all's well,
    Looks into the straw
    To see there's no flaw,
    Goes once round the house,[5]
    Half afraid of a mouse,
    Then sinks calmly to rest
    On the top of her nest,
First doubling up each of her legs.
Time rolled away, and so did every shell,
  "Small by degrees and beautifully less,"
As the sage mother with a powerful spell [6]
  Forced each in turn its contents to "express," [7]
But ah! "imperfect is expression,"
  Some poet said, I don't care who,
  If you want to know you must go elsewhere,
  One fact I can tell, if you're willing to hear,
  He never attended a Parliament Session,
  For I'm certain that if he had ever been there,
  Full quickly would he have changed his ideas,
  With the hissings, the hootings, the groans and the cheers,
  And as to his name it is pretty clear
  That it wasn't me and it wasn't you!

And so it fell upon a day,
    (That is, it never rose again,)
A chick was found upon the hay,
Its little life had ebbed away,
No longer frolicsome and gay,
No longer could it run or play,
  "And must we, chicken, must we part?

[3] at the rate of a stroke and two thirds in a second.
[4] unless the hen was a poacher, which is unlikely.
[5] the hen house.
[6] beak and claw.
[7] press out.

It's master [8] cried with bursting heart,
    And voice of agony and pain
So one, whose ticket's marked "Return," [9]
    When to the lonely road side station
    He flies in fear and perturbation,
    Thinks of his home—the hissing urn—
    Then runs with flying hat and hair,
    And, entering, finds to his despair
        He's missed the very latest train! [10]

Too long it were to tell of each conjecture
    Of chicken suicide, and poultry victim,
The deadly frown, the stern and dreary lecture,
    The timid guess, "perhaps some needle pricked him!"
The din of voice, the words both loud and many,
    The sob, the tear, the sigh that none could smother,
Till all agreed "a shilling to a penny
    It killed it self, and we acquit the mother!"
        Scarce was the verdict spoken,
        When that still calm was broken,
    A childish form hath burst into the throng,
        With tears and looks of sadness,
        That bring no news of gladness,
But tell too surely something hath gone wrong.
    "The sight that I have come upon
    "The stoutest [11] heart would sicken,
    "That nasty hen has been and gone
    "And, killed another chicken!"

THE TWO BROTHERS [12]

There were two brothers at Twyford school,
    And when they had left the place,
It was, "Will ye learn Greek and Latin?
    Or will ye run me a race?
Or will ye go up to yonder bridge,
    And there we will angle for dace?"

"I'm too stupid for Greek and for Latin,
    I'm too lazy by half for a race,

[8] probably one of the two stalwart youths.
[9] the system of return tickets is an excellent one. People are conveyed, on particular days, there and back again for one fare.
[10] an additional vexation would be that his "Return" ticket would be no use the next day.
[11] perhaps even the "bursting heart of its master."
[12] From *Misch-Masch.—McD.*

So I'll even go up to yonder bridge,
And there we will angle for dace."

He has fitted together two joints of his rod,
And to them he has added another,
And then a great hook he took from his book,
And ran it right into his brother.

Oh much is the noise that is made among boys
When playfully pelting a pig,
But a far greater pother was made by his brother
When flung from the top of the brigg.

The fish hurried up by the dozens,
All ready and eager to bite,
For the lad that he flung was so tender and young,
It quite gave them an appetite.

Said, "Thus shall he wallop about
And the fish take him quite at their ease,
For me to annoy it was ever his joy,
Now I'll teach him the meaning of 'Tees'!"

The wind to his ear brought a voice,
"My brother you didn't had ought ter!
And what have I done that you think it such fun
To indulge in the pleasure of slaughter?

"A good nibble or bite is my chiefest delight,
When I'm merely expected to *see*,
But a bite from a fish is not quite what I wish,
When I get it performed upon *me;*
And just now here's a swarm of dace at my arm,
And a perch has got hold of my knee

"For water my thirst was not great at the first,
And of fish I have quite sufficien—"
"Oh fear not!" he cried, "for whatever betide,
We are both in the selfsame condition!

"I am sure that our state's very nearly alike
(Not considering the question of slaughter)
For I have my perch on the top of the bridge,
And you have your perch in the water.

"I stick to my perch and your perch sticks to you,
We are really extremely alike;
I've a turn pike up here, and I very much fear
You may soon have a turn with a pike."

"Oh grant but one wish! If I'm took by a fish
(For your bait is your brother, good man!),
Pull him up if you like, but I hope you will strike
As gently as ever you can."

"If the fish be a trout, I'm afraid there's no doubt
I must strike him like lightning that's greased;
If the fish be a pike, I'll engage not to strike,
Till I've waited ten minutes at least."

"But in those ten minutes to desolate Fate
Your brother a victim may fall!"
"I'll reduce it to five, so *perhaps* you'll survive,
But the chance is exceedingly small."

"Oh hard is your heart for to act such a part;
Is it iron, or granite, or steel?"
"Why, I really can't say—it is many a day
Since my heart was accustomed to feel.

" 'Twas my heart-cherished wish for to slay many fish,
Each day did my malice grow worse,
For my heart didn't soften with doing it so often,
But rather, I should say, the reverse."

"Oh would I were back at Twyford school,
Learning lessons in fear of the birch!"
"Nay, brother!" he cried, "for whatever betide,
You are better off here with your perch!

"I am sure you'll allow you are happier now,
With nothing to do but to play;
And this single line here, it is perfectly clear,
Is much better than thirty a day!

"And as to the rod hanging over your head,
And apparently ready to fall,
That, you know, was the case, when you lived in that place,
So it need not be reckoned at all.

"Do you see that old trout with a turn-up-nose snout?
(Just to speak on a pleasanter theme,)
Observe, my dear brother, our love for each other—
He's the one I like best in the stream.

"To-morrow I mean to invite him to dine
(We shall all of us think it a treat,)
If the day should be fine, I'll just *drop him a line*,
And we'll settle what time we're to meet.

"He hasn't been into society yet,
    And his manners are not of the best,
So I think it quite fair that it should be *my* care,
    To see that he's properly dressed."

Many words brought the wind of "cruel" and "kind,"
    And that "man suffers more than the brute":
Each several word with patience he heard,
    And answered with wisdom to boot.

"What? prettier swimming in the stream,
    Than lying all snugly and flat?
Do but look at that dish filled with glittering fish,
    Has Nature a picture like that?

"What? a higher delight to be drawn from the sight
    Of fish full of life and glee?
What a noodle you are! 'tis delightfuller far
    To kill them than let them go free!

"I know there are people who prate by the hour,
    Of the beauty of earth, sky, and ocean;
Of the birds as they fly, of the fish darting by,
    Rejoicing in Life and in Motion.

"As to any delight to be got from the sight,
    It is all very well for a flat,
But I think it all gammon, for hooking a salmon
    Is better than twenty of that!

"They say that a man of a right-thinking mind
    Will *love* the dumb creatures he sees—
What's the use of his mind, if he's never inclined
    To pull a fish out of the Tees?

"Take my friends and my home—as an outcast I'll roam:
    Take the money I have in the Bank—
It is just what I wish, but deprive me of *fish*,
    And my life would indeed be a blank!"

Forth from the house his sister came,
    Her brothers for to see,
But when she saw that sight of awe,
    The tear stood in her ee.

"Oh what bait's that upon your hook,
    My brother, tell to me?"
"It is but the fantailed pigeon,
    He would not sing for me."

"Whoe'er would expect a pigeon to sing,
   A simpleton he must be!
But a pigeon-cote is a different thing
   To the coat that there I see!"

"Oh what bait's that upon your hook,
   My brother, tell to me?"
"It is but the black-capped bantam,
   He would not dance for me."

"And a pretty dance you are leading him now!"
   In anger answered she,
"But a bantam's cap is different thing
   To the cap that there I see!"

"Oh what bait's that upon your hook,
   Dear brother, tell to me?"
"It is my younger brother," he cried,
   "Oh woe and dole is me!

"I's mighty wicked, that I is!
   Or how could such things be?
Farewell, farewell, sweet sister,
   I'm going o'er the sea."

"And when will you come back again,
   My brother, tell to me?"
"When chub is good for human food,
   And that will never be!"

She turned herself right round about,
   And her heart brake into three,
Said, "One of the two will be wet through and through,
   And 'tother'll be late for his tea!"

Croft, 1853.

SHE'S ALL MY FANCY PAINTED HIM [13]

A Poem

[This affecting fragment was found in MS. among the papers of the well-known author of "Was it You or I?" a tragedy, and the two popular novels, "Sister and Son," and "The Niece's Legacy, or the Grateful Grandfather."]

   She's all my fancy painted him
      (I make no idle boast);
   If he or you had lost a limb,
      Which would have suffered most?

[13] From *Misch-Masch.—McD.*

He said that you had been to her,
    And seen me here before;
But, in another character,
    She was the same of yore.

There was not one that spoke to us,
    Of all that thronged the street;
So he sadly got into a 'bus,
    And pattered with his feet.

They sent him word I had not gone
    (We know it to be true);
If she should push the matter on,
    What would become of you?

They gave her one, they gave me two,
    They gave us three or more;
They all returned from him to you,
    Though they were mine before.

If I or she should chance to be
    Involved in this affair,
He trusts to you to set them free,
    Exactly as we were.

It seemed to me that you had been
    (Before she had this fit)
An obstacle, that came between
    Him, and ourselves, and it.

Don't let him know she liked them best,
    For this must ever be
A secret, kept from all the rest,
    Between yourself and me.

LAYS OF MYSTERY, IMAGINATION, AND HUMOUR [14]

No. 1

The Palace of Humburg.   (For the end of 1855.)

I dreamt I dwelt in marble halls,
And each damp thing that creeps and crawls
Went wobble-wobble on the walls.

Faint odours of departed cheese,
Blown on the dank, unwholesome breeze,
Awoke the never-ending sneeze.

[14] From *Misch-Masch.—McD.*

Strange pictures decked the arras drear,
Strange characters of woe and fear,
The humbugs of the social sphere.

One showed a vain and noisy prig,
That shouted empty words and big
At him that nodded in a wig.

And one, a dotard grim and grey,
Who wasteth childhood's happy day
In work more profitless than play.

Whose icy breast no pity warms,
Whose little victims sit in swarms,
And slowly sob on lower forms.

And one, a green thyme-honoured Bank,
Where flowers are growing wild and rank,
Like weeds that fringe a poisoned tank.

All birds of evil omen there
Flood with rich Notes the tainted air,
The witless wanderer to snare.

The fatal Notes neglected fall,
No creature heeds the treacherous call,
For all those goodly Strawn Baits Pall.

The wandering phantom broke and fled,
Straightway I saw within my head
A Vision of a ghostly bed,

Where lay two worn decrepit men,
The fictions of a lawyer's pen,
Who never more might breathe again.

The serving-man of Richard Roe
Wept, inarticulate with woe:
She wept, that waited on John Doe.

"Oh rouse," I urged, "the waning sense
"With tales of tangled evidence,
"Of suit, demurrer, and defence."

"Vain," she replied, "such mockeries:
"For morbid fancies, such as these,
"No suits can suit, no plea can please."

And bending o'er that man of straw,
She cried in grief and sudden awe,
Not inappropriately, "Law!"

The well-remembered voice he knew,
He smiled, he faintly muttered "Sue!"
(Her very name was legal too.)

The night was fled, the dawn was nigh:
A hurricane went raving by,
And swept the Vision from mine eye.

Vanished that dim and ghostly bed,
(The hangings, tape; the tape was red:)
'Tis o'er, and Doe and Roe are dead!

Oh yet my spirit inly crawls,
What time it shudderingly recalls
That horrid dream of marble halls!

                                        Oxford, 1855.

FINIS

A CATALOGUE OF SELECTED DOVER BOOKS
IN ALL FIELDS OF INTEREST

THE DEVIL'S DICTIONARY, Ambrose Bierce. Barbed, bitter, brilliant witticisms in the form of a dictionary. Best, most ferocious satire America has produced. 145pp. 20487-1 Pa. $1.75

ABSOLUTELY MAD INVENTIONS, A.E. Brown, H.A. Jeffcott. Hilarious, useless, or merely absurd inventions all granted patents by the U.S. Patent Office. Edible tie pin, mechanical hat tipper, etc. 57 illustrations. 125pp. 22596-8 Pa. $1.50

AMERICAN WILD FLOWERS COLORING BOOK, Paul Kennedy. Planned coverage of 48 most important wildflowers, from Rickett's collection; instructive as well as entertaining. Color versions on covers. 48pp. 8¼ x 11. 20095-7 Pa. $1.50

BIRDS OF AMERICA COLORING BOOK, John James Audubon. Rendered for coloring by Paul Kennedy. 46 of Audubon's noted illustrations: red-winged blackbird, cardinal, purple finch, towhee, etc. Original plates reproduced in full color on the covers. 48pp. 8¼ x 11. 23049-X Pa. $1.50

NORTH AMERICAN INDIAN DESIGN COLORING BOOK, Paul Kennedy. The finest examples from Indian masks, beadwork, pottery, etc. — selected and redrawn for coloring (with identifications) by well-known illustrator Paul Kennedy. 48pp. 8¼ x 11. 21125-8 Pa. $1.50

UNIFORMS OF THE AMERICAN REVOLUTION COLORING BOOK, Peter Copeland. 31 lively drawings reproduce whole panorama of military attire; each uniform has complete instructions for accurate coloring. (Not in the Pictorial Archives Series). 64pp. 8¼ x 11. 21850-3 Pa. $1.50

THE WONDERFUL WIZARD OF OZ COLORING BOOK, L. Frank Baum. Color the Yellow Brick Road and much more in 61 drawings adapted from W.W. Denslow's originals, accompanied by abridged version of text. Dorothy, Toto, Oz and the Emerald City. 61 illustrations. 64pp. 8¼ x 11. 20452-9 Pa. $1.50

CUT AND COLOR PAPER MASKS, Michael Grater. Clowns, animals, funny faces . . . simply color them in, cut them out, and put them together, and you have 9 paper masks to play with and enjoy. Complete instructions. Assembled masks shown in full color on the covers. 32pp. 8¼ x 11. 23171-2 Pa. $1.50

STAINED GLASS CHRISTMAS ORNAMENT COLORING BOOK, Carol Belanger Grafton. Brighten your Christmas season with over 100 Christmas ornaments done in a stained glass effect on translucent paper. Color them in and then hang at windows, from lights, anywhere. 32pp. 8¼ x 11. 20707-2 Pa. $1.75

CREATIVE LITHOGRAPHY AND HOW TO DO IT, Grant Arnold. Lithography as art form: working directly on stone, transfer of drawings, lithotint, mezzotint, color printing; also metal plates. Detailed, thorough. 27 illustrations. 214pp.
21208-4 Pa. $3.00

DESIGN MOTIFS OF ANCIENT MEXICO, Jorge Enciso. Vigorous, powerful ceramic stamp impressions — Maya, Aztec, Toltec, Olmec. Serpents, gods, priests, dancers, etc. 153pp. 6⅛ x 9¼.
20084-1 Pa. $2.50

AMERICAN INDIAN DESIGN AND DECORATION, Leroy Appleton. Full text, plus more than 700 precise drawings of Inca, Maya, Aztec, Pueblo, Plains, NW Coast basketry, sculpture, painting, pottery, sand paintings, metal, etc. 4 plates in color. 279pp. 8⅜ x 11¼.
22704-9 Pa. $4.50

CHINESE LATTICE DESIGNS, Daniel S. Dye. Incredibly beautiful geometric designs: circles, voluted, simple dissections, etc. Inexhaustible source of ideas, motifs. 1239 illustrations. 469pp. 6⅛ x 9¼.
23096-1 Pa. $5.00

JAPANESE DESIGN MOTIFS, Matsuya Co. Mon, or heraldic designs. Over 4000 typical, beautiful designs: birds, animals, flowers, swords, fans, geometric; all beautifully stylized. 213pp. 11⅜ x 8¼.
22874-6 Pa. $5.00

PERSPECTIVE, Jan Vredeman de Vries. 73 perspective plates from 1604 edition; buildings, townscapes, stairways, fantastic scenes. Remarkable for beauty, surrealistic atmosphere; real eye-catchers. Introduction by Adolf Placzek. 74pp. 11⅜ x 8¼.
20186-4 Pa. $2.75

EARLY AMERICAN DESIGN MOTIFS, Suzanne E. Chapman. 497 motifs, designs, from painting on wood, ceramics, appliqué, glassware, samplers, metal work, etc. Florals, landscapes, birds and animals, geometrics, letters, etc. Inexhaustible. Enlarged edition. 138pp. 8⅜ x 11¼.
22985-8 Pa. $3.50
23084-8 Clothbd. $7.95

VICTORIAN STENCILS FOR DESIGN AND DECORATION, edited by E.V. Gillon, Jr. 113 wonderful ornate Victorian pieces from German sources; florals, geometrics; borders, corner pieces; bird motifs, etc. 64pp. 9⅜ x 12¼.
21995-X Pa. $2.75

ART NOUVEAU: AN ANTHOLOGY OF DESIGN AND ILLUSTRATION FROM THE STUDIO, edited by E.V. Gillon, Jr. Graphic arts: book jackets, posters, engravings, illustrations, decorations; Crane, Beardsley, Bradley and many others. Inexhaustible. 92pp. 8⅛ x 11.
22388-4 Pa. $2.50

ORIGINAL ART DECO DESIGNS, William Rowe. First-rate, highly imaginative modern Art Deco frames, borders, compositions, alphabets, florals, insectals, Wurlitzer-types, etc. Much finest modern Art Deco. 80 plates, 8 in color. 8⅜ x 11¼.
22567-4 Pa. $3.50

HANDBOOK OF DESIGNS AND DEVICES, Clarence P. Hornung. Over 1800 basic geometric designs based on circle, triangle, square, scroll, cross, etc. Largest such collection in existence. 261pp.
20125-2 Pa. $2.75

VICTORIAN HOUSES: A TREASURY OF LESSER-KNOWN EXAMPLES, Edmund Gillon and Clay Lancaster. 116 photographs, excellent commentary illustrate distinct characteristics, many borrowings of local Victorian architecture. Octagonal houses, Americanized chalets, grand country estates, small cottages, etc. Rich heritage often overlooked. 116 plates. 11⅜ x 10.   22966-1 Pa. $4.00

STICKS AND STONES, Lewis Mumford. Great classic of American cultural history; architecture from medieval-inspired earliest forms to 20th century; evolution of structure and style, influence of environment. 21 illustrations. 113pp.
20202-X Pa. $2.50

ON THE LAWS OF JAPANESE PAINTING, Henry P. Bowie. Best substitute for training with genius Oriental master, based on years of study in Kano school. Philosophy, brushes, inks, style, etc. 66 illustrations. 117pp. 6⅛ x 9¼.   20030-2 Pa. $4.50

A HANDBOOK OF ANATOMY FOR ART STUDENTS, Arthur Thomson. Virtually exhaustive. Skeletal structure, muscles, heads, special features. Full text, anatomical figures, undraped photos. Male and female. 337 illustrations. 459pp.
21163-0 Pa. $5.00

AN ATLAS OF ANATOMY FOR ARTISTS, Fritz Schider. Finest text, working book. Full text, plus anatomical illustrations; plates by great artists showing anatomy. 593 illustrations. 192pp. 7⅞ x 10¾.   20241-0 Clothbd. $6.95

THE HUMAN FIGURE IN MOTION, Eadweard Muybridge. More than 4500 stopped-action photos, in action series, showing undraped men, women, children jumping, lying down, throwing, sitting, wrestling, carrying, etc. "Unparalleled dictionary for artists," American Artist. Taken by great 19th century photographer. 390pp. 7⅞ x 10⅝.   20204-6 Clothbd. $12.50

AN ATLAS OF ANIMAL ANATOMY FOR ARTISTS, W. Ellenberger et al. Horses, dogs, cats, lions, cattle, deer, etc. Muscles, skeleton, surface features. The basic work. Enlarged edition. 288 illustrations. 151pp. 9⅜ x 12¼.   20082-5 Pa. $4.50

LETTER FORMS: 110 COMPLETE ALPHABETS, Frederick Lambert. 110 sets of capital letters; 16 lower case alphabets; 70 sets of numbers and other symbols. Edited and expanded by Theodore Menten. 110pp. 8⅛ x 11.   22872-X Pa. $3.00

THE METHODS OF CONSTRUCTION OF CELTIC ART, George Bain. Simple geometric techniques for making wonderful Celtic interlacements, spirals, Kells-type initials, animals, humans, etc. Unique for artists, craftsmen. Over 500 illustrations. 160pp. 9 x 12.   USO 22923-8 Pa. $4.00

SCULPTURE, PRINCIPLES AND PRACTICE, Louis Slobodkin. Step by step approach to clay, plaster, metals, stone; classical and modern. 253 drawings, photos. 255pp. 8⅛ x 11.   22960-2 Pa. $5.00

THE ART OF ETCHING, E.S. Lumsden. Clear, detailed instructions for etching, drypoint, softground, aquatint; from 1st sketch to print. Very detailed, thorough. 200 illustrations. 376pp.   20049-3 Pa. $3.75

CONSTRUCTION OF AMERICAN FURNITURE TREASURES, Lester Margon. 344 detail drawings, complete text on constructing exact reproductions of 38 early American masterpieces: Hepplewhite sideboard, Duncan Phyfe drop-leaf table, mantel clock, gate-leg dining table, Pa. German cupboard, more. 38 plates. 54 photographs. 168pp. 8⅜ x 11¼. 23056-2 Pa. $4.00

JEWELRY MAKING AND DESIGN, Augustus F. Rose, Antonio Cirino. Professional secrets revealed in thorough, practical guide: tools, materials, processes; rings, brooches, chains, cast pieces, enamelling, setting stones, etc. Do not confuse with skimpy introductions: beginner can use, professional can learn from it. Over 200 illustrations. 306pp. 21750-7 Pa. $3.00

METALWORK AND ENAMELLING, Herbert Maryon. Generally conceded best all-around book. Countless trade secrets: materials, tools, soldering, filigree, setting, inlay, niello, repoussé, casting, polishing, etc. For beginner or expert. Author was foremost British expert. 330 illustrations. 335pp. 22702-2 Pa. $3.50

WEAVING WITH FOOT-POWER LOOMS, Edward F. Worst. Setting up a loom, beginning to weave, constructing equipment, using dyes, more, plus over 285 drafts of traditional patterns including Colonial and Swedish weaves. More than 200 other figures. For beginning and advanced. 275pp. 8¾ x 6⅜. 23064-3 Pa. $4.50

WEAVING A NAVAJO BLANKET, Gladys A. Reichard. Foremost anthropologist studied under Navajo women, reveals every step in process from wool, dyeing, spinning, setting up loom, designing, weaving. Much history, symbolism. With this book you could make one yourself. 97 illustrations. 222pp. 22992-0 Pa. $3.00

NATURAL DYES AND HOME DYEING, Rita J. Adrosko. Use natural ingredients: bark, flowers, leaves, lichens, insects etc. Over 135 specific recipes from historical sources for cotton, wool, other fabrics. Genuine premodern handicrafts. 12 illustrations. 160pp. 22688-3 Pa. $2.00

THE HAND DECORATION OF FABRICS, Francis J. Kafka. Outstanding, profusely illustrated guide to stenciling, batik, block printing, tie dyeing, freehand painting, silk screen printing, and novelty decoration. 356 illustrations. 198pp. 6 x 9. 21401-X Pa. $3.00

THOMAS NAST: CARTOONS AND ILLUSTRATIONS, with text by Thomas Nast St. Hill. Father of American political cartooning. Cartoons that destroyed Tweed Ring; inflation, free love, church and state; original Republican elephant and Democratic donkey; Santa Claus; more. 117 illustrations. 146pp. 9 x 12.
22983-1 Pa. $4.00
23067-8 Clothbd. $8.50

FREDERIC REMINGTON: 173 DRAWINGS AND ILLUSTRATIONS. Most famous of the Western artists, most responsible for our myths about the American West in its untamed days. Complete reprinting of Drawings of Frederic Remington (1897), plus other selections. 4 additional drawings in color on covers. 140pp. 9 x 12. 20714-5 Pa. $3.95

EARLY NEW ENGLAND GRAVESTONE RUBBINGS, Edmund V. Gillon, Jr. 43 photographs, 226 rubbings show heavily symbolic, macabre, sometimes humorous primitive American art. Up to early 19th century. 207pp. 8⅜ x 11¼.
21380-3 Pa. $4.00

L.J.M. DAGUERRE: THE HISTORY OF THE DIORAMA AND THE DAGUERREOTYPE, Helmut and Alison Gernsheim. Definitive account. Early history, life and work of Daguerre; discovery of daguerreotype process; diffusion abroad; other early photography. 124 illustrations. 226pp. 6⅙ x 9¼.
22290-X Pa. $4.00

PHOTOGRAPHY AND THE AMERICAN SCENE, Robert Taft. The basic book on American photography as art, recording form, 1839-1889. Development, influence on society, great photographers, types (portraits, war, frontier, etc.), whatever else needed. Inexhaustible. Illustrated with 322 early photos, daguerreotypes, tintypes, stereo slides, etc. 546pp. 6⅛ x 9¼.
21201-7 Pa. $5.95

PHOTOGRAPHIC SKETCHBOOK OF THE CIVIL WAR, Alexander Gardner. Reproduction of 1866 volume with 100 on-the-field photographs: Manassas, Lincoln on battlefield, slave pens, etc. Introduction by E.F. Bleiler. 224pp. 10¾ x 9.
22731-6 Pa. $5.00

THE MOVIES: A PICTURE QUIZ BOOK, Stanley Appelbaum & Hayward Cirker. Match stars with their movies, name actors and actresses, test your movie skill with 241 stills from 236 great movies, 1902-1959. Indexes of performers and films. 128pp. 8⅜ x 9¼.
20222-4 Pa. $2.50

THE TALKIES, Richard Griffith. Anthology of features, articles from Photoplay, 1928-1940, reproduced complete. Stars, famous movies, technical features, fabulous ads, etc.; Garbo, Chaplin, King Kong, Lubitsch, etc. 4 color plates, scores of illustrations. 327pp. 8⅜ x 11¼.
22762-6 Pa. $6.95

THE MOVIE MUSICAL FROM VITAPHONE TO "42ND STREET," edited by Miles Kreuger. Relive the rise of the movie musical as reported in the pages of Photoplay magazine (1926-1933): every movie review, cast list, ad, and record review; every significant feature article, production still, biography, forecast, and gossip story. Profusely illustrated. 367pp. 8⅜ x 11¼.
23154-2 Pa. $7.95

JOHANN SEBASTIAN BACH, Philipp Spitta. Great classic of biography, musical commentary, with hundreds of pieces analyzed. Also good for Bach's contemporaries. 450 musical examples. Total of 1799pp.
EUK 22278-0, 22279-9 Clothbd., Two vol. set $25.00

BEETHOVEN AND HIS NINE SYMPHONIES, Sir George Grove. Thorough history, analysis, commentary on symphonies and some related pieces. For either beginner or advanced student. 436 musical passages. 407pp.
20334-4 Pa. $4.00

MOZART AND HIS PIANO CONCERTOS, Cuthbert Girdlestone. The only full-length study. Detailed analyses of all 21 concertos, sources; 417 musical examples. 509pp.
21271-8 Pa. $6.00

THE FITZWILLIAM VIRGINAL BOOK, edited by J. Fuller Maitland, W.B. Squire. Famous early 17th century collection of keyboard music, 300 works by Morley, Byrd, Bull, Gibbons, etc. Modern notation. Total of 938pp. 8⅜ x 11.
ECE 21068-5, 21069-3 Pa., Two vol. set $15.00

COMPLETE STRING QUARTETS, Wolfgang A. Mozart. Breitkopf and Härtel edition. All 23 string quartets plus alternate slow movement to K156. Study score. 277pp. 9⅜ x 12¼. 22372-8 Pa. $6.00

COMPLETE SONG CYCLES, Franz Schubert. Complete piano, vocal music of Die Schöne Müllerin, Die Winterreise, Schwanengesang. Also Drinker English singing translations. Breitkopf and Härtel edition. 217pp. 9⅜ x 12¼.
22649-2 Pa. $4.50

THE COMPLETE PRELUDES AND ETUDES FOR PIANOFORTE SOLO, Alexander Scriabin. All the preludes and etudes including many perfectly spun miniatures. Edited by K.N. Igumnov and Y.I. Mil'shteyn. 250pp. 9 x 12. 22919-X Pa. $5.00

TRISTAN UND ISOLDE, Richard Wagner. Full orchestral score with complete instrumentation. Do not confuse with piano reduction. Commentary by Felix Mottl, great Wagnerian conductor and scholar. Study score. 655pp. 8⅛ x 11.
22915-7 Pa. $11.95

FAVORITE SONGS OF THE NINETIES, ed. Robert Fremont. Full reproduction, including covers, of 88 favorites: Ta-Ra-Ra-Boom-De-Aye, The Band Played On, Bird in a Gilded Cage, Under the Bamboo Tree, After the Ball, etc. 401pp. 9 x 12.
EBE 21536-9 Pa. $6.95

SOUSA'S GREAT MARCHES IN PIANO TRANSCRIPTION: ORIGINAL SHEET MUSIC OF 23 WORKS, John Philip Sousa. Selected by Lester S. Levy. Playing edition includes: The Stars and Stripes Forever, The Thunderer, The Gladiator, King Cotton, Washington Post, much more. 24 illustrations. 111pp. 9 x 12.
USO 23132-1 Pa. $3.50

CLASSIC PIANO RAGS, selected with an introduction by Rudi Blesh. Best ragtime music (1897-1922) by Scott Joplin, James Scott, Joseph F. Lamb, Tom Turpin, 9 others. Printed from best original sheet music, plus covers. 364pp. 9 x 12.
EBE 20469-3 Pa. $6.95

ANALYSIS OF CHINESE CHARACTERS, C.D. Wilder, J.H. Ingram. 1000 most important characters analyzed according to primitives, phonetics, historical development. Traditional method offers mnemonic aid to beginner, intermediate student of Chinese, Japanese. 365pp. 23045-7 Pa. $4.00

MODERN CHINESE: A BASIC COURSE, Faculty of Peking University. Self study, classroom course in modern Mandarin. Records contain phonetics, vocabulary, sentences, lessons. 249 page book contains all recorded text, translations, grammar, vocabulary, exercises. Best course on market. 3 12" 33⅓ monaural records, book, album. 98832-5 Set $12.50

THE BEST DR. THORNDYKE DETECTIVE STORIES, R. Austin Freeman. The Case of Oscar Brodski, The Moabite Cipher, and 5 other favorites featuring the great scientific detective, plus his long-believed-lost first adventure — 31 New Inn — reprinted here for the first time. Edited by E.F. Bleiler. USO 20388-3 Pa. $3.00

BEST "THINKING MACHINE" DETECTIVE STORIES, Jacques Futrelle. The Problem of Cell 13 and 11 other stories about Prof. Augustus S.F.X. Van Dusen, including two "lost" stories. First reprinting of several. Edited by E.F. Bleiler. 241pp.
20537-1 Pa. $3.00

UNCLE SILAS, J. Sheridan LeFanu. Victorian Gothic mystery novel, considered by many best of period, even better than Collins or Dickens. Wonderful psychological terror. Introduction by Frederick Shroyer. 436pp. 21715-9 Pa. $4.00

BEST DR. POGGIOLI DETECTIVE STORIES, T.S. Stribling. 15 best stories from EQMM and The Saint offer new adventures in Mexico, Florida, Tennessee hills as Poggioli unravels mysteries and combats Count Jalacki. 217pp. 23227-1 Pa. $3.00

EIGHT DIME NOVELS, selected with an introduction by E.F. Bleiler. Adventures of Old King Brady, Frank James, Nick Carter, Deadwood Dick, Buffalo Bill, The Steam Man, Frank Merriwell, and Horatio Alger — 1877 to 1905. Important, entertaining popular literature in facsimile reprint, with original covers. 190pp. 9 x 12. 22975-0 Pa. $3.50

ALICE'S ADVENTURES UNDER GROUND, Lewis Carroll. Facsimile of ms. Carroll gave Alice Liddell in 1864. Different in many ways from final Alice. Handlettered, illustrated by Carroll. Introduction by Martin Gardner. 128pp. 21482-6 Pa. $1.50

ALICE IN WONDERLAND COLORING BOOK, Lewis Carroll. Pictures by John Tenniel. Large-size versions of the famous illustrations of Alice, Cheshire Cat, Mad Hatter and all the others, waiting for your crayons. Abridged text. 36 illustrations. 64pp. 8¼ x 11. 22853-3 Pa. $1.50

AVENTURES D'ALICE AU PAYS DES MERVEILLES, Lewis Carroll. Bué's translation of "Alice" into French, supervised by Carroll himself. Novel way to learn language. (No English text.) 42 Tenniel illustrations. 196pp. 22836-3 Pa. $2.50

MYTHS AND FOLK TALES OF IRELAND, Jeremiah Curtin. 11 stories that are Irish versions of European fairy tales and 9 stories from the Fenian cycle — 20 tales of legend and magic that comprise an essential work in the history of folklore. 256pp. 22430-9 Pa. $3.00

EAST O' THE SUN AND WEST O' THE MOON, George W. Dasent. Only full edition of favorite, wonderful Norwegian fairytales — Why the Sea is Salt, Boots and the Troll, etc. — with 77 illustrations by Kittelsen & Werenskiöld. 418pp.
22521-6 Pa. $4.00

PERRAULT'S FAIRY TALES, Charles Perrault and Gustave Doré. Original versions of Cinderella, Sleeping Beauty, Little Red Riding Hood, etc. in best translation, with 34 wonderful illustrations by Gustave Doré. 117pp. 8⅛ x 11. 22311-6 Pa. $2.50

MOTHER GOOSE'S MELODIES. Facsimile of fabulously rare Munroe and Francis "copyright 1833" Boston edition. Familiar and unusual rhymes, wonderful old woodcut illustrations. Edited by E.F. Bleiler. 128pp. 4½ x 6⅜. 22577-1 Pa. $1.50

MOTHER GOOSE IN HIEROGLYPHICS. Favorite nursery rhymes presented in rebus form for children. Fascinating 1849 edition reproduced in toto, with key. Introduction by E.F. Bleiler. About 400 woodcuts. 64pp. 6⅞ x 5¼. 20745-5 Pa. $1.00

PETER PIPER'S PRACTICAL PRINCIPLES OF PLAIN & PERFECT PRONUNCIATION. Alliterative jingles and tongue-twisters. Reproduction in full of 1830 first American edition. 25 spirited woodcuts. 32pp. 4½ x 6⅜. 22560-7 Pa. $1.00

MARMADUKE MULTIPLY'S MERRY METHOD OF MAKING MINOR MATHEMATICIANS. Fellow to Peter Piper, it teaches multiplication table by catchy rhymes and woodcuts. 1841 Munroe & Francis edition. Edited by E.F. Bleiler. 103pp. 4⅝ x 6.
22773-1 Pa. $1.25
20171-6 Clothbd. $3.00

THE NIGHT BEFORE CHRISTMAS, Clement Moore. Full text, and woodcuts from original 1848 book. Also critical, historical material. 19 illustrations. 40pp. 4⅝ x 6. 22797-9 Pa. $1.25

THE KING OF THE GOLDEN RIVER, John Ruskin. Victorian children's classic of three brothers, their attempts to reach the Golden River, what becomes of them. Facsimile of original 1889 edition. 22 illustrations. 56pp. 4⅝ x 6⅜.
20066-3 Pa. $1.50

DREAMS OF THE RAREBIT FIEND, Winsor McCay. Pioneer cartoon strip, unexcelled for beauty, imagination, in 60 full sequences. Incredible technical virtuosity, wonderful visual wit. Historical introduction. 62pp. 8⅜ x 11¼. 21347-1 Pa. $2.50

THE KATZENJAMMER KIDS, Rudolf Dirks. In full color, 14 strips from 1906-7; full of imagination, characteristic humor. Classic of great historical importance. Introduction by August Derleth. 32pp. 9¼ x 12¼. 23005-8 Pa. $2.00

LITTLE ORPHAN ANNIE AND LITTLE ORPHAN ANNIE IN COSMIC CITY, Harold Gray. Two great sequences from the early strips: our curly-haired heroine defends the Warbucks' financial empire and, then, takes on meanie Phineas P. Pinchpenny. Leapin' lizards! 178pp. 6⅛ x 8⅜. 23107-0 Pa. $2.00

THE BEST OF GLUYAS WILLIAMS. 100 drawings by one of America's finest cartoonists: The Day a Cake of Ivory Soap Sank at Proctor & Gamble's, At the Life Insurance Agents' Banquet, and many other gems from the 20's and 30's. 118pp. 8⅜ x 11¼. 22737-5 Pa. $2.50

THE MAGIC MOVING PICTURE BOOK, Bliss, Sands & Co. The pictures in this book move! Volcanoes erupt, a house burns, a serpentine dancer wiggles her way through a number. By using a specially ruled acetate screen provided, you can obtain these and 15 other startling effects. Originally "The Motograph Moving Picture Book." 32pp. 8¼ x 11. 23224-7 Pa. $1.75

STRING FIGURES AND HOW TO MAKE THEM, Caroline F. Jayne. Fullest, clearest instructions on string figures from around world: Eskimo, Navajo, Lapp, Europe, more. Cats cradle, moving spear, lightning, stars. Introduction by A.C. Haddon. 950 illustrations. 407pp. 20152-X Pa. $3.50

PAPER FOLDING FOR BEGINNERS, William D. Murray and Francis J. Rigney. Clearest book on market for making origami sail boats, roosters, frogs that move legs, cups, bonbon boxes. 40 projects. More than 275 illustrations. Photographs. 94pp. 20713-7 Pa. $1.25

INDIAN SIGN LANGUAGE, William Tomkins. Over 525 signs developed by Sioux, Blackfoot, Cheyenne, Arapahoe and other tribes. Written instructions and diagrams: how to make words, construct sentences. Also 290 pictographs of Sioux and Ojibway tribes. 111pp. 6⅛ x 9¼. 22029-X Pa. $1.50

BOOMERANGS: HOW TO MAKE AND THROW THEM, Bernard S. Mason. Easy to make and throw, dozens of designs: cross-stick, pinwheel, boomabird, tumblestick, Australian curved stick boomerang. Complete throwing instructions. All safe. 99pp. 23028-7 Pa. $1.75

25 KITES THAT FLY, Leslie Hunt. Full, easy to follow instructions for kites made from inexpensive materials. Many novelties. Reeling, raising, designing your own. 70 illustrations. 110pp. 22550-X Pa. $1.25

TRICKS AND GAMES ON THE POOL TABLE, Fred Herrmann. 79 tricks and games, some solitaires, some for 2 or more players, some competitive; mystifying shots and throws, unusual carom, tricks involving cork, coins, a hat, more. 77 figures. 95pp. 21814-7 Pa. $1.25

WOODCRAFT AND CAMPING, Bernard S. Mason. How to make a quick emergency shelter, select woods that will burn immediately, make do with limited supplies, etc. Also making many things out of wood, rawhide, bark, at camp. Formerly titled Woodcraft. 295 illustrations. 580pp. 21951-8 Pa. $4.00

AN INTRODUCTION TO CHESS MOVES AND TACTICS SIMPLY EXPLAINED, Leonard Barden. Informal intermediate introduction: reasons for moves, tactics, openings, traps, positional play, endgame. Isolates patterns. 102pp. USO 21210-6 Pa. $1.35

LASKER'S MANUAL OF CHESS, Dr. Emanuel Lasker. Great world champion offers very thorough coverage of all aspects of chess. Combinations, position play, openings, endgame, aesthetics of chess, philosophy of struggle, much more. Filled with analyzed games. 390pp. 20640-8 Pa. $4.00

DRIED FLOWERS, Sarah Whitlock and Martha Rankin. Concise, clear, practical guide to dehydration, glycerinizing, pressing plant material, and more. Covers use of silica gel. 12 drawings. Originally titled "New Techniques with Dried Flowers." 32pp. 21802-3 Pa. $1.00

ABC OF POULTRY RAISING, J.H. Florea. Poultry expert, editor tells how to raise chickens on home or small business basis. Breeds, feeding, housing, laying, etc. Very concrete, practical. 50 illustrations. 256pp. 23201-8 Pa. $3.00

HOW INDIANS USE WILD PLANTS FOR FOOD, MEDICINE & CRAFTS, Frances Densmore. Smithsonian, Bureau of American Ethnology report presents wealth of material on nearly 200 plants used by Chippewas of Minnesota and Wisconsin. 33 plates plus 122pp. of text. 6⅛ x 9¼. 23019-8 Pa. $2.50

THE HERBAL OR GENERAL HISTORY OF PLANTS, John Gerard. The 1633 edition revised and enlarged by Thomas Johnson. Containing almost 2850 plant descriptions and 2705 superb illustrations, Gerard's Herbal is a monumental work, the book all modern English herbals are derived from, and the one herbal every serious enthusiast should have in its entirety. Original editions are worth perhaps $750. 1678pp. 8½ x 12¼. 23147-X Clothbd. $50.00

A MODERN HERBAL, Margaret Grieve. Much the fullest, most exact, most useful compilation of herbal material. Gigantic alphabetical encyclopedia, from aconite to zedoary, gives botanical information, medical properties, folklore, economic uses, and much else. Indispensable to serious reader. 161 illustrations. 888pp. 6½ x 9¼. USO 22798-7, 22799-5 Pa., Two vol. set $10.00

HOW TO KNOW THE FERNS, Frances T. Parsons. Delightful classic. Identification, fern lore, for Eastern and Central U.S.A. Has introduced thousands to interesting life form. 99 illustrations. 215pp. 20740-4 Pa. $2.75

THE MUSHROOM HANDBOOK, Louis C.C. Krieger. Still the best popular handbook. Full descriptions of 259 species, extremely thorough text, habitats, luminescence, poisons, folklore, etc. 32 color plates; 126 other illustrations. 560pp. 21861-9 Pa. $4.50

HOW TO KNOW THE WILD FRUITS, Maude G. Peterson. Classic guide covers nearly 200 trees, shrubs, smaller plants of the U.S. arranged by color of fruit and then by family. Full text provides names, descriptions, edibility, uses. 80 illustrations. 400pp. 22943-2 Pa. $4.00

COMMON WEEDS OF THE UNITED STATES, U.S. Department of Agriculture. Covers 220 important weeds with illustration, maps, botanical information, plant lore for each. Over 225 illustrations. 463pp. 6⅛ x 9¼. 20504-5 Pa. $4.50

HOW TO KNOW THE WILD FLOWERS, Mrs. William S. Dana. Still best popular book for East and Central USA. Over 500 plants easily identified, with plant lore; arranged according to color and flowering time. 174 plates. 459pp. 20332-8 Pa. $3.50

DRIED FLOWERS, Sarah Whitlock and Martha Rankin. Concise, clear, practical guide to dehydration, glycerinizing, pressing plant material, and more. Covers use of silica gel. 12 drawings. Originally titled "New Techniques with Dried Flowers." 32pp. 21802-3 Pa. $1.00

ABC OF POULTRY RAISING, J.H. Florea. Poultry expert, editor tells how to raise chickens on home or small business basis. Breeds, feeding, housing, laying, etc. Very concrete, practical. 50 illustrations. 256pp. 23201-8 Pa. $3.00

HOW INDIANS USE WILD PLANTS FOR FOOD, MEDICINE & CRAFTS, Frances Densmore. Smithsonian, Bureau of American Ethnology report presents wealth of material on nearly 200 plants used by Chippewas of Minnesota and Wisconsin. 33 plates plus 122pp. of text. 6⅛ x 9¼. 23019-8 Pa. $2.50

THE HERBAL OR GENERAL HISTORY OF PLANTS, John Gerard. The 1633 edition revised and enlarged by Thomas Johnson. Containing almost 2850 plant descriptions and 2705 superb illustrations, Gerard's Herbal is a monumental work, the book all modern English herbals are derived from, and the one herbal every serious enthusiast should have in its entirety. Original editions are worth perhaps $750. 1678pp. 8½ x 12¼. 23147-X Clothbd. $50.00

A MODERN HERBAL, Margaret Grieve. Much the fullest, most exact, most useful compilation of herbal material. Gigantic alphabetical encyclopedia, from aconite to zedoary, gives botanical information, medical properties, folklore, economic uses, and much else. Indispensable to serious reader. 161 illustrations. 888pp. 6½ x 9¼. USO 22798-7, 22799-5 Pa., Two vol. set $10.00

HOW TO KNOW THE FERNS, Frances T. Parsons. Delightful classic. Identification, fern lore, for Eastern and Central U.S.A. Has introduced thousands to interesting life form. 99 illustrations. 215pp. 20740-4 Pa. $2.75

THE MUSHROOM HANDBOOK, Louis C.C. Krieger. Still the best popular handbook. Full descriptions of 259 species, extremely thorough text, habitats, luminescence, poisons, folklore, etc. 32 color plates; 126 other illustrations. 560pp. 21861-9 Pa. $4.50

HOW TO KNOW THE WILD FRUITS, Maude G. Peterson. Classic guide covers nearly 200 trees, shrubs, smaller plants of the U.S. arranged by color of fruit and then by family. Full text provides names, descriptions, edibility, uses. 80 illustrations. 400pp. 22943-2 Pa. $4.00

COMMON WEEDS OF THE UNITED STATES, U.S. Department of Agriculture. Covers 220 important weeds with illustration, maps, botanical information, plant lore for each. Over 225 illustrations. 463pp. 6⅛ x 9¼. 20504-5 Pa. $4.50

HOW TO KNOW THE WILD FLOWERS, Mrs. William S. Dana. Still best popular book for East and Central USA. Over 500 plants easily identified, with plant lore; arranged according to color and flowering time. 174 plates. 459pp. 20332-8 Pa. $3.50

THE STYLE OF PALESTRINA AND THE DISSONANCE, Knud Jeppesen. Standard analysis of rhythm, line, harmony, accented and unaccented dissonances. Also pre-Palestrina dissonances. 306pp. 22386-8 Pa. $4.50

DOVER OPERA GUIDE AND LIBRETTO SERIES prepared by Ellen H. Bleiler. Each volume contains everything needed for background, complete enjoyment: complete libretto, new English translation with all repeats, biography of composer and librettist, early performance history, musical lore, much else. All volumes lavishly illustrated with performance photos, portraits, similar material. Do not confuse with skimpy performance booklets.

CARMEN, Georges Bizet. 66 illustrations. 222pp. 22111-3 Pa. $3.00
DON GIOVANNI, Wolfgang A. Mozart. 92 illustrations. 209pp. 21134-7 Pa. $2.50
LA BOHÈME, Giacomo Puccini. 73 illustrations. 124pp. USO 20404-9 Pa. $1.75
ÄIDA, Giuseppe Verdi. 76 illustrations. 181pp. 20405-7 Pa. $2.25
LUCIA DI LAMMERMOOR, Gaetano Donizetti. 44 illustrations. 186pp. 22110-5 Pa. $2.00

ANTONIO STRADIVARI: HIS LIFE AND WORK, W. H. Hill, et al. Great work of musicology. Construction methods, woods, varnishes, known instruments, types of instruments, life, special features. Introduction by Sydney Beck. 98 illustrations, plus 4 color plates. 315pp. 20425-1 Pa. $4.00

MUSIC FOR THE PIANO, James Friskin, Irwin Freundlich. Both famous, little-known compositions; 1500 to 1950's. Listing, description, classification, technical aspects for student, teacher, performer. Indispensable for enlarging repertory. 448pp. 22918-1 Pa. $4.00

PIANOS AND THEIR MAKERS, Alfred Dolge. Leading inventor offers full history of piano technology, earliest models to 1910. Types, makers, components, mechanisms, musical aspects. Very strong on offtrail models, inventions; also player pianos. 300 illustrations. 581pp. 22856-8 Pa. $5.00

KEYBOARD MUSIC, J.S. Bach. Bach-Gesellschaft edition. For harpsichord, piano, other keyboard instruments. English Suites, French Suites, Six Partitas, Goldberg Variations, Two-Part Inventions, Three-Part Sinfonias. 312pp. 8⅛ x 11. 22360-4 Pa. $5.00

COMPLETE STRING QUARTETS, Ludwig van Beethoven. Breitkopf and Härtel edition. 6 quartets of Opus 18; 3 quartets of Opus 59; Opera 74, 95, 127, 130, 131, 132, 135 and Grosse Fuge. Study score. 434pp. 9⅜ x 12¼. 22361-2 Pa. $7.95

COMPLETE PIANO SONATAS AND VARIATIONS FOR SOLO PIANO, Johannes Brahms. All sonatas, five variations on themes from Schumann, Paganini, Handel, etc. Vienna Gesellschaft der Musikfreunde edition. 178pp. 9 x 12. 22650-6 Pa. $4.50

PIANO MUSIC 1888-1905, Claude Debussy. Deux Arabesques, Suite Bergamesque, Masques, 1st series of Images, etc. 9 others, in corrected editions. 175pp. 9⅜ x 12¼. 22771-5 Pa. $4.00

INCIDENTS OF TRAVEL IN YUCATAN, John L. Stephens. Classic (1843) exploration of jungles of Yucatan, looking for evidences of Maya civilization. Travel adventures, Mexican and Indian culture, etc. Total of 669pp.
20926-1, 20927-X Pa., Two vol. set $6.00

LIVING MY LIFE, Emma Goldman. Candid, no holds barred account by foremost American anarchist: her own life, anarchist movement, famous contemporaries, ideas and their impact. Struggles and confrontations in America, plus deportation to U.S.S.R. Shocking inside account of persecution of anarchists under Lenin. 13 plates. Total of 944pp.
22543-7, 22544-5 Pa., Two vol. set $9.00

AMERICAN INDIANS, George Catlin. Classic account of life among Plains Indians: ceremonies, hunt, warfare, etc. Dover edition reproduces for first time all original paintings. 312 plates. 572pp. of text. 6⅛ x 9¼.
22118-0, 22119-9 Pa., Two vol. set $8.00
22140-7, 22144-X Clothbd., Two vol. set $16.00

THE INDIANS BOOK, Natalie Curtis. Lore, music, narratives, drawings by Indians, collected from cultures of U.S.A. 149 songs in full notation. 45 illustrations. 583pp. 6⅝ x 9⅜.
21939-9 Pa. $6.95

INDIAN BLANKETS AND THEIR MAKERS, George Wharton James. History, old style wool blankets, changes brought about by traders, symbolism of design and color, a Navajo weaver at work, outline blanket, Kachina blankets, more. Emphasis on Navajo. 130 illustrations, 32 in color. 230pp. 6⅛ x 9¼.
22996-3 Pa. $5.00
23068-6 Clothbd. $10.00

AN INTRODUCTION TO THE STUDY OF THE MAYA HIEROGLYPHS, Sylvanus Griswold Morley. Classic study by one of the truly great figures in hieroglyph research. Still the best introduction for the student for reading Maya hieroglyphs. New introduction by J. Eric S. Thompson. 117 illustrations. 284pp.
23108-9 Pa. $4.00

THE ANALECTS OF CONFUCIUS, THE GREAT LEARNING, DOCTRINE OF THE MEAN, Confucius. Edited by James Legge. Full Chinese text, standard English translation on same page, Chinese commentators, editor's annotations; dictionary of characters at rear, plus grammatical comment. Finest edition anywhere of one of world's greatest thinkers. 503pp.
22746-4 Pa. $5.00

THE I CHING (THE BOOK OF CHANGES), translated by James Legge. Complete translation of basic text plus appendices by Confucius, and Chinese commentary of most penetrating divination manual ever prepared. Indispensable to study of early Oriental civilizations, to modern inquiring reader. 448pp.
21062-6 Pa. $3.50

THE EGYPTIAN BOOK OF THE DEAD, E.A. Wallis Budge. Complete reproduction of Ani's papyrus, finest ever found. Full hieroglyphic text, interlinear transliteration, word for word translation, smooth translation. Basic work, for Egyptology, for modern study of psychic matters. Total of 533pp. 6½ x 9¼.
EBE 21866-X Pa. $4.95

CATALOGUE OF DOVER BOOKS

BUILD YOUR OWN LOW-COST HOME, L.O. Anderson, H.F. Zornig. U.S. Dept. of Agriculture sets of plans, full, detailed, for 11 houses: A-Frame, circular, conventional. Also construction manual. Save hundreds of dollars. 204pp. 11 x 16.
21525-3 Pa. $6.00

HOW TO BUILD A WOOD-FRAME HOUSE, L.O. Anderson. Comprehensive, easy to follow U.S. Government manual: placement, foundations, framing, sheathing, roof, insulation, plaster, finishing — almost everything else. 179 illustrations. 223pp. 7⅞ x 10¾.
22954-8 Pa. $3.50

CONCRETE, MASONRY AND BRICKWORK, U.S. Department of the Army. Practical handbook for the home owner and small builder, manual contains basic principles, techniques, and important background information on construction with concrete, concrete blocks, and brick. 177 figures, 37 tables. 200pp. 6½ x 9¼.
23203-4 Pa. $4.00

THE STANDARD BOOK OF QUILT MAKING AND COLLECTING, Marguerite Ickis. Full information, full-sized patterns for making 46 traditional quilts, also 150 other patterns. Quilted cloths, lamé, satin quilts, etc. 483 illustrations. 273pp. 6⅞ x 9⅝.
20582-7 Pa. $3.50

101 PATCHWORK PATTERNS, Ruby S. McKim. 101 beautiful, immediately useable patterns, full-size, modern and traditional. Also general information, estimating, quilt lore. 124pp. 7⅞ x 10¾.
20773-0 Pa. $2.50

KNIT YOUR OWN NORWEGIAN SWEATERS, Dale Yarn Company. Complete instructions for 50 authentic sweaters, hats, mittens, gloves, caps, etc. Thoroughly modern designs that command high prices in stores. 24 patterns, 24 color photographs. Nearly 100 charts and other illustrations. 58pp. 8⅜ x 11¼.
23031-7 Pa. $2.50

IRON-ON TRANSFER PATTERNS FOR CREWEL AND EMBROIDERY FROM EARLY AMERICAN SOURCES, edited by Rita Weiss. 75 designs, borders, alphabets, from traditional American sources printed on translucent paper in transfer ink. Reuseable. Instructions. Test patterns. 24pp. 8¼ x 11.
23162-3 Pa. $1.50

AMERICAN INDIAN NEEDLEPOINT DESIGNS FOR PILLOWS, BELTS, HANDBAGS AND OTHER PROJECTS, Roslyn Epstein. 37 authentic American Indian designs adapted for modern needlepoint projects. Grid backing makes designs easily transferable to canvas. 48pp. 8¼ x 11.
22973-4 Pa. $1.50

CHARTED FOLK DESIGNS FOR CROSS-STITCH EMBROIDERY, Maria Foris & Andreas Foris. 278 charted folk designs, most in 2 colors, from Danube region: florals, fantastic beasts, geometrics, traditional symbols, more. Border and central patterns. 77pp. 8¼ x 11.
USO 23191-7 Pa. $2.00

Prices subject to change without notice.
Available at your book dealer or write for free catalogue to Dept. GI, Dover Publications, Inc., 180 Varick St., N.Y., N.Y. 10014. Dover publishes more than 150 books each year on science, elementary and advanced mathematics, biology, music, art, literary history, social sciences and other areas.